Spending
OF MIDDLE-INCOME FAMILIES

Issued under the Auspices of the
Heller Committee for Research in Social Economics
University of California

Spending

OF MIDDLE-INCOME FAMILIES

Incomes and Expenditures of Salaried Workers
in the San Francisco Bay Area in 1950

EMILY H. HUNTINGTON

With the assistance of
Mary H. Hawes and Esther Oswalt

1957
University of California Press · Berkeley · Los Angeles

University of California Press
Berkeley and Los Angeles, California

Cambridge University Press
London, England

© 1957
By The Regents of the University of California

Library of Congress Catalog Card Number: 57-7592

ISBN 978-0-520-30726-1

THE
HELLER COMMITTEE

For Research in Social Economics of the University of California
1956

Emily H. Huntington, <u>Chairman</u>
Barbara N. Armstrong
Sidney S. Hoos
Harvey Leibenstein
Davis McEntire
Ruth Okey

PREFACE

This study, published under the auspices of the Heller Committee for Research in Social Economics, is the most recent of a series of Heller Committee studies of incomes and expenditures. Its special contribution is that it provides detailed evidence as to the patterns of consumption of salaried workers in occupations above routine clerical workers but below the executive class. Many other income and expenditure studies have been made, but none have segregated this socioeconomic group for special study.

As is always true of statistical studies, the results are based on the work of many people. Special gratitude is due two persons on the Heller Committee staff—Mary H. Hawes and Esther Oswalt, who were responsible not only for the preparation of the original drafts of many sections, but were largely responsible for some of the chapters which appear in the final manuscript. Miss Hawes and Mrs. Oswalt also contributed suggestions as to the methods of analysis to be used. I should like to thank also Vera Hopkins, whose careful supervision of the field work resulted in a high degree of accuracy of the raw materials. Thanks are also expressed to Lucille Bonsack, secretary of the Heller Committee for the laborious task of typing the manuscript, and to Maria Draeger, who worked long and carefully in checking computations. Others who contributed are too numerous to name, but appreciation is due those who assisted in securing the names of firms to be visited, to the firms who coöperated, to the field workers whose long hours of careful work made the raw materials available, and finally, of course, to the 159 families who gave the necessary detailed information about their incomes and expenditures.

As stated in chapter 1, Professor Jerzy Neyman, head of the Department of Statistics, University of California, Berkeley, suggested a method which tested the extent to which the sample of 159 families may be representative of other families. I am grateful to Professor Neyman for his advice as to the techniques and procedures to be used and also to members of his staff who made the laborious calculations which were required.

This study was financed in the main by the regular annual donation from Mrs. E. S. Heller and by funds granted by the University to the Heller Committee. Some additional funds were made available by the Bureau of Business and Economic Research and by the Institute of Social Sciences of the University of California.

The question always arises whether to place a summary chapter at the beginning or end of such a study as this. Since the body of this manuscript includes details in which some readers may not be interested, the decision was made to follow the chapter on "Scope and Method" with the summary. The reader who prefers to examine the detail first may wish at once to read through the later chapters.

Emily H. Huntington

CONTENTS

Chapter I
SCOPE AND METHOD

This study of family income and expenditures of middle-income[1] salaried workers in occupations above routine clerical work but who are below the executive class[2] was undertaken for two reasons. First, the Heller Committee decided to price a budget for the family of a salaried worker in this socio-economic group, and thus data were required from an income and expenditure study in order to determine the items and quantities of goods to be included in this budget.[3] The second and broader purpose was to provide information about the spending patterns of an important but often neglected segment of the population. This Heller Committee study, as well as detailed tabulations of the Bureau of Labor Statistics 1950 expenditure study, to be published shortly by the Wharton School of the University of Pennsylvania, will provide empirical data which will be useful in further analytical studies of consumers' economic behavior and in the development of income and expenditure theory.

Many income and expenditure studies have been made during the past several decades, and since the latter part of the nineteenth century several have been published by the Bureau of Labor Statistics of the United States Department of Labor. The earliest B.L.S. studies were limited to wage-earning families,[4] whereas those made in 1918-1919 and 1934-1936 also included

---

[1] Although the income of the group studied is well above the statistical middle of the general income distribution, it is probable that the incomes of the families studied represent a middle group between wage earners and the executive class, if retired persons, beginning workers, and broken families could be eliminated from the distribution.

[2] See p. 3 for description of eligibility requirements.

[3] Included in the annual Quantity and Cost Budgets for Two Income Levels, prices for the San Francisco Bay area. The new budget was first priced in September, 1953.

[4] U.S. Department of Labor, Bureau of Labor Statistics, Cost of Living in the United States, Bulletin 357, Washington D.C., 1924, p. 1, fn. 1.

[1]

families of clerical workers, but with strict eligibility requirements as to their incomes; both excluded salaried workers with incomes above $2,000.[5]

More recent Bureau of Labor Statistics studies, covering the years 1941-1942 and 1945 through 1950, included all occupational and income groups.[6] The 1941-1942 and 1945-1949 studies classified expenditures by income levels but not by occupational groups. In contrast, the 1950 survey presented expenditure data for wage-earning families as well as for all families combined, but did not classify the information by income level.[7] Since none of these studies provided data on the incomes and expenditures of the occupational group surveyed by the Heller Committee, it is believed that the present inquiry will be a useful addition to what is known about consumption habits.

This Heller Committee study was designed to collect information on the consumption patterns of a group fairly homogeneous both as to occupations and income. The definition of the salaried workers to be included in terms of occupations presented difficulties. The types of occupations to be represented were found within four of the U. S. Census classifications: professional, technical, and kindred workers; managers, officials, and proprietors; clerical and kindred workers; and sales workers. One difficulty which arises in connection with the use of job titles is that of varying job responsibilities: the term "bookkeeper," for example, may be the title given to a person who merely operates a bookkeeping machine or makes routine bookkeeping entries, but it also applies to someone highly trained in bookkeeping theory and practice; the term "manager" may designate the head of a small department or section, or it may refer to a person responsible for the general management of a large establishment. Moreover, a study which included everyone within these four Census classifications would cover persons at widely varying economic levels. For example, the classification "professional, technical and kindred workers" includes blueprint tracers, architects, internes, and surgeons; "managers, officials, and proprietors" includes section heads and floor walkers in retail establishments, as well as

---

[5]U. S. Department of Labor, Bureau of Labor Statistics: schedule used in the 1918-1919 study, p. 1; and Money Disbursements of Wage Earners and Clerical Workers, 1934-36, Bulletin 638, Washington, D. C., 1941, p. 1.

[6]U. S. Department of Labor, Bureau of Labor Statistics, Family Spending and Saving in Wartime, Bulletin 822, Washington, D. C., 1945; Family Income, Expenditures and Savings in 1945, Bulletin 956, Washington, D. C., 1949; Family Income, Expenditures, and Savings in 10 Cities (1946-1949), Bulletin 1065, Washington, D. C., 1952; Family Income, Expenditures and Savings in 1950, Bulletin 1097 (revised), Washington, D. C., 1953.

[7]Further analyses of the 1950 data have been since made by the Wharton School of Finance and Commerce, University of Pennsylvania, but were not available at the time the Heller Committee study went to press.

presidents of banks and industrial establishments; "clerical and kindred workers" includes messengers and typists in addition to bookkeepers; and "sales workers" includes not only salesmen in retail establishments, but also insurance, real estate, and stock and bond salesmen.

Because of the difficulties in using job titles as the basis for selecting a homogeneous economic group, it was necessary also to use some other criterion if persons very high and very low in the economic scale were to be omitted. An income qualification appeared to be the only practical method of accomplishing this job.

At the time the study was being planned, there was very little current information which analyzed incomes by any occupational classifications above those of wage earners. However, some data for the United States as a whole were available in the Survey of Consumer Finances published annually in the Federal Reserve Bulletin. These data classified salaried workers as professional and semiprofessional, managerial and self-employed, and clerical and sales personnel. This study showed that in 1949, in the professional and managerial classes, which probably contained a large part of the occupations to be studied by the Heller Committee, the majority of spending units had incomes before taxes of $4,000 or more.[8] This group of spending units was distributed in three income classes ($4,000-$4,999, $5,000-$7,499, $7,500 and over), with the largest number of cases in the $5,000-$7,499 class. As would be expected, among the clerical and sales personnel the majority of spending units had incomes of less than $4,000. Of the 30 per cent with incomes above that figure, 14 per cent were between $4,000 and $5,000, 13 per cent from $5,000 to $7,500, and only 3 per cent were in the highest income class. In the light of these Federal Reserve figures, it was decided to limit the Heller Committee study to families in which the chief breadwinners had 1950 salaries between $4,800 and $7,500, and to put a ceiling of $10,000 on total family income in 1950.[9] Although these limitations gave some flexibility to the qualifications for inclusion in the study, they also insured considerable similarity of family incomes.

The study was further limited to families in which (1) both the husband and wife had been in the household all year; (2) there was at least 1 child under twenty-one who had been a member of the family for not less than

---

[8]Federal Reserve Bulletin, August 1950, p. 950.

[9]Originally the lower limit for salaries was set at $5,000. This was reduced to $4,800 when employers indicated that standard rates for employees in some of the classifications to be included were more frequently $4,800 than $5,000. Since salary was the only available guide to income in selecting the sample, and many families have some income in addition to the breadwinner's salary, an upper limit for total family income was arbitrarily set at $10,000.

eight months in 1950; and (3) at least 1 child was dependent upon family funds for more than half of his living expenses.

The sample.—On the basis of available funds it was decided that about 200 families could be studied. The most desirable method of selecting this group would have been to draw a random sample from among all eligible families living in the geographic area covered by the study. However, this would have required locating and listing all such family units—an impossible task for the Heller Committee. Therefore it was necessary to use an alternative and far less satisfactory method of selecting the families to be interviewed. A list of San Francisco Bay area[10] firms was obtained from a large employers' organization whose membership included companies in most of the major industries found in the area. From this list a 10 per cent random sample was drawn. A few firms in this sample were dropped because they were very small and would have yielded few persons eligible for the study; substitutions were made from among firms which had not fallen into the original sample. The names of sixty-nine companies were obtained from this source, forty-seven in San Francisco and twenty-two in the East Bay area, representing manufacturing, wholesale and retail trade, finance and insurance, and service industries. Originally it had been planned to ask all sixty-nine companies for lists of employees who appeared to be eligible for the study. However, it soon became evident that it would be impossible for the chairman to visit every firm, and therefore seventeen companies, chosen to include diverse industries, were visited. Nine of these coöperated by providing lists of 165 presumably eligible persons. The firms that did not assist gave no specific reasons for their actions, and telephone calls and letters brought no results.

Since it was necessary to find some other method of adding to the lists of eligible persons, eleven additional firms were chosen after consultation with various members of the business community. In most instances the firms selected in this second group were substitutions for firms of the same type in the original sample. However, though no public utility was drawn in the original sample, one such establishment was added since utilities employ large numbers of salaried workers, and it was hoped that a considerable number of eligible persons could be found in this way. Eight of the second group of firms coöperated, providing the names of 150 persons presumably meeting the eligibility requirements. Thus a total of 315 names was obtained from seventeen Bay area companies.

---

[10] The "Bay area" for this listing of firms was limited to San Francisco, San Mateo County south to and including South San Francisco, Oakland, Alameda, Emeryville, Piedmont, Berkeley, Albany, El Cerrito, and Richmond. The firms in the final sample were all situated in San Francisco, Oakland, Emeryville, or Berkeley.

Since professional services and public administration did not have membership in the employers' organization, it was necessary to secure lists
from other sources of persons employed in these fields. It would, of course,
have been desirable to include all types of professional services; however,
lists were most easily available from the educational services, and therefore this classification was selected as the chief source for supplementing
the original group of industries. A 12 per cent sample of all faculty members who were thought to be eligible at the University of California, Berkeley, plus a sample of teachers and administrators in the San Francisco and
Oakland school systems, yielded a total of 51 persons. (Professional services were also represented by the 6 eligible employees of one law firm and
one architect's office.) Public administration was represented by a list of 5
persons who were presumably eligible, all of whom worked for one department of the federal government.

Of the original sample of 371 presumably eligible families, only 222 were
found to be actually eligible. This group of 222 yielded 159 usable schedules;
2 families could not give sufficiently accurate information, and 61 refused
to coöperate, resulting in a refusal rate of 27.5 per cent of the eligible families. This is a high rate compared to the experience of other income sur-
veys, in which 15 per cent appears normal for all families regardless of
income.[11] The refusal rate in the Heller Committee study was probably
high because of the economic group being studied. Families higher in the
economic scale are generally less willing to give income and expenditure
information than are those with lower incomes.[12]

It is not entirely clear what effect the refusals may have had on the
results of this study. In order to throw some light on this problem, those
who refused were asked to give certain information concerning income, the
employment status of family members, home tenure, size of family, and
the age and occupation of the head. In most cases this information was
secured, but a few families refused to reveal anything.

Although the incomes reported by families that refused were considerably lower than those of the families studied, this cannot be given too much
weight in analyzing the effect of the refusals. Experience shows that all
families tend to underestimate their income in studies of this kind, but it
is believed that there was probably a greater degree of underestimation of
income among families who refused than among those who coöperated in

---

[11]U.S. Department of Labor, Bureau of Labor Statistics, Family Spending and Saving in Wartime, Bulletin 822, Washington D.C., 1945, p. 22.

[12]In its 1941-1942 study the B.L.S. found that "The refusal rates rise
from 1 per cent at the under $500 level to 17 per cent at the $5,000 to
$10,000 level, and to 35 per cent at the over $10,000 level." Ibid., pp. 23-24.

this survey. Families unwilling to coöperate could be asked only to give total income, and could not be asked for details of the amounts and sources of such income—a procedure essential for obtaining reasonably accurate total income figures. It is also possible that, although income before taxes was requested, some may have estimated their incomes on the basis of monthly salaries after tax deductions. However, there is one piece of evidence which does suggest that the income data in this study may have been affected by the refusals. Of the 56 refusals for which employment information was available, there were 7 families in which 2 persons were employed full time, in contrast to only 1 such family in the group from whom schedules were obtained. It is possible that families with 2 full-time workers may have been underrepresented in the final sample, and the 7 families of this type who refused may have exerted some downward bias on the study's income data.

The refusal rate was 19 per cent among families in which the heads were employed in professional or technical occupations, and between 30 and 40 per cent in the managerial, clerical, and sales groups. Since the incomes of the occupational groups included in this study did not differ greatly, the variations in their refusal rates probably did not significantly bias the sample.

The remaining information secured from those who refused indicated no significant differences between this group and the families interviewed. About three-quarters of both the refusals and those who coöperated were home owners. Since home ownership is an indication of the economic status of families, the fact that the refusals contained about the same proportions of renters and owners as were found in the final sample is at least some indication that the economic status of the two groups was similar.

The other items obtained from those who refused which might have affected income and expenditure patterns in the study were family size and the age of the head of the family. With respect to these two characteristics there were no significant differences between the refusals and the final sample. In both, the average size of the family was 4; the average age of the husbands was forty-two among the refusals, and forty in the group which coöperated.

As stated earlier, the families whose incomes and expenditures were analyzed in this study were not a random sample of all families within the specified income and occupational groups in the Bay area. It therefore cannot be safely assumed that the families studied represented the universe of families with similar incomes and occupations. It may, however, be possible to arrive at some rough estimates as to whether or not the families studied may be representative of other families with similar incomes and occupations.

Although the industries included in this study did not represent all industries in the community, it does not seem probable that this would have a serious biasing effect on the results. It is not likely that the spending habits of a chief clerk or bookkeeper would be affected by whether he is employed by an insurance company or by a manufacturing concern making steel or shoes. It is, of course, possible that the fact that 27.5 per cent of the eligible families refused to coöperate may have biased the results as shown by the responses of the 72.5 per cent from whom income and expenditure data were obtained. The available evidence from the nonresponders did not, however, indicate any marked differences between those who refused and those who coöperated. In this, as in other studies where coöperation is not compulsory, it is impossible to measure the degree to which nonresponse may have affected the results. In the analysis which follows, generalizations are limited to inference about a hypothetical population of families which might have been expected to respond in a larger population from which we may have a random sample.

The method used to estimate the degree to which the sample of families studied may represent other families in the same income and occupational groups in this area was suggested by Jerzy Neyman, and the following analysis is based on a memorandum from Professor Neyman. In general, this analysis seems to suggest that the expenditure patterns of the families studied may quite closely represent the expenditure patterns of other families of salaried workers in the Bay area with incomes in the neighborhood of $6,000 who might have responded in a larger study. These specific procedures and results will be described in the following paragraphs.

In order to determine whether there were large differences in the expenditure patterns within the group of 159 families, the sample was divided into five groups according to the industries in which the breadwinners were employed.[13] The size of these groups varied from 26 to 39 families. The expenditures of each of these five groups for four major items were analyzed—food, clothing, transportation, and housing, which together accounted for nearly two-thirds of all consumption expenditures.

A priori it might be expected that within any group of families there will be a considerable variation in patterns of expenditure, and that the two most

---

[13]Many bases for choosing the groups were possible. The grouping in accordance with industry was used to determine whether or not employment in a particular industry affected seriously the pattern of expenditure. If large differences in the patterns of expenditure had been found, this would have been an indication against generalizing from the figures obtained from a few nonrandomly selected industries to the population of employees at large. The actual findings appear to be favorable to such generalizations. The industry groups are G_1 Food; G_2 Insurance; G_3 Educational and Professional; G_4 Manufacturing, G_5 Transportation, Utilities, and Miscellaneous.

TABLE 1

Average Actual and Estimated Expenditures of Families in Five Industry Groups

Industry group number[a]	Income after taxes	Family size	Items of expenditure							
			Clothing		Food		Housing		Transportation	
			Actual	Estimated	Actual	Estimated	Actual	Estimated	Actual	Estimated
G_1 39	$6,041	3.92	$626	$632	$1,612	$1,617	$654	$654	$1,100	$1,102
G_2 26	5,887	3.92	615	652	1,548	1,572	645	653	1,009	1,015
G_3 36	6,486	4.22	571	529	1,540	1,444	747	655	911	961
G_4 32	5,982	3.53	620	615	1,616	1,625	819	779	727	718
G_5 26	5,868	4.27	702	739	1,833	1,809	680	744	834	862
$G_1 + G_2 + G_4$ 97	5,980	3.79			1,596	1,610				
$G_3 + G_5$ 62	6,227	4.24			1,663	1,600				
Average all groups	6,077	3.97	623		1,622		711		924	

[a]G_1 Food; G_2 Insurance; G_3 Educational and Professional; G_4 Manufacturing; G_5 Transportation, Utilities, and Miscellaneous.

important influences upon expenditures would be income and size of family. The analysis which follows will attempt to answer the question: Given a family with an income equal to the average of all groups combined, and of a family size equal to the average of the total sample, what is the estimated average family expenditure in each group for each of the items studied—food, clothing, housing, transportation. (See table 1.)

The first step in this analysis was to compute partial regression coefficients of each item of expenditure on total income and on total members of the family, labeled "Family Size" (table 2).

The next step was to compute estimates of expenditures for food, clothing, housing, and transportation for each of the five groups using the regression coefficients from table 2 to correct the differences in income and family size. The estimated expenditures shown on table 2 are therefore based on an assumed income of $6,077, the average income of all five groups combined, and on a fixed family size of 3.97.

Table 1 shows that the estimated expenditures for each category of expenditure by the five groups, holding income and family size constant, varied substantially and sometimes quite substantially. This suggests the possibility that the pattern of expenditure in different industry groups was not the same. Unfortunately, the lack of normality in the distribution of expenditures does not permit too much faith to be placed in the application of classical tests. Nevertheless, such tests were performed.[14] There appeared to be no sign of a significant differentiation among the five groups in the general level of their expenditures for the categories of food, clothing, housing, and transportation, with income and family size held constant.

Table 2 shows the effect of income and family size on expenditures for each of the five groups and for all groups combined. The level of income influenced in a positive direction the expenditures for clothing, 11 per cent; for food, 14 per cent; for housing, 17 per cent; but for this group of families the level of income did not influence the expenditures for transportation. Furthermore, there appeared to be no significant variation among the five groups with respect to changes in expenditure for clothing, housing, and transportation with each $100 addition to income, holding the family size constant. Contrary to this, there appeared to be a highly significant differentiation among the groups in expenditures for food with each $100 addition to income. This suggested a closer analysis of the effect on expenditures of a unit increase in family size. With the possible exception of housing, an additional member of the family had no apparent effect on any of the items of expenditure except food in Groups III and V. It is possible that Groups III and V and Groups I, II, and IV had something in their patterns of life which

---

[14]Standard regression analysis with the application of the F. test.

TABLE 2

Partial Regression Coefficients of Four Categories of Expenditure on Income and Family Size

Industry group number[a]	Clothing		Food		Housing		Transportation	
	Income[b] after taxes (per cent)	Family[c] size (dollars)	Income[b] after taxes (per cent)	Family[c] size (dollars)	Income[b] after taxes (per cent)	Family[c] size (dollars)	Income[b] after taxes (per cent)	Family[c] size (dollars)
G₁ 39	+8.4	$+48.2	+7.9	$+34.7	+3.6	$-40.3	11.3	$-38.4
G₂ 26	-17.2	+83.0	+11.9	+21.9	+4.8	-4.6	13.0	-356.3
G₃ 36	+6.3	+66.1	+16.5	+111.0	+25.4	-47.4	-13.6	+20.8
G₄ 32	+17.1	-48.9	+17.5	-17.8	+30.5	-155.1	+7.1	-35.9
G₅ 26	+9.2	-60.7	+15.6	+190.8	+16.0	-100.0	-6.5	-137.6
G₁ + G₂ + G₄ 97			+11.9 ± 3.4	+14.3 ± 39.6				
G₃ + G₅ 62			+16.1 ± 4.6	+144.2 ± 49.5				
Average all groups	+11.0 ± 2.4	+22.5 ± 26.7	+13.6 ± 2.8	+72.3 ± 30.7	+16.7 ± 3.8	-70.6 ± 42.6	+1.2 ± 7.6	-88.1 ± 84.5

[a] G₁ Food; G₂ Insurance; G₃ Educational and Professional; G₄ Manufacturing; G₅ Transportation, Utilities, and Professional.

[b] The average change in per cent spent which accompanies each $100 addition to income.

[c] The average dollar change in expenditure which accompanies each unit increase in family size.

made their food expenditures react differently to differences in family size. It is impossible to say whether differences of this sort might exist among various segments of any population group.

The regression coefficients of housing expenditures on family size show that there were differences among the five industrial groups. However, the test does not indicate that these differences were significant, and the regression coefficient on family size is less than twice the standard error. These negative results do not, however, insure that family size actually had no effect on housing expenditures. The consistently negative signs of these regression coefficients appear to indicate that on the average an additional member of the family meant a lesser expenditure on housing. It must be recognized, however, that the conclusion must not be drawn that the negative regression coefficients indicate that a negative relation exists between family size and housing expenditures. An analysis of the housing expenditures of renters and owners shows that the housing costs of renters increased with family size whereas the opposite was true of owners. Since nearly 70 per cent of the families studied were owners, the result was that housing costs for the entire group decreased with family size. Further analysis of the housing costs of owners indicates that the reason the larger families had lower costs was that their interest payments were lower, because they usually lived in older houses which had been purchased for smaller sums. The tax payments of the larger families were also lower. Whether or not these lower expenditures were also related to family size or to other factors it is impossible to say.

It is important to recognize that within any group of families there will always be considerable variation in patterns of expenditure. For example, some families will prefer to spend more generously on food and live in relatively inexpensive housing; others may choose to economize on food and spend more on housing. The expenditures of some families may also be affected in one way and some in another by income or size of family. There are, of course, innumerable possibilities as to the final effects of the choices by various strata within any group of families on over-all expenditure patterns. It is possible that there was more variation among the several strata of families included in the total of 159 in this study than would be expected if the sample had been selected in a truly random fashion. The fact, however, that in many respects the expenditures of the five groups varied within reasonable limits, at least suggests that the total group may quite closely represent the expenditure patterns of a larger sample drawn in accordance with the principles of random selection.

Chapter II

SUMMARY

TOTAL RECEIPTS AND DISBURSEMENTS

The families in this study reported average total receipts of $9,992. This sum included money income before taxes which averaged $6,637, other money receipts or "windfall" money (such as inheritances and large gifts) of $324, and $3,031 in money made available by withdrawing previously accumulated assets or increasing obligations of various kinds.

Total disbursements averaged $10,202; of this sum $5,957 was spent for current consumption, and $1,271 for nonconsumption expenditures (personal insurance, gifts and contributions, and taxes). Disbursements also included $2,974 which was either added to assets or used to decrease obligations of various kinds. Almost all families reported some surpluses and some deficits. Nearly half had an average net surplus at the end of the year of $1,069, whereas just over half reported a net deficit which averaged $1,127. (One family had neither a net surplus or net deficit.) For the families as a whole, total deficits were in large part canceled by total surpluses, and thus the average net deficit for the entire group of families was the very small sum of $57.

MONEY INCOME

These families had an average money income before taxes of $6,637. The lowest family income before taxes was $4,917, the highest was $9,304, and the median was $6,588. Clearly these families belonged to an upper income group in the population, since the U.S. Census reported that in 1949 only 33 per cent of the families in the San Francisco-Oakland urbanized area had incomes of $5,000 or more, and the median income of all families was $3,958.[1]

---

[1]U.S. Bureau of the Census, U.S. Census of Population: 1950. Vol. II, Characteristics of the Population, Part 5, California, Chapter B, p. 128. U.S. Government Printing Office, Washington, D.C., 1952.

TABLE 3

Average Receipts and Disbursements

All Families

Total receipts	$9,991.98		Total disbursements	$10,202.32
Money income before			Total expenditures	7,227.88
taxes	6,637.10		Consumption	5,957.25
Other money receipts	323.90		Nonconsumption	1,270.63
Decrease in assets and/or			Increase in assets and/or	
increase in liabilities . . .	3,030.98		decrease in liabilities . . .	2,974.44

Balancing Difference -$210.34

Families with Incomes Under $6,000

Total receipts	$8,668.03		Total disbursements	$ 8,888.80
Money income before			Total expenditures	6,512.69
taxes	5,788.20		Consumption	5,424.23
Other money receipts	315.80		Nonconsumption	1,088.46
Decrease in assets and/or			Increase in assets and/or	
increase in liabilities . . .	2,564.03		decrease in liabilities . . .	2,376.11

Balancing Difference -$220.77

Families with Incomes $6,000 and Over

Total receipts	$11,204.25		Total disbursements	$11,405.07
Money income before			Total expenditures	7,882.76
taxes	7,414.40		Consumption	6,445.32
Other money receipts	331.31		Nonconsumption	1,437.44
Decrease in assets and/or			Increase in assets and/or	
increase in liabilities . .	3,458.54		decrease in liabilities . . .	3,522.31

Balancing Difference -$200.82

Ninety-one per cent of the income before taxes of these families came
from the earnings of the head of the family; although most families had
some other sources of income, the average additional sum was only $592.
When income taxes were deducted, the average spendable income from
regular sources was $6,077, and nearly three-quarters of the families had
incomes between $5,000 and $7,000.

EXPENDITURES FOR CURRENT CONSUMPTION

These families reported average total expenditures of $7,228, of which
$5,957, or 82 per cent, was for consumption items. The sums spent for
the various consumption categories varied widely: in order of size the
largest was of course food, which was followed by transportation, housing,
and clothing. These four categories combined accounted for 65 per cent of
all consumption expenditures. Families spent between $350 and approxi-
mately $450 for house operation, housefurnishings, medical care, and

TABLE 4

Summary of Income and Expenditures, All Families

Categories of consumption	Average expenditures	Total expenditures (per cent)	Consumption expenditures (per cent)
Total expenditures................	$7,227.88	100.0	....
Current consumption expenditures, total...	5,957.25	82.4	100.0
Food.................................	1,622.28	22.4	27.2
Alcoholic beverages	90.66	1.3	1.5
Housing	711.21	9.8	11.9
House operation, total	459.09	6.4	7.7
Fuel, light, refrigeration, water	135.41	1.9	2.3
Miscellaneous.....................	323.68	4.5	5.4
Housefurnishings and equipment, total..	444.85	6.2	7.5
Household textiles	49.69	.7	.8
Furniture........................	115.38	1.6	1.9
Floor covering	57.40	.8	1.0
Kitchen, cleaning, and laundry equipment......................	145.72	2.0	2.4
All other........................	76.66	1.1	1.3
Clothing, total	622.98	8.6	10.5
Purchase, total...................	548.70	7.6	9.2
Women and girls	295.48	4.1	5.0
Men and boys	243.09	3.4	4.1
Children under 2................	10.14	.1	.2
Services, total	74.27	1.0	1.2
Transportation, total	923.52	12.8	15.5
Automobile.......................	822.04	11.4	13.8
Other	101.48	1.4	1.7
Medical care........................	374.63	5.2	6.3
Personal care	110.57	1.5	1.9
Recreation	355.35	4.9	6.0
Tobacco............................	57.30	.8	1.0
Reading	48.63	.7	.8
Education ....\.................	65.62	.9	1.1
Miscellaneous......................	70.56	1.0	1.2
Nonconsumption expenditures, total.......	1,270.63	17.6	....
Insurance and retirement	533.27	7.4	....
Gifts and contributions	176.79	2.4	....
Personal taxes	560.57	7.8	....

Money income after taxes............................	$6,076.53
Other money receipts	323.90
Net decrease in assets and/or increase in liabilities.....	56.54
Balancing difference	-210.34
Total families in sample	159
Average family size..................................	3.9

recreation, and a little more than $100 for personal care. For no other current consumption category was the average expenditure as much as $100.

Food and alcoholic beverages.—The average expenditure for food was $1,622, or 27.2 per cent of the amount spent for all current consumption items. Sixty-two per cent of the families spent between $1,500 and $2,686; 82 per cent spent from one-fifth to 35 per cent of their total consumption expenditures for food; and about one-eighth spent 35 to 43 per cent. Families with incomes over $6,000 spent more money for food than did those in the lower income brackets, but the two income groups spent almost the same proportion of their total consumption expenditures for food: 27.8 per cent and 26.8 per cent respectively.

Eighty-nine per cent of the families bought some beer, wine, or liquor. The average expense for the entire group of families was $91 or 1.5 per cent of total consumption expenditures. The average sums spent by families in both the income group under $6,000 and the higher bracket were very similar: $97 and $106 respectively.

Transportation.—Second in order of size were transportation expenditures, which averaged $924, or 15.5 per cent of total consumption expenditures. Since all but 8 of these families owned cars, it is not surprising to find that $822 of the $924 was spent for automobile transportation. Unlike the situation in most categories of expenditure, the families with incomes less than $6,000 not only spent more money on total transportation than did the higher income group, but these expenses represented a larger proportion of all their current consumption expenditures: 17.8 in contrast with 13.7 per cent. Since both income groups spent almost identical sums for nonautomobile transportation, the difference in their total expenditures came solely from their car expenses and reflected the greater necessity of replacing old cars, which the lower income families faced in 1950.

Over-all automobile costs were, of course, higher for those who purchased cars; 27 per cent of the families spent a thousand dollars or more for automobile transportation, and most of this group bought cars in 1950. All families spent an average of $458 for car purchase and $364 for operation and upkeep.[2] For those who actually bought cars, the average cost was $1,323 after the trade-in allowance. Fifty-two per cent of these cars were purchased new, and the average expenditure for new cars was $1,839 whereas used cars cost the buyers an average of $720. Forty-seven per cent of the families who bought cars paid cash for them; another 22 per cent made these purchases on installment; and 31 per cent borrowed money which was probably used to buy a car.[3] Only 44 per cent of the buyers with incomes of $6,000 or more used any credit in making car purchases, in contrast with 59 per cent of those in the lower income group.

In the main these were one-car families, and most of the automobiles they owned were in the low or moderate priced classes. The average price before trade-in of all the cars purchased in 1950 was $1,660, including any

---

[2] Automobile expenditures are those made for nonbusiness use of car. Operation, upkeep, and purchase costs as given have been adjusted to exclude business use of car by 4 families.

[3] See fn. 3, p. 164.

financing charge and all extras bought at the time of purchase; the average price of new cars was $2,347, and second-hand cars $922.

Clearly the families in this study used automobiles as their chief mode of transportation, since they spent an average of only $101 for all other transportation. Only 3 families spent more than $300, and these expenses were largely for vacation travel.

Housing.—Housing expenditures average $711 per family, which was 11.9 per cent of total consumption expenditures. Of this sum $676 was spent for the family home, and the remainder chiefly for vacation housing. Families with incomes under $6,000 spent $582 for all their housing, whereas those in the higher income brackets spent $829. These expenditures for the two income groups represented 10.7 and 12.9 per cent, respectively, of their total consumption expenditures.

Sixty-nine per cent of the families lived in owned homes, and not quite one-quarter lived in rented homes, during all of 1950.[4] The owners usually lived in 5- to 7-room houses, and the renters in 4- or 5-room houses or apartments; the full-year owners' average cash expenditure[5] for the family home was $568, whereas the renters spent $774. However, if the net value of occupancy (N.V.O., the difference between the estimated rental value of an owned home and the actual cash expense for that home) had been added to the cash outlay, the family home would have cost the full-year owners an average of $1,338.

Clothing.—Clothing expenditures were very moderate; the average family expense for clothing and clothing services combined was $623, or 10.5 per cent of the average of all expenditures for current consumption. Families with incomes less than $6,000 spent an average of $542, or 10 per cent of all consumption expenditures, whereas the higher income group spent $697, which was 10.8 per cent of their consumption expenses.

Clothing purchases averaged $549 per family. Wives spent an average of $194; their husbands spent $162; boys more than two years $89; girls in the same age bracket $117; and the average cost of infants' clothing was $47. In general the higher-income families spent more for clothing purchases than those in the lower income group. Clothing upkeep and repair cost an average of $74 per family, and expenditures for these services varied little with income.

Household operation.—The average expenditure for all household operation was $459, or 7.7 per cent of total consumption expenditures. Families

---

[4]Thirteen families lived part of the year in an owned home and were renters for the rest of the year.

[5]Excluding down payments on homes bought in 1950, principal payments on mortgages, special assessments, and the cost of home improvements.

with incomes less than $6,000 spent an average of $391, which was 7.2 per cent of consumption expenses, whereas those with higher incomes spent $521, or 8.1 per cent. Since fuel, light, refrigeration, and water took very similar amounts from both income groups, the difference in their expenditures is largely attributable to all other expenses for house operation.

Fuel, light, refrigeration, and water accounted for 30 per cent of all household operation expenses and cost all families an average of $135; of this amount, gas took 40 per cent, electricity one-third, and water nearly one-quarter. The main factor governing the size of expenditures for gas and electricity appeared to be the size of the dwelling units.

Among the innumerable other household expenses, the largest were for telephone and telegraph service and for wages, which averaged about $70 each and together accounted for 43 per cent of these miscellaneous household operation costs. Laundry sent out, plus laundry and cleaning supplies, accounted for almost another quarter of these costs. For all household operation except fuel, light, refrigeration, and water, all families spent an average of $324; families with incomes below $6,000 spent $262, whereas the higher income brackets spent $380.

Housefurnishings.—Expenditures for housefurnishings represented 7.5 per cent of the average cost of all current consumption items. The average cash outlay was $445; families with incomes less than $6,000 spent $385, and the higher income families spent $500. For the lower group this represented 7.1 per cent of all consumption expenditures; for the upper bracket it was 7.8 per cent.

Since the size and nature of housefurnishings purchases varied so widely, it is impossible to describe the typical family expenditure pattern. Full-year home owners spent an average of $397, whereas those who rented all year spent $395; however, the 13 families that were both renters and owners during the year spent $984.

Kitchen, cleaning, and laundry equipment accounted for one-third of the total cost of housefurnishings; furniture took just over one-fourth of the money, and floor coverings and textiles together represented almost another fourth of the housefurnishings dollar.

The majority of families bought their housefurnishings for cash, but 29 per cent of the sample reported purchasing some furnishings on installment —26 families purchased one item, and 20 bought two or more items with this type of credit. The 2 families with the largest installment expenditures became home owners during the study year.

Medical and dental care.—Medical and dental care cost the families in this study an average of $375, or 6.3 per cent of all their consumption expenditures. Of the total, $270 went for medical care, and dentistry took $101. There was no consistent relationship between the size of the bills for total health care and family income; although families with incomes of less than $6,000 spent an average of $339, and those with higher incomes spent $407, large and small bills appeared in both income groups. The proportions of total consumption expenditures were virtually identical in the two groups (6.2 and 6.3 per cent).

An average of $199 was spent by all families for all medical care except the cost of prepayment plans. Fifty-five per cent of this amount went for physicians' bills; drugs and medicines accounted for another 26 per cent; laboratory tests and X rays took 7 per cent; and eye care 6 per cent of the total. Ninety-four per cent of the individuals in the study reported receiving some kind of medical care, at an average cost of $54. The average cost for those persons whose expenses could be allocated to family members was $66. The expenditures of the family heads averaged $46; their wives spent $124; and the children under 18 years, $45.

Ninety-three per cent of the families reported that at least 1 family member belonged to some kind of a prepaid medical care plan during 1950, and more than three-quarters of the memberships covered the entire family for a full year. There was little difference in the proportions of husbands, wives, and children who were members of prepayment plans, but memberships were somewhat more frequent among the husbands.

The average premium paid for prepayment plans by all families in the study was $74, which represented slightly more than one-fourth of the average total medical care expenditure. The average cost of full-year family coverage for those families reporting such coverage was $77. Almost three-quarters of the families who reported full-year coverage belonged to plans which provided hospital, surgical, and medical care; 24 per cent had plans which gave hospital and surgical care; and 2 per cent belonged to plans providing only hospital care. However, within each of these three broad types of coverage, the extent of care provided by the various policies varied considerably.

Of the total of 412 individuals who reported receiving some medical care and who were full-year members of a prepayment plan, 159 or 39 per cent received some service from their prepayment plans. Those who used their prepayment plans when hospitalized received substantial assistance in paying their hospital bills, and a large majority of the prepayment plan members who received services from their plans for nonhospitalized illnesses had relatively small bills. However, there were some prepayment plan members who had high hospital or nonhospital bills in addition to what was paid by the prepayment plans.

Ten families had no expenditures for dental care in 1950. The average family expenditure for dentistry for the entire sample was $101. Families with incomes under $6,000 spent an average of $86, whereas those in the higher brackets spent $116, but there were both large and small bills at every income level. The average cost of dentistry for all individuals in the sample was $26. Dental service was reported by 65 per cent of the husbands, 77 per cent of the wives, 79 per cent of the children six to seventeen, and by slightly more than one-fourth of the children under six. The average dental cost for those individuals who received care was $40; the wives spent $6 more than this, and the average for children under six was $18.

Recreation.—Every family spent something for recreation, and the average outlay was $355, or 6 per cent of all consumption expenditures. Those families with incomes below $6,000 spent considerably less than the higher income brackets—$290 in contrast with $415. The proportions of total consumption expenditures were also relatively far apart: 5.3 and 6.4 per cent, respectively.

The largest expenditures were for the purchase and repair of television sets, radios, and musical instruments, which as a group absorbed 43 per cent of the average recreation expenditure for all families in the sample. Those who reported expenditures in this category spent an average of $240 per family, and almost half of all the money spent went for television sets. The only recreation items bought on installment were in this category. Installment credit was used in the purchase of 38 per cent of the television sets and 42 per cent of the radio phonographs, as well as to buy three of the seven pianos, an organ, and an accordian.

The money spent for all other types of recreation purchased a wide variety of items. The average expenditures for any of these categories were never large—ranging from $13 to $42—and the vast majority of purchases in any category were less than $50.

Personal care.—All families reported expenditures for personal care, and they spent an average of $111, almost equally divided between services and supplies. Expenditures did not vary consistently with income, and in families with incomes either under or over $6,000, the per capita expenditure was $28. The lower income families spent 2 per cent of all current consumption expenditures for personal care, whereas the upper bracket spent 1.8 per cent.

Two families managed to spend nothing for personal services by having home haircuts, shampoos, etc. The average expenditure for these services among the other 157 families was $55. Husbands spent 45 per cent of all the money going for services, with an average expenditure of $25. Wives accounted for slightly less than one-third of the total spent, and the average for those spending was $20. Services for the children averaged $12 a family among all families and $16 for those families that reported expenditures. Seventy-two per cent of all the boys spent something for personal services,

TABLE 5

Number of Families Reporting Expenditures and Proportion of Total Consumption Expenditures Allocated to Each Category of Consumption

Categories of consumption	Total families reporting expenditures		Proportion of total consumption expenditures													
			Total		Under 5 per cent				5 to 9.9		10 to 14.9		15 to 29.92		30 and over	
					Under 2.5		2.5 to 4.9									
	Number	Per cent	Number	Per cent	Number	Per cent	Number	Per cent	Number	Per cent	Number	Per cent	Number	Per cent	Number	Per cent
Food...........	159	100.0	0	.0	0	.0	0	.0	0	.0	1	.6	102	64.2	56	35.2
Alcohol.........	142	100.0	133	93.7	107	75.4	26	18.3	8	5.6	1	.7	0	.0	0	.0
Housing.........	159	100.0	15	9.4	2	1.3	13	8.2	60	37.7	38	23.9	43	27.0	3	1.9
Housing operation																
Total.........	159	100.0	24	15.1	0	.0	24	15.1	109	68.6	17	10.7	9	5.7	0	.0
Utilities......	157	100.0	157	100.0	87	55.7	70	44.3	0	.0	0	.0	0	.0	0	.0
Other.........	159	100.0	84	52.8	14	8.8	70	44.0	61	38.4	12	7.5	2	1.3	0	.0
House furnishings.	159	100.0	71	44.7	36	22.6	35	22.0	49	30.8	26	16.4	12	7.6	1	.6
Clothing																
Total.........	159	100.0	11	6.9	1	.6	10	6.3	61	38.4	72	45.3	15	9.5	0	.0
Purchase......	159	100.0	18	11.3	4	2.5	14	8.8	76	47.8	56	35.2	9	5.6	0	.0
Upkeep........	159	100.0	159	100.0	152	95.6	7	4.4	0	.0	0	.0	0	.0	0	.0
Transportation																
Total.........	159	100.0	16	10.1	2	1.3	14	8.8	57	35.8	39	24.5	24	15.1	23	14.5
Auto.........	151	100.0	22	14.5	0	.0	22	14.5	64	42.4	20	13.2	27	17.8	18	12.0
Other........	148	100.0	145	98.0	104	70.9	41	27.0	1	.7	2	1.4	0	.0	0	.0
Medical care																
Total.........	159	100.0	66	41.5	15	9.4	51	32.1	78	49.1	11	6.9	3	1.9	1	.6
Medical.......	158[a]	100.0[a]	110	69.6	39	24.7	71	44.9	39	24.7	6	3.8	2	1.3	1	.6
Dental........	147[a]	100.0[a]	135	91.8	111	75.5	24	16.3	11	7.5	1	.7	0	.0	0	.0
Personal care....	159	100.0	158	99.4	128	80.5	30	18.9	1	.6	0	.0	0	.0	0	.0
Recreation......	159	100.0	90	56.6	34	21.4	56	35.2	46	28.9	14	8.8	7	4.4	2	1.2
Tobacco........	114	100.0	114	100.0	99	86.8	15	13.1	0	.0	0	.0	0	.0	0	.0
Reading........	159	100.0	159	100.0	156	98.1	3	1.9	0	.0	0	.0	0	.0	0	.0
Education.......	118	100.0	110	93.2	103	87.3	7	5.9	8	6.8	0	.0	0	.0	0	.0
Miscellaneous....	147	100.0	137	93.2	126	85.7	11	7.5	9	6.1	1	.7	0	.0	0	.0

[a] In one schedule where total medical care was 7.4 per cent of all consumption expenditures, the distribution between medical and dental care was unknown. Therefore, the percentage distribution of families with expenditures by per cent of consumption expense is based upon 147 for dental care and 158 for medical care (number spending less one).

at an average cost of $13. Only 41 per cent of the girls had any expenditures, and their average expense was $6.

Every family bought some personal care supplies, spending an average of $56. In contrast to the situation in personal services, it seems likely that more of the supplies dollar was allocated to the women than to the men.

Education, reading, tobacco, and miscellaneous expenditures.—The average expenditure of all families for each of these categories amounted to 1.2 per cent or less of the average cost of all consumption items.

About three-quarters of the sample had some expense for education, and these expenses averaged $66 for all families, and $88 for those with expenses. Such expenses were generally for tuition, or for music, dancing, or other private lessons.

Every family spent something for reading material; the average was $49, and most families spent only enough to have a daily paper, one or two magazine subscriptions, and perhaps an occasional book.

Seventy-two per cent of the families bought tobacco, at an average cost of $57 for all families, and $80 for those who reported purchases.

Among the miscellaneous expenses, the most numerous or largest were for real estate other than occupied homes, interest on loans, bank service charges, and safe deposit box rental. For the combined items in this heterogeneous category the average expense for all families was $71; those families who actually had expenses reported an average of $76.

NONCONSUMPTION EXPENDITURES

In addition to current consumption expenditures, all families reported outlays for personal insurance, gifts and contributions, and personal taxes. The combined average expenditure for these items was $1,271, or 18 per cent of their total expenditures. Forty-two per cent of these nonconsumption expenditures went for personal insurance, 14 per cent for gifts and contributions, and 44 per cent for taxes.

The average cost of personal insurance was $533, or 7.4 per cent of the average of all consumption and nonconsumption expenditures. Families with incomes under $6,000 spent 7 per cent of all their expenditures, or $457, and those with higher incomes 7.7 per cent, or $603. Slightly more than half of the average paid for all personal insurance was spent on commercial insurance, which averaged $278 for the entire sample. The remaining insurance payments went to state, federal, or company retirement or disability plans.

The average family expense for gifts and contributions was $177, or 2.4 per cent of the total of all consumption and nonconsumption items. Those with incomes less than $6,000 spent 2.6 per cent of their total expenditures on gifts and contributions whereas the higher income brackets spent 2.3 per

TABLE 6

Comparison of Family Expenditures in the Heller Committee and Bureau of Labor Statistics

(1950 expenditure studies[a])

Categories of consumption	Heller	B.L.S.	Per cent Heller above B.L.S.	Per cent of total expenditures	
				Heller	B.L.S.
Total expenditures	$7,228	$5,228	36.8	100.0	100.0
Current consumption, total	5,957	4,477	33.1	82.4	84.8
Food, housing, clothing, total	3,951	3,052	29.5	54.7	57.8
Food	1,622	1,313	23.5	22.4	24.9
Housing, utilities, household operation and housefurnishings	1,615	1,166	38.5	22.3	22.1
Clothing	623	494	26.1	8.6	9.4
All other consumption expenditures, total	2,007	1,425	40.8	27.8	27.0
Transportation	923	634	45.7	12.8	12.0
Medical care	375	269	39.4	5.2	5.1
Personal care	111	98	13.3	1.5	1.9
Recreation	355	207	71.5	4.9	3.9
Education	66	28	135.7	.9	.5
All other	268	268	....	3.7	5.1
Nonconsumption, total	1,270	805	57.8	17.6	15.2
Personal insurance	533	213	150.2	7.4	4.0
Gifts and contributions	177	156	13.5	2.4	2.9
Personal taxes	560	436	28.7	7.8	8.3

[a]U. S. Department of Labor, Bureau of Labor Statistics, Family Income, Expenditures, and Savings in 1950, Bulletin 1097, Washington, D.C., 1953, p.18.

cent. Church contributions and gifts of cash or goods to persons outside the economic family were the chief expenditures. Support of persons outside the economic family also took relatively large sums from one-quarter of the families who had such responsibilities.

Personal taxes cost this group of families an average of $561, or 7.8 per cent of all consumption and nonconsumption expenditures. Ninety-seven per cent of this expense was for federal income taxes, which averaged $546, in contrast to an average state income tax of $14 for those reporting. Families with incomes under $6,000 paid an average for all taxes of $463, or 7.1 per cent of all their expenditures, whereas the upper bracket families paid $650, which was 8.2 per cent of their total expenditures.

COMPARISON WITH B.L.S. SURVEY OF
CONSUMER EXPENDITURES IN 1950

A great deal has been written about the differences in family expenditure patterns at various income levels. It is possible to present further evidence on this subject by comparing the results of the Heller Committee study with the data for the San Francisco Bay area in the 1950 B.L.S. study of family income and expenditures. The B.L.S. study included all occupational and income groups; it reported an average Bay area income after taxes of $4,584, and an average total family expenditure of $5,282. The selected group of salaried worker families studied by the Heller Committee reported an average income after taxes of $6,077 and average total expenditures of $7,228. In other words, the average Heller Committee family income was 33 per cent above the average B.L.S. family, and the average expenditures were higher by $1,946, or 37 per cent.[6]

The following generalizations have been made concerning the differences which are likely to be found at various income levels in the proportions of total expenditures allocated for various categories of expense. First, the higher the income, the smaller is the proportion spent for food. Second, the higher the income, the larger is the proportion spent for clothing, automobiles, recreation, and education. This is also true for nonconsumption items (personal insurance, gifts and contributions, and personal taxes). Third, the proportion spent for housing (including utilities, furnishings,

---

[6]The average family size in the B.L.S. study was 3.2, and in the Heller Committee study, 3.9. Since it is not possible to estimate the effect of family size on each category of expenditure this factor has been ignored in the following analysis. It should, however, be pointed out that the average per capita total expenditure in the Heller Committee was $1,853 and in the B.L.S. study, $1,651; in other words, the average Heller Committee per capita total expenditure was 12.2 per cent above that reported in the B.L.S. study.

and house operation) tends to be much the same at all income levels, which is also generally the case with both medical and personal care.[7]

In many categories of goods and services the purchases of the Heller Committee families conformed with these generalizations. They allocated 22 per cent of their total expenditures to food, in contrast to the 25 per cent spent by the B.L.S. families. Both groups of families spent 22 per cent of their total costs for housing, utilities, furnishings, and house operation combined, and 5 per cent for medical care. The Heller Committee families, on the other hand, spent a larger proportion of total expenditures than did the B.L.S. families for transportation, recreation, education, and for all nonconsumption items combined.

There were two types of expenditures for which the Heller Committee families spent less than might have been expected—they spent a smaller proportion for clothing and for personal care than did the B.L.S. families. This was somewhat surprising in view of the fact that the Heller Committee families not only had more money to spend, but belonged to an occupational group in which the importance of personal appearance might have led to larger expenditures for these items.

The variation in the expenditure patterns of the Heller Committee and B.L.S. families can be seen even more clearly by comparing the differences in the size of their average expenditures. In every major category the average expenditure of the Heller Committee families was larger than that reported by the B.L.S. families. The average total expenditure in the Heller Committee study was 37 per cent above that reported by B.L.S. If the expenditure patterns of the two groups had been identical, the average Heller Committee family expenditure for each category of goods and services would also have been 37 per cent larger; this, however, was not always true. The Heller Committee families' average expenditure for food was only 24 per cent larger than that of the B.L.S. families. Their average expenditure for the combined category of housing, utilities, household opera-

---

[7]Some of the generalizations regarding patterns of expenditures for various income groups do not always apply to families at the extremes of the income scale. For example, in a 1948 B.L.S. study in Denver, medical care expenditures were a much higher proportion of total expenditures for families with incomes below $3,000 than they were for those with higher incomes, and to a lesser extent this was also true of housing. For families above the $10,000 level, the proportion spent for automobile transportation tended to decline and household operation expenses rose quite sharply. U.S. Bureau of Labor Statistics, Family Income, Expenditures, and Savings in Ten Cities, Bulletin 1065, Washington, D.C., 1952, pp. 18-21. Also see discussion in E.E. Hoyt, M.G. Reid, J.L. McConnell, and J.M. Hooks, American Income and Its Uses, New York: Harper Bros., 1954, p. 217; and H.G. Canoyer and R.S. Vaile. Economics of Income and Consumption, New York: The Ronald Press Co., 1951, pp. 133 ff.

tion, and housefurnishings was larger by 38 per cent—a figure close to the amount by which their total expenditures exceeded B.L.S. —and this was also true of medical expenditures. The average expenditures in the Heller Committee study were larger than those of the B.L.S. families by 46 per cent for transportation, 72 per cent for recreation, 136 per cent for education, and 58 per cent for all nonconsumption items combined. Contrary to expectations, the Heller Committee families spent only 26 per cent more than the B.L.S. families for clothing, and only 13 per cent more for personal care.

Another comparison of these two groups of families can be made by examining their expenditures for two broad categories of consumption items: the first satisfying basic needs and including food, clothing, housing, utilities, household operation, and housefurnishings; and the second made up of all other consumption expenditures. Although the average over-all expenditures of the Heller Committee families were 37 per cent above the B.L.S. figure, their expenditures for basic needs were only 30 per cent higher, whereas for all other consumption items they spent 41 per cent more than the B.L.S. families.

The Heller Committee families spent only 33 per cent more for consumption items as a whole, than did those in the B.L.S. sample. In contrast, the expenditures of the Heller Committee families for all nonconsumption items combined were 58 per cent above the B.L.S. families. The chief factor in this difference was the amount spent for personal insurance. The Heller Committee families apparently valued such protection more than the satisfactions to be obtained from the purchase of certain consumption items, and they spent two and one-half times as much for such insurance as did the B.L.S. families. There were many families in both groups, of course, which were covered by one or more types of compulsory insurance (including O.A.S.I., C.D.I., and employer retirement plans) but the Heller Committee families spent an average of $278 for commercial insurance alone, or more than the average spent for all personal insurance by the B.L.S. families.

Chapter III

FAMILY CHARACTERISTICS
AND INCOME

FAMILY CHARACTERISTICS

The characteristics of the 159 families whose income and expenditure patterns are analyzed in this study are in large measure a reflection of the conditions of eligibility. Family size was affected by the fact that childless families and those in which there was only one parent were excluded. Largely as a result of limiting the families to those in which there was at least 1 child under twenty-one, there were no parents over sixty. The income qualifications excluded very young couples, and the occupations of the chief breadwinners were of major importance in determining the educational level of the husbands and probably also of the wives.

Family size and composition.[1]—In this study the average family size was 3.9, and only 4 per cent of all the families contained 6 or more persons. Although the average number of children per family was 1.9, 1-child families made up almost a third of the total, and 24 per cent had 3 or more children. Most households consisted of the immediate family only—a husband and wife plus 1 or more children—but 9 families also included at least 1 dependent adult relative. All but 1 of the 10 dependent adult relatives were parents of either the head of the family or his wife. The 1 exception was a wife's brother, living with the family while he completed his studies. Clearly, dependent relatives were not an important factor in this group of families.

Age of family members.—The average age of the husbands was forty, and their wives were three years younger. Seventy-two per cent of the husbands and 79 per cent of the wives were between thirty and forty-five. Only 3 per cent of the husbands and 9 per cent of the wives were less than thirty, and

---

[1]Family or household as used in this study refers to a group of persons living together and drawing from a common or pooled fund for all their major expenses.

TABLE 7

Family Composition and Average Family Size

	Number of families	Per cent of all families
All families	159	100.0

Size of family[a]		
3 persons	46	28.9
4 persons	71	44.7
5 persons	36	22.6
6 persons	5	3.1
7 persons	1	.6

Number of children[a]		
1 child ··················	51	32.1
2 children	70	44.0
3 children	33	20.8
4 children	4	2.5
5 children	1	.6

Number of dependent relatives[a]		
No dependent relatives	150	94.3
1 relative	8	5.0
2 relatives................	1	.6

Average family size and number of children per family[b]	Mean	Median
Family size...............	4.0	4.0
Children per family........	2.0	2.0

[a]Persons in family at any time of the year.
[b]Averages are based on the number of persons who were members of the economic
family at any time during the year. In terms of full-year equivalent persons (fifty-two
weeks of family membership equivalent to 1 person, twenty-six weeks equivalent to .5
person, etc.) the mean family size was 3.9, and the mean children per family, 1.9. The
medians are the same, both for persons present at any time and for full-year equivalents.
(See table 18 in the chapter on food for the distribution of families by full-year equivalents.)

the number over fifty were about these same proportions in reverse.   No
husbands or wives were more than sixty.

A majority of the children were of preschool or primary school age. The
average age of the entire group of 311 was eight; just over one-third were
under five and another third between five and nine. Thus a large proportion
of the families had children of an age which did not allow the mother a great
deal of freedom for activities outside the home. All but 2 of the adult dependents were at least sixty-five years of age.

Country of birth and race.—All families were of the white race, and 87
per cent of the husbands and 96 per cent of the wives were born in continen-
tal United States. Eight per cent of the husbands and wives were born out-

TABLE 8

Age of Family Members

Age and sex of parents

Age of parents[a]	Parents		Male		Female	
	Number	Per cent	Number	Per cent	Number	Per cent
All parents	318	100.0	159	100.0	159	100.0
Under 30	20	6.3	5	3.1	15	9.4
30 to 34	77	24.2	35	22.0	42	26.4
35 to 39	101	31.8	47	29.6	54	34.0
40 to 44	62	19.5	32	20.1	30	18.9
45 to 49	37	11.6	22	13.8	15	9.4
50 to 59	21	6.6	18	11.3	3	1.9

Age of other family members[a]

Age of children and dependents[a]	Number	Per cent
All children	311	100.0
Under 5	106	34.1
5 to 9	105	33.8
10 to 14	55	17.7
15 to 19	35	11.3
20 to 24	10	3.2
All dependent relatives	10	100.0
35 to 64	2	20.0
65 and over	8	80.0

Average ages and ranges

Family members	Mean	Median	Range
All parents	38.3	37	24 to 58
Male	39.7	39	27 to 58
Female	36.8	36	24 to 52
All children	7.6	7	1 month to 24
All dependent relatives	67.0	67.5	35 to 88

[a]Including both full- and part-year members.

TABLE 9

Occupations of Heads of Families

Occupation	Number	Per cent
All family heads	159	100.0
Professional, technical, and kindred	82	51.6
Accountants and auditors	13	8.2
Engineers.............................	12	7.5
Teachers and school administrators	28	17.6
All other	29	18.2
Managers, officials, proprietors	46	28.9
Clerical and kindred workers	25	15.7
Sales workers	6	3.8

side the United States: about 5 per cent in Europe (almost entirely in the northwestern countries), 2 per cent in Canada, and 3 parents in Hawaii, the Philippine Islands, or China. No attempt was made to confine the sample to white and primarily native born, but the eligibility requirements for both occupations and incomes tended to exclude the nonwhite and foreign-born populations.

Occupation of the head of the family. — The eligibility requirements concerning general occupational classes and income limits determined the kinds of jobs in which the chief breadwinners were employed. By definition they were always salaried workers, either in professional or technical jobs or in various office occupations involving a considerable degree of responsibility, but not at the top executive level. Eighty-two of the 159 men were employed in professional or technical occupations. Of this group roughly one-third were teachers or administrators either in colleges or public schools, and two-thirds worked in a variety of occupations including 12 engineers, approximately the same number of accountants and auditors, and smaller numbers in about a dozen other classifications within the professional and technical group.

The remaining breadwinners were employed in many types of office, administrative, or sales jobs. Sixty per cent of this group held positions which included some managerial functions such as department heads, superintendents, or purchasing agents. Almost one-third were in a variety of office and clerical jobs involving some administrative or supervisory functions; and 8 per cent were employed as salesmen.

In addition to the chief breadwinners, there were a few other family members who reported some employment in a variety of occupations which will be discussed in the section on family income. Only 1 of this group, a wife, was employed full time.

Education. — In view of the occupations represented in this study, a relatively high educational level among parents would be expected. There were only 5 husbands and 1 wife without some high school education, and of the remaining parents, only 1 husband and 13 wives had left school before completion of twelve years. Ninety-six per cent of the husbands and 91 per cent of the wives had either completed high school or continued their education beyond this level. Some college education was reported by 65 per cent of the husbands and 54 per cent of the wives. A small number did not complete their college courses, but approximately a quarter of all the men and women in the sample did complete four years, and about a quarter of the men and 9 per cent of the women carried their education beyond college graduation. This last is not surprising, since a considerable number of the occupations represented in this study — particularly the teaching profession — require further education.

INCOME

Since the primary concern of this study is family expenditures, the income analysis is made, in the main, in terms of money income from regular sources. "Windfall" receipts are shown separately, and are not used in the classification of families by economic levels. Nonmoney income is also shown separately and is omitted in classifying families for the expenditure analysis. This type of income covers all goods or services received without cost, such as gifts of food, clothing, housefurnishings, opera tickets, and the like; free medical care; free lunches or transportation provided by an employer; as well as the net value of occupancy of owned homes. The value of such items is often difficult to estimate, and therefore the inclusion of nonmoney income might reduce the accuracy of the analysis. If nonmoney were added to money income, it would also have to be taken into account in family expenditures. It is possible that the addition of nonmoney to money expenses might distort the expenditure patterns, since a coat or a piece of furniture received as a gift might well be more expensive or of a different type than the family itself would buy, and some things received as gifts might otherwise never be purchased.

Money income.—Money income as used in this study conforms with the 1950 definition of the U.S. Bureau of Labor Statistics.[2] Money income includes wages and salaries after the deduction of occupational expenses, income from unincorporated businesses or professions,[3] net receipts from rented properties and roomers and boarders, net profits from the sale of stocks and bonds bought in 1950,[4] and money from a variety of other sources. In order to arrive at spendable income, personal taxes were deducted from money income, and this spendable income is used throughout the study to classify the families. However, money income before taxes is presented in table 5 in order to give a more complete picture of the general economic level of the families in the study.

Size of money income.— The 159 families included in this study reported an average money income before taxes of $6,637. Two-thirds of the family incomes before taxes were between $5,500 and $7,500 and only 9 per cent were between $8,000 and the $10,000 maximum set for eligibility. Income

---

[2]U.S. Department of Labor, Bureau of Labor Statistics, Family Income, Expenditures, and Savings in 1950, Bulletin 1097, Washington, 1953, pp. 2 and 10.

[3]Net profits or earnings from unincorporated business or profession are classified as income. However, net losses from such businesses or professions are not considered as deductions from income, but rather as decreases in business investments.

[4]Total proceeds from stocks and bonds purchased before 1950 and sold in 1950 are considered decreases in assets, even though the selling price was greater than the purchase price. (See chap. xvi, pp. 166 ff.)

TABLE 10

Years of School Completed by Parents

Years of school completed	All parents		Male		Female	
	Number	Per cent	Number	Per cent	Number	Per cent
Number of years known, total	316	100.0	158	100.0	158	100.0
8	6	1.9	5	3.2	1	.6
9 to 11	14	4.4	1	.6	13	8.2
12	108	34.2	49	31.0	59	37.3
13 to 15	51	16.1	20	12.7	31	19.6
16	81	25.6	41	25.9	40	25.3
Over 16	56	17.7	42	26.6	14	8.9
Years unknown	2	....	1	....	1	....

TABLE 11

Size of Money Income

Income	Money income before taxes		Money income after taxes	
	Number of families	Per cent of families	Number of families	Per cent of families
All families	159	100.0	159	100.0
Under $5,000	4	2.5	20	12.6
$5,000 to $5,499	17	10.7	28	17.6
$5,500 to $5,999	28	17.6	28	17.6
$6,000 to $6,499	28	17.6	34	21.4
$6,500 to $6,999	20	12.6	27	17.0
$7,000 to $7,499	30	18.9	9	5.7
$7,500 to $7,999	18	11.3	9	5.7
$8,000 to $8,499	8	5.0	3	1.9
$8,500 to $8,999	1	.6	1	.6
$9,000 to $9,499	5	3.1	0	.0

Average incomes and ranges

All families		
Mean	$6,637.10	$6,076.53
Median	6,587.89	6,040.33
Range	$4,917.25 to $9,304.25	$4,427.83 to $8,597.89
Incomes under $6,000		
Mean	5,788.20	5,325.29
Median	5,580.00	5,375.74
Incomes $6,000 and over		
Mean	7,414.40	6,764.40
Median	7,069.88	6,598.69

and all other personal taxes averaged $560, making the average income
after taxes $6,077. Almost three-quarters of the incomes after taxes were
between $5,000 and $7,000 and only 2 per cent were $8,000 or more. Because
of the eligibility requirements, the families in the study fell into a relatively
narrow income range. Within this range there was, of course, considerable

TABLE 12

Money Income Before Taxes, by Source of Income

Source of income	All families		Families reporting				
	Mean	Per cent	Number	Per cent of all families	Mean	Median	Range
Money income, total	$6,637.10	100.0	159	100.0	$6,637.10	$6,587.89	$4,917.25 to $9,304.25
Net earnings, total[a]	6,154.41	92.7	159	100.0	6,154.41	6,050.90	$4,826.90 to $8,959.90
Man	6,044.66	91.1	159	100.0	6,044.66	5,928.75	$4,826.90 to $8,563.00
Woman	66.71	1.0	19	11.9	558.25	254.04	$3.75 to $2,400.00
All others	43.05	.6	26	16.4	263.26	129.29	$12.00 to $1,058.74
Income except earnings, total ...	482.68	7.3	144	90.6	532.96	376.00	$3.00 to $3,820.17
Receipts from military service ...	131.99	2.0	57	35.8	368.19	340.00	$10.00 to $996.00
Dividends..................	90.85	1.4	49	30.8	294.80	120.00	$1.00 to $2,750.00
Interest	29.07	.4	75	47.2	61.62	24.00	$0.49 to $462.00
Cash gifts	48.29	.7	71	44.7	108.13	50.00	$3.00 to $900.00
Annuities and trusts	47.91	.7	15	9.4	507.80	150.00	$10.00 to $2,872.19
Net real estate rentals[b]	27.17	.4	15[b]	9.4	288.00	67.01	-$60.52 to $1,020.00
Receipts from roomers and boarders .	22.95	.3	15	9.4	243.26	180.00	$68.64 to $720.00
Unincorporated business	33.47	.5	9	5.7	591.27	714.50	$25.00 to $1,235.96
All other net money income[c]	50.99	.8	30[c]	17.6	270.25	110.00	-$389.32 to $1,325.67

[a] Gross earnings minus occupational expenses. Seventy-six families reported some occupational expense, averaging $37.34 for those reporting, and $17.85 for all families.

[b] Of the 15 families reporting real estate rentals, 14 reported a profit, and 1 had a loss of $60.52. The average profit for the 14 reporting a profit was $312.89, or $27.55 for all families.

[c] Includes 1 family with a profit from stocks and bonds of $1,325.67, and 3 families with losses from stocks and bonds, averaging $179.77 for those with losses, and $3.39 for all families.

dispersion, but the group studied represented primarily families with spend-able incomes concentrated between $5,000 and $7,000.[5]

In this study, no conclusions based on sound evidence can be drawn concerning the relation between income and size of family. As in similar studies, this relationship is difficult to determine because income is the result of so many factors, including the age of the breadwinner and the type of job at which he is employed. The fact that families with less than 3.5 full-year equivalent members had somewhat lower incomes than larger families in this study cannot be interpreted as showing a cause and effect relationship between these two variables,[6] since the incomes of the smaller families may have been lower for many reasons not related to size of family.

Money income from earnings.—Ninety-one per cent of all income came from the earnings of the head of the family. In most instances these earnings were solely from one full-time job; these full-time earnings averaged $5,921, with 82 per cent ranging from $5,000 to $7,000. There were 31 families, or about one-fifth of the total, in which the husband increased the family income by supplementary earnings; these earnings added only $123 to the average income of all families, but the increase for those who had subsidiary jobs was substantial, averaging $633. Just over half the extra earnings were less than $400, but slightly more than a fourth were between $1,000 and $2,500. The supplementary jobs were varied: 29 per cent of the men reported earnings from Army or Navy reserve duty or the National Guard, and nearly a fifth earned extra income by teaching, usually in summer school or extension division classes. The remaining men did many kinds of work, including such jobs as gas station attendant, sales clerk, and insurance salesman.

In addition to the earnings of the chief breadwinner, in 42 families 19 wives and 34 other family members reported some earnings. For the entire sample the employment of wives added only $67 to income, but the average earnings of those who worked was $558. There was only 1 wife who worked full time, earning $2,400 as a typist clerk. All other employed wives were

---

[5]One type of bias which undoubtedly occurred in this, as in similar studies, is the underreporting of income. The Bureau of Labor Statistics (Family Income, Expenditures, and Savings in 1950. Bulletin 1097, p. 7) concludes that such underreporting "apparently is based on inability or unwillingness on the part of many families to give a complete report of income." It is impossible in the present study to estimate the effect of such underreporting, although some studies have indicated that income may be underestimated by at least 10 per cent.

[6]The average net income after taxes of the 49 families with from 2.50 to 3.49 members was $5,904, whereas the two groups of families with 3.50 to 4.49 and 4.50 to 5.49 members had average incomes of $6,125 and $6,144 respectively. There were only 5 larger families—too small a number for any significance to be attached to their average incomes.

TABLE 13

Net Earnings of the Heads of Families, by Type of Jobs

	Total earnings		Full-time jobs		Supplementary jobs	
	Family heads reporting					
Earnings class[a]	Number	Per cent	Number	Per cent	Number	Per cent
All family heads..........	159	100.0	159	100.0	31	100.0
Under $5,000...........	12	7.5	15	9.4	31	100.0
$5,000 to $5,499........	35	22.0	38	23.9	0	.0
$5,500 to $5,999........	37	23.3	38	23.9	0	.0
$6,000 to $6,499........	23	14.5	27	17.0	0	.0
$6,500 to $6,999........	29	18.2	27	17.0	0	.0
$7,000 to $7,499........	19	11.9	12	7.5	0	.0
$7,500 and over........	4	2.5	2[b]	1.2	0	.0

Average earnings and ranges

	Total earnings	Full-time jobs	Supplementary jobs
All family heads			
Mean ··················	$6,044.66	$5,921.21	$123.45
Median ··············	5,928.75	5,847.10	....
Family heads reporting			
Mean ··················	6,044.66	5,921.21	633.16
Median ··············	5,928.75	5,847.10	398.43
Range ················	4,826.90 to 8,563.00	4,702.23 to 8,563.00	20.00 to 2,500.00

[a]Total earnings less occupational expenses (including non-reimbursed expenses for business use of personal cars).

[b]The two top salaries were higher than the $7,500 eligibility maximum only because one man was over-reimbursed for meals while traveling and the other for the business use of his car. Such over-reimbursement has been added to their base salaries of $7,490 and $6,212, making their final salaries $8,563 and $7,662 respectively.

part-time workers with earnings varying from a few dollars to $1,970; 9 of all those who worked earned less than $200, and only 3 made more than $1,000. The types of occupations which these women reported covered a wide range, including election clerks, sales workers, part-time teachers, and a miscellany of other jobs.

The 34 other family members who had some part-time earnings were all children with the exception of a brother-in-law (a student living with the family and contributing his part-time earnings of $325 to the family purse), and 1 mother-in-law who earned $170 baby sitting. One-fifth of the 158 children seven years of age and older reported earnings from part-time employment. Only 2 were as young as seven, and 69 per cent were between eleven and eighteen. In most cases the sums earned were small, often as low as $15 or $20. Twenty-eight per cent of all the children who had jobs earned less than $50, and about 72 per cent less than $250. The 3 children with the highest earnings made between $700 and $825 each; all 3 were in families in which the combined earnings of 2 or more children ran from $1,000 to $1,059. As would be expected, the younger children earned the smaller sums, usually from newspaper routes or baby sitting. The older group was employed in a variety of occupations, including summer work in manufacturing establishments, and such jobs as grass cutting, comparison shopping for a department store, and clerking in a drug store.

For the entire sample the additional income from the earnings of children or in-laws averaged only $43. However, in the families in which this type of income was reported, the average earnings amounted to $263, and in a few cases these earnings were substantially larger.

Money income from sources other than earnings.—Ninety-one per cent of the families had some income in addition to earnings, but such supplementary cash made up only 7 per cent of the average income before taxes. The average amount received from sources other than earnings was $483 for all families and $533 for the 144 cases which reported such incomes. The sums varied widely from $3 to $3,820; about one-fifth were less than $100, 37 per cent were less than $250, and slightly more than three-fifths were below $500. Of the 55 families whose income from such sources was more than $500, nearly two-thirds were less than $1,000.

Between 30 and 50 per cent of all families received some income from interest, dividends, cash gifts, or veterans' payments. Most important in terms of the amount of money received were the various types of veterans' allowances. For the entire sample these payments averaged $132 per family, but for those receiving such income the average was $368. Although payments varied from $10 to $996, 63 per cent were between $250 and $500, and 84 per cent were less than $500.

Dividends averaged $91 for all families and $295 for the 49 cases reporting them. Family income from this source ranged from $1 to $2,750, but 43 per cent of the families received less than $100, and payments to another 24 per cent were between $100 and $200. Only 3 families reported receiving more than $1,000 in dividends.

The two sources other than earnings from which the largest proportions of the sample received some income were gifts of money and interest, reported by 45 per cent and 47 per cent of the families. However, the average income received was relatively small in both instances. Cash gifts averaged $48 for the entire sample, and $108 for those who received them. Slightly less than half the families who reported these gifts received less than $50, and 87 per cent of such gifts were less than $250. The average interest received by all families was $29, and a little more than twice that amount for those who reported such income. Fifty-three per cent of the families reporting received less than $25, and 29 per cent received sums between $25 and $100.

Receipts from roomers and boarders, real estate rentals, and income from annuities and trusts were each reported by 15 families, and 9 families received profits from an unincorporated business or profession. Although

TABLE 14

Size of Nonmoney Income, by Type of Income

Nonmoney income class	Total non-money income		Food		Clothing		Housing[a]		House furnishings		All other	
	Number	Per cent	Number	Per cent	Number	Per cent	Number	Per cent	Number	Per cent	Number	Per cent
All families	158	100.0	117	100.0	138	100.0	122	100.0	99[b]	100.0	134[c]	100.0
Negative income	7	4.4	0	.0	0	.0	10	8.2	0	.0	0	.0
Positive income	151	95.6	117	100.0	138	100.0	112	91.8	99	100.0	134	100.0
Families with positive												
income, total	151	100.0	117	100.0	138	100.0	112	100.0	99[b]	100.0	134[c]	100.0
Under $50	2	1.3	72	61.5	55	39.9	0	.0	70	70.7	83	61.9
$50 to $99.99	6	4.0	10	8.5	44	31.9	2	1.8	11	11.1	26	19.4
$100 to $199.99	14	9.3	6	5.1	33	23.9	4	3.6	12	12.1	18	13.4
$200 to $299.99	13	8.6	27	23.1	3	2.2	5	4.5	4	4.0	3	2.2
$300 to $399.99	7	4.6	1	.9	0	.0	4	3.6	0	.0	0	.0
$400 to $499.99	5	3.3	0	.0	1	1.4	5	4.5	0	.0	2	1.5
$500 to $999.99	48	31.8	1	.9	2	.7	66	58.9	2	2.0	2	1.5
$1,000 and over	56	37.1	0	.0	0	.0	26	23.2	0	.0	0	.0

Families reporting nonmoney income by size of nonmoney income

Average nonmoney income, ranges

All families						
Mean	$751.35	$58.69	$74.91	$528.01[a]	$35.79	$53.94
Negative	-21.79	.00	.00	-36.58[a]	.00	.00
Positive	773.14	58.69	74.91	558.59	35.79	53.94
Median	806.91	11.00	52.12	635.24	8.03	21.00
Families reporting						
Mean	756.10	79.76	86.31	688.14[a]	57.49	64.01
Negative	-494.99	.00	.00	-486.20[a]	.00	.00
Positive	814.10	79.76	86.31	792.99	57.49	64.01
Median	808.24	26.00	62.79	747.24	25.00	32.70
Range	-948.90 to +2,302.87	1.00 to 570.20	4.50 to 535.47	-990.65 to +1,527.89	1.50 to 650.00	1.50 to 556.10
Per cent reporting	99.4	73.6	86.8	76.7	62.3	84.3

[a] Nonmoney income in the form of housing was made up almost entirely of the net value of occupancy of owned homes. However, 1 family not only reported a negative NVO of $768, but free housing valued at $162. Therefore its net money housing income was minus $606, which is the figure used in the calculations for this table.

[b] One family reported receiving some housefurnishings without cost, but their value was lumped with miscellaneous nonmoney income. Therefore this family is not included in the 99 cases.

[c] One family reported receiving some miscellaneous items without cost, but did not report the value. Therefore this family is not included in the 134 cases.

the average income from these four sources combined was only $132 for the
entire sample, there were a few quite substantial amounts among the families that reported such receipts.

The remaining income before taxes came from a variety of other sources,
reported by 30 families. The amounts reported per family were usually
small, but in some cases they were sufficiently large to be an important
addition to the family exchequer.

It is important to recognize that the average income received from any
of the sources other than earnings was inflated by the few families who received relatively large sums. Although the economic position of such families was often considerably improved, slightly more than one-quarter of
the sample had nothing, or less than $100, over and above earnings, and 43
per cent had less than $300 as a supplement to wage and salary income.

Nonmoney income.—Nonmoney income is defined as the value of any goods
or services received by the family without money outlay. It includes gifts of
all kinds, other free goods or services such as meals or transportation furnished by an employer, the net value of occupancy of owned homes (N.V.O.),[7]
and any housing received without cost.

There was only 1 family which reported nothing received without cost,
and many families were the recipients of several types of nonmoney income
in sizable amounts. Total nonmoney income averaged $751 per family for
all families in the study, with $528, or 70 per cent of this sum, from N.V.O.
and free housing. The range of total nonmoney income was wide—from $18
to $2,303—but there was considerable concentration at the higher levels.
Eight families received less than $100 in nonmoney income; approximately
one-quarter of the families with positive nonmoney income received between
$100 and $500; nearly one-third had between $500 and $1,000; and 37 per
cent reported $1,000 or more. The evidence clearly indicates that the eco-
nomic position of a large majority of these families was substantially improved by their nonmoney income. Seven families reported negative total
nonmoney income which in every case resulted from a negative N.V.O. position. Three other cases with negative N.V.O. had sufficient nonmoney income from other sources to produce a positive total nonmoney income position.

Housing.—N.V.O. represents the difference between a family's estimate
of the rental value of its home (an estimate generally based on the rent
charged in the neighborhood for similar housing), and annual expenditure
for taxes, mortgage interest, insurance, repairs, and so on.[8] Payments

---

[7]N.V.O. is the difference between the estimated rental value of an owned
home (during the months it was occupied) and the cash outlay for current
housing expenses.

[8]For a further discussion of N.V.O., see the housing chapter, p. 53.

on principal are not involved in this calculation since they are treated as an increase in assets.

Ninety-two per cent of those families who were home owners at any time in 1950 had some positive nonmoney income from this source; they received an average of $793, with N.V.O. for individual families ranging from $60 to $1,528. Almost one-quarter of those who had positive N.V.O. income received more than $1,000, and 82 per cent received $500 or more. Ten families, or 8 per cent of all full- or part-year home owners, had expenses for their homes in excess of the estimated rental values, and consequently showed negative figures for N.V.O. This situation resulted from unusually large repairs made in 1950, or, for some who bought homes during the year, from relatively large expenses in connection with their house purchases. Two of these negative figures were very small, but the rest ranged from about $100 to nearly $1,000.[9] For all families who occupied owned homes at any time in 1950, including those with negative as well as positive nonmoney income from their homes, the average N.V.O. and free housing was $688, whereas for all 159 families, both owners and renters, this average was $528. Since these figures are made up almost entirely of N.V.O., home ownership certainly appeared to be advantageous for the group studied.

Clothing without cost.—Eighty-seven per cent of the families received some clothing without cost. The average value of this clothing was $75 for all families, and $86 for those who received it. Seventy-two per cent of such gifts were valued at less than $100 per family (with more than half of these valued at less than $50), and about 95 per cent of the families reported clothing gifts worth less than $200. Three families reported receiving clothing, either as gifts or without cost, which was valued from $410 to $535. One of these was a case in which the husband reported he used his mother's charge account, and obviously the family secured most of its clothing free, since its money expenditures for these items totaled only $20 (plus another $50 for clothing upkeep and repair). The second family received such items as a $75 coat and a $15 hat for the husband, plus a $60 suit and a $50 dress for the wife, yet their money outlay for clothing purchases was $120 above the average for all families. The third family, in spite of more than $500 worth of gifts, spent 82 per cent more on clothing purchases than the average for the entire sample. Although these 3 families were unusual, 28 per cent of the total group received gifts of clothing valued at $100 or more, representing quite substantial additions to their wardrobes.

Food without cost.—Nearly three-quarters of the sample received nonmoney income in the form of food, averaging $59 for all families, and for

---

[9]In addition to reporting negative N.V.O., 1 family also received housing without cost, with an estimated value of $160. This free housing reduced the family's negative nonmoney housing income from minus $768 to minus $606.

those who received it, $80.[10] Sixty-two per cent of the families receiving gifts of food valued them at less than $50; 8 per cent were given food worth between $50 and $100; and slightly less than one-quarter received from $200 to $300 in nonmoney income from this source. With one exception the chief breadwinners in this last group were employed by a company which provided free lunches for its employees. The value of these lunches was set by the Heller Committee at 88 cents, the average cost of restaurant lunches purchased by the men who did not work for this company.[11] Since most companies did not give lunches to their employees, the fact that this firm was included in the sample and had a relatively large number of the cases in the study, resulted in an upward bias in the value of food received without cost.[12] Without these free lunches, there would have been only 3 families with nonmoney income of $200 or more from food, and the average value of food received without cost by the entire sample would have been about $25 instead of $59. Finally, the 2 families receiving the largest amounts of free food valued that food at $362 and $570. In one of these cases the husband reported that his customers took him out to lunch, and in the other the employer paid for three expensive meals per week.

With the exception of those families in which the chief breadwinner received free lunches, family food purchases were not greatly supplemented by free food. Most such food came as gifts at Christmas and other holidays and was usually relatively small in value. (In a related field, about one-sixth of all families reported gifts of alcoholic beverages. Out of a total of 26 such cases almost half were valued at less than $20, and only 1 was more than $100.)

Housefurnishings without cost.—Housefurnishings were received by 62 per cent of the families. These gifts were generally small, averaging $36 for all families and $57 for those who received them. Seventy-one per cent were valued at less than $50 per family, another 11 per cent between $50 and $100, and 94 per cent were less than $200. The larger gifts included appliances such as vacuum cleaners and sewing machines, as well as rugs and davenports. One of the two largest consisted of dining room furniture and three chairs worth $545; the other was a rug valued at $650. Although

---

[10]Only one family reported home-grown food which was valued at $152.

[11]It is, of course, possible that the cost to the company varied from this amount, and the quantity of food provided may have been more than would have been purchased in restaurants. However, it seemed reasonable to assume that the addition to income would be about what lunches cost the other men in this study.

[12]This bias would have disappeared in a very large sample, but in this small study, the number of workers who received free lunches is clearly too large a proportion of the total.

only 18 per cent of the entire sample received gifts of housefurnishings worth $100 or more, such gifts did provide some fairly important equipment or furniture, even at prevailing high prices.

Miscellaneous items without cost.—Sixty per cent of all families received gifts in the areas of recreation, reading, and education. Included were such things as television sets, radios, records, tickets for theaters or sport events, books, subscriptions to magazines, and music lessons. Thirty-two per cent of these gifts were valued at less than $10 per family; 88 per cent at less than $100; and the four highest were worth between $200 and $550. The eleven gifts valued at $100 or more included four television sets ranging in cost from $100 to more than $500, two radio phonographs, a piano, and various combinations of things such as books and toys. For the total sample, gifts in these categories were not important, but for a few families they were significant additions to available goods or services.

Approximately half of the families received gifts of perfume, soap, powder, lipsticks, and other personal care items. Sixty-three per cent of these gifts were valued at less than $10 per family, and only 1 family received items worth as much as $100. The average value of such gifts was $11 for those who received them, and for the entire group about half that amount.

Twenty-eight cases or 18 per cent of the sample received some nonmoney income in the form of transportation. Again the amounts were small: 17 families received less than $50, 8 between $50 and $100, and the highest amount reported was $125. This type of nonmoney income appeared most frequently in the form of free transportation to work, often in a car provided by the employer. In general such income was not important, but in a few cases it was of real assistance in covering commutation expenses.

Finally, about one-fourth of the sample received a wide variety of other gifts, mostly of small value, such as stationery, fuel, tobacco, and flowers. Forty-eight per cent of these gifts were worth less than $10 per family, and 88 per cent less than $50. There were only 2 with values of more than $90: 1 family received free utilities, amounting to $200 as part pay for a secondary job; another had moving expenses of $350 which were paid by the employer.

Other money receipts.—In addition to money income from relatively regular sources, 14 families or 9 per cent of the sample received some windfall money which in this study had been listed separately in order to differentiate it from regular income. Moreover, such additional receipts were not considered as income for family classification purposes. They included inheritances, gifts of $1,000 or more, lump sum settlements from property insurance, and similar items; they varied so greatly—from $9 to $14,000— that the only significant average is the $324 for all families in the study. Ten families received $1,000 or more, and the other 4 ranged from $9 to

$400. The two largest receipts were inheritances of $10,842 and $14,000; next in size was a government settlement of $7,006 given a family head who had been in an internment camp in the last war; and 7 families received sums between $1,000 and $4,000, which in all but 1 case were specified as gifts or inheritances.

Chapter IV

EXPENDITURES FOR FOOD
AND ALCOHOLIC BEVERAGES

TOTAL FOOD EXPENDITURES

Expenditures for food accounted for 27.2 per cent of the total consumption expenditures by the 159 families included in this study.[1] These families spent an average of $1,622 for all food purchased; $1,288, or 79 per cent, was for food prepared at home. Most of the remaining $334 was spent for meals in restaurants, although it also included small sums for snacks, such as ice cream, soft drinks, or coffee.

Forty-six per cent of the families spent between $1,5000 and $2,000 for all their food, and 16 per cent reported sums between $2,000 and $2,686. Slightly more than one-third spent between $1,000 and $1,500, and 4 families reported expenditures below $1,000.

---

[1] This proportion is a little lower than that found by the U.S. Bureau of Labor Statistics in its 1950 survey of family income and expenditures. The 226 families included in the B.L.S. San Francisco-Oakland area sample spent 29.4 per cent of their current consumption expenditures for food—a higher proportion in spite of the fact that the B.L.S. survey families had an average size of 3.2, whereas the average Heller Committee family consisted of 3.9 persons. From size of family alone it would be expected that the Heller Committee families would show a larger part of their expenditures allocated to food, since food is a category of expenditure which may be expected to increase more directly with each addition to the family than would some others such as housing, recreation, or transportation. However, the average total current consumption expenditure for the B.L.S. families was $4,477 whereas the salaried worker families in the Heller Committee survey spent $5,957. If data for a higher income group were available from the B.L.S. survey, the percentages found in the two studies would probably be more similar. Bureau of Labor Statistics, U.S. Department of Labor, Washington, D.C., 1953, Family Income, Expenditures, and Savings in 1950, Bulletin No. 1097 (Revised), p. 18.

TABLE 15

Expenditures for Food, Families Reporting, by Type of Expenditure

	Total		At home		Away from home	

Families reporting expenditures

Expenditure class	Number	Per cent	Number	Per cent	Number	Per cent
Families reporting, total ...	159	100.0	159	100.0	158	100.0
Under $500, total	0	.0	0	.0	131	82.9
Under $100	0	.0	0	.0	20	12.7
$100 to $199	0	.0	0	.0	25	15.8
$200 to $299	0	.0	0	.0	34	21.5
$300 to $399	0	.0	0	.0	31	19.6
$400 to $499	0	.0	0	.0	21	13.3
$500 to $999	4	2.5	26	16.4	24	15.2
$1,000 to $1,499	56	35.2	101	63.5	3	1.9
$1,500 to $1,999	74	46.5	27	17.0	0	.0
$2,000 and over	25	15.7	5	3.1	0	.0

Average expenditures and ranges

Families reporting.........			
Mean	$1,622.28	$1,288.35	$336.05
Median................	1,603.90	1,275.00	301.85
Range	850.70 to	714.00 to	24.00 to
	2,685.70	2,438.33	1,399.40

The concentration of total food expenditures within relatively narrow limits is also indicated by the fact that the sums spent for food by 58 per cent of the families were between 20 and 30 per cent of their total consumption expenditures, and the costs of 23 per cent of the sample were between 30 and 35 per cent of total consumption. For 6 per cent of the families food costs were less than one-fifth of consumption expenditures, whereas for nearly one-eighth of the sample they were 35 per cent or more.

The family with the lowest expenditure ($851) spent roughly half as much as the average family, and the family with the largest expenditure ($2,686) spent 66 per cent more than the average. These 2 families illustrate some of the reasons why differences in food expenditures occur. The family with the lowest expenses for food had a net money income after taxes of $4,993 and 4 persons to support—2 adults and 2 small children. This family spent 17 per cent of total consumption costs for food, and clearly was exercising careful economies in food purchases. Its expenditures were 57 per cent of the average sum spent by other families in the income group below $5,000, and on a per capita basis were 54 per cent of the per capita expenditures of other families with similar incomes. The family with the highest expenditure included 4 adults and 2 children, and reported an income of $6,040, or about the average for all families studied. Forty-three per cent of this family's consumption expenditures went for food, and it spent twice as

TABLE 16

Family and Per Capita Expenditures for Food, by Family Size, Income Class, and Type of Expenditure

	Family size							
	Per family				Per capita			
	All families	Under 3.49	3.50 to 4.49	4.50 to 6.49	All families	Under 3.49	3.50 to 4.49	4.50 to 6.49
Average expenditures for food								
All families, total food	$1,622.28	$1,574.97	$1,592.81	$1,735.40	$410.84	$524.38	$401.75	$339.80
At home	1,288.35	1,181.88	1,260.86	1,472.16	326.27	393.50	318.02	288.26
Away from home	333.93	393.09	331.95	263.24	84.57	130.88	83.73	51.54
Families with incomes under $6,000								
Total food	1,507.19	1,505.79	1,450.16	1,623.68	394.20	501.81	364.39	327.97
At home	1,240.79	1,214.82	1,185.43	1,396.95	324.52	404.84	297.87	282.17
Away from home	266.40	290.97	264.73	226.73	69.68	96.97	66.52	45.80
Families with incomes $6,000 and over								
Total food	1,727.68	1,667.20	1,709.85	1,813.12	425.18	554.41	432.62	347.60
At home	1,331.90	1,137.96	1,322.75	1,524.48	327.78	378.42	334.68	292.26
Away from home	395.78	529.24	387.10	288.64	97.40	175.99	97.94	55.34
	Number of families				Number of persons[a]			
All families	159	49	71	39	627.8	147.2	281.5	199.2
Income under $6,000	76	28	32	16	290.6	84.0	127.4	79.2
Income $6,000 and over	83	21	39	23	337.3	63.2	154.1	120.0

[a]Full-year equivalent family members.

TABLE 17

Expenditures for Food, All Families, by Income Class and Type of Expenditure

Income class	Number of families	Expenditures					
			Mean			Median	
		Total	At home	Away from home	Total	At home	Away from home
All families	159	$1,622.28	$1,288.35	$333.93	$1,603.90	$1,275.00	$291.20
Under $5,000	20	1,496.37	1,244.08	252.29	1,253.52	1,287.50	226.83
$5,000 to $5,499	28	1,525.19	1,275.42	249.77	1,474.68	1,264.10	183.99
$5,500 to $5,999	28	1,496.91	1,203.82	293.09	1,502.42	1,147.12	268.00
$6,000 to $6,499	34	1,675.95	1,282.33	393.62	1,636.25	1,232.75	379.94
$6,500 to $6,999	27	1,783.60	1,462.21	321.39	1,770.40	1,412.78	275.85
$7,000 and over	22	1,738.98	1,248.57	490.41	1,686.44	1,222.59	431.90
Under $6,000	76	1,507.19	1,240.79	266.40	1,484.93	1,252.34	235.25
$6,000 and over	83	1,727.68	1,331.90	395.78	1,687.00	1,305.37	369.85

much per capita as did the family described above. Its per capita expenditures, however, were only $20 a year higher than the average for other families with incomes between $6,000 and $6,500. This family's large food expenditure was primarily the result of its above-average size.

Food expenditures were of course affected by family size. The larger the family, the greater the expenditure for total food. Three-person families[2] spent an average of $1,575; those with 4 persons only slightly more, or $1,593; and the larger families spent $1,735. This last group, however, in spite of a larger average expenditure for total food, spent less per family member than the smaller families. Three-person families spent an average of $524 per person; 4-person families spent $402; and 5- and 6-person families spent only $340 per person. This decrease in per capita expenditures with increase in family size was probably in the main accounted for by the fact that the larger families found it necessary to be more economical in food expenditures, since they had more persons to feed on approximately the same incomes. They may also have been able to use food at home with somewhat less waste.

There was some tendency for total food expenditures to increase from the lower to the higher income groups. Families with incomes less than $6,000 spent an average of $1,507, and those with incomes of $6,000 or more spent $1,728, or 15 per cent more. When these averages are expressed as per cents of total consumption expenditures, the difference between the two groups is very slight. The families with incomes less than $6,000 spent 27.8 per cent, and the higher income group, 26.8 per cent of their total consumption expenditures for food.

Families were somewhat larger in the income group of $6,000 and over, than in the groups with lower incomes—4.1 persons in comparison with 3.8. Thus some of the extra money spent for food by the higher income families was required to feed more people. When per capita food expenditures were compared, it was found that families with incomes less than $6,000 spent an average of $394 per person, whereas the higher income group spent $425, or 8 per cent more than those with the smaller incomes. This suggests that the additional money which the upper income families spent for food overstates the difference in expenditures between the two income groups. Part of this difference was the result of larger family size, which also affected the proportion of total consumption expenditures going for food. When the per cent of total family expenditures which went for food

---

[2] Family sizes are stated in terms of full-year equivalent family members. An infant or other person in the family some fractional part of a year is counted as that fraction of "one." For brevity, the families are referred to in this discussion as 3, 4, etc. person families although each of these family-size groups includes a few families slightly larger or smaller.

TABLE 18

Per Cent of Total Consumption Expenditures for Food, by Income Class and Type of Expenditure

Income class	Number of families	Average family size	Per cent of total consumption expenditures					
			Per family			Per cent per family member[a]		
			Total food	At home	Away from home	Total food	At home	Away from home
All families	159	3.9	27.2	21.6	5.6	7.0	5.6	1.4
Under $5,000....	20	3.8	26.4	22.0	4.5	7.0	5.8	1.2
$5,000 to $5,499..	28	3.7	28.3	23.7	4.6	7.6	6.4	1.2
$5,500 to $5,999..	28	4.0	28.3	22.8	5.5	7.1	5.7	1.4
$6,000 to $6,499..	34	3.9	27.8	21.3	6.5	7.1	5.4	1.7
$6,500 to $6,999..	27	4.3	27.2	22.3	4.9	6.3	5.2	1.1
$7,000 and over..	22	3.9	25.0	17.9	7.1	6.4	4.6	1.8
Under $6,000....	76	3.8	27.8	22.9	4.9	7.3	6.0	1.3
$6,000 and over ..	83	4.1	26.8	20.7	6.1	6.5	5.0	1.5

[a]Proportion spent per family divided by average family size.

TABLE 19

Expenditures for Food Away from Home, by Type of Expenditure

	All families		Families reporting expenditures				
	Mean expenditures	Per cent	Number	Per cent all families	Expenditures		Range
					Mean	Median	
Food away from home, total ..	$333.94	100.0	158	99.4	$336.05	$301.85	$24.00 to $1,399.40
Meals, total[a]	303.93	91.0	157	98.7	307.80	275.37	$19.92 to $1,366.60
Work	154.85	46.4	118	74.2	208.66	168.00	$6.00 to $1,127.50
School	16.72	5.0	66	41.5	40.28	18.10	$1.20 to $459.00
Vacation	57.36	17.2	116	73.0	78.62	59.00	$10.00 to $333.02
Other	74.99	22.5	148	93.1	80.57	61.30	$4.50 to $626.80
Snacks	30.01	9.0	138	86.8	34.57	25.25	$0.50 to $240.00

[a]Includes supplements to meals such as soup, dessert, and coffee, bought to eat with a lunch brought from home.

was apportioned among family members, it was found that the per cent spent for food per family member was 7.3 for the lower income group and 6.5 for the upper group. If both groups of families had contained 4 persons, those with lower incomes probably would have spent an average of about 29 per cent for food, and the upper group about 26 per cent.

Food at home.—The average family expenditure for food at home was $1,288, and 64 per cent of the sample spent sums between $1,000 and $1,500. The amount spent for food at home did not vary significantly with size of income. The average expenditure of families with incomes less than $6,000 was $1,241, and those with higher incomes spent 7 per cent more, or $1,332. More important, however, is the fact that the per capita expenditures by the two income groups were almost identical—$325 for those with incomes below $6,000, and $328 for those with the higher incomes. Thus most of the additional money spent by the higher income group for food at home was the result of larger families. As was true for total food expenditures, the sums spent for food at home varied with family size, and the larger families spent less per capita. The smallest families spent $1,182 ($394 per capita); 4-person families spent $1,261 ($318 per capita); and the largest families spent $1,472 ($288 per capita).

Food away from home.—All but 1 family reported some expenditure for food purchased away from home. Ninety-one per cent of the average expenditure of $334 went for meals, and the remainder was spent on miscellaneous snacks. Half the cost of meals was for lunches purchased by the husbands, and the average expenditures of those who bought lunches was $209. However, one-fourth of the families reported no such expenses, either because the head of the family went home for lunch, carried a packed lunch, or received free lunch from his employer. The remainder of the money spent for meals was about equally divided between meals for various members of the family while shopping or out for the evening, and meals on vacation or school lunches. In addition to meals, most families bought some miscellaneous snacks, with an average expenditure of $35.

Families varied greatly in the sums spent for food away from home, although there was considerable concentration in the lower expenditure brackets. Eighty-three per cent spent less than $500, and 3 families spent more than $1,000. The 2 highest spenders were families in which the husband was away part of the year, and while he was away he ate all his meals in restaurants;[3] 1 of the 2 also had a daughter away at college, thus further increasing the cost of food away from home.

There was a substantial difference in the expenditures for food away from home by families with incomes below and above $6,000. The lower of

---

[3] Expenditures for these meals were reimbursed. This amount is added both to income and to expenditures for food for each family concerned.

these groups spent an average of $266 and the upper group spent $396, or 49 per cent more. Although this difference is narrowed when per capita expenditures are considered, the higher income group still spent 40 per cent more than those with lower incomes: $97 in contrast with $70.

Although expenditures for food at home varied directly with size of family, the reverse was true in the case of expenditures for food away from home. Three-person families spent an average of $393 per family; 4-person families spent $332; and the largest families spent $263.

Expenditures for food away from home had considerable effect on total food costs. Expenditures per person for food at home did not differ greatly between the two income groups. Since the group with incomes above $6,000 spent more for food away from home than the families in the lower income bracket, they had relatively larger total food expenditures. Thus the real difference in their spending habits was the much greater amount spent for food away from home.[4]

ALCOHOLIC BEVERAGES

Although alcoholic beverages are not classified as food, they are included in this chapter because they are more closely related to food than to any other expenditure item. Eighty-nine per cent of the families reported some expenditure for beer, wine, or liquor. The total group of 159 families spent an average of $91 or 1.5 per cent of all consumption expenditures; for the 142 who reported buying alcoholic beverages, the average amount spent was $102. Family expenditures varied greatly, but just over two-thirds were less than $100, and 41 per cent were less than $50. Nearly one-quarter of the families spent between $100 and $300, and the remaining 8 per cent spent larger sums, the highest of which was $500.

On the whole, alcoholic beverages were a small part of the total expenses of these families, but a few spent relatively large amounts. The 142 families who bought beer, wine, or liquor spent an average of 1.7 per cent of their total consumption expenditures for this purpose; for 61 per cent of those

---

[4]One company in the sample provided free meals to all its employees with an estimated average value of $208 per year. Since the families whose breadwinners were employees of this company made up one-fifth of the lower income group, and only slightly more than one-eighth of the higher income bracket, the underspending for food away from home by these employees might have biased the results. When these families were omitted from both income groups, it was found that the per capita expenditures for total food remained 8 per cent higher for those with incomes of $6,000 and more, and the proportions spent for food at home and food away from home changed very little. Therefore, the inclusion of this particular group of families does not invalidate the point that although the lower income group spent similar amounts for food at home, they spent less for food away from home than the upper income group.

TABLE 20

Expenditures for Alcoholic Beverages

Families reporting expenditures		
Expenditure class	Number	Per cent
Families reporting, total	142	100.0
Under $100, total	96	67.6
Under $25	28	19.7
$25 to $49	30	21.1
$50 to $74	22	15.5
$75 to $99	16	11.3
$100 to $199	22	15.5
$200 to $299	12	8.5
$300 to $399	8	5.6
$400 to $499	3	2.1
$500 to $599	1	.7

Average expenditures, ranges, and per cent reporting expenditures

All families
  Mean $90.66
  Median 56.08
Families reporting
  Mean 101.51
  Median 65.68
  Range .... $2.00 to 500.34
Per cent reporting 89.3

buying, the proportion was less than 1.5 per cent. Two families, however, reported spending 10.7 and 7.7 per cent respectively of all their consumption expenditures for alcoholic beverages. Apparently the amount families spent in this category depended on other factors besides size of their incomes. There were both small and large expenditures at every level of income, and the average sums spent by families with expenditures, in both the income group under $6,000 and the higher bracket, were very similar —$97 and $106, respectively.

Chapter V

EXPENDITURES
FOR HOUSING

EXPENDITURES OF ALL FAMILIES

Housing[1] ranked third in relative importance among the money expenses for family living. The average cash outlay for all housing was $711, a sum exceeded only by food and transportation.

Ninety-five per cent of the total housing expense, or $676, went for the family home. Two-thirds of the families also spent something for housing away from home, averaging $36 for all families and $53 for those who reported such expense. Eighty-four per cent of these additional expenditures were less than $100, and all were less than $300. Vacation housing accounted for the largest part of such costs, but there were a few cases with housing expenses while family members were away either at school, at work, or on personal business.

The proportion of total consumption expenditures which went for all housing averaged 11.9 per cent. (See table 4, p. 13.) Almost four-fifths of the families spent between 5 and 20 per cent, but here, as in dollar expenditures, the range was wide. Fifteen families spent less than 5 per cent, with all but 1 in this group owning their homes outright and consequently free of interest payments on mortgages. Eighteen families spent 20 per cent or more, chiefly because of high repair and replacement costs or large expenses in connection with sales of homes.

Families with incomes over $6,000 spent an average of $829 for all their housing requirements, whereas those in the lower income bracket spent

---

[1]Includes rents, expenses for housing away from home, current maintenance costs for home owners (interest on mortages, taxes, insurance, and expenses for repairs and replacements). Excludes down payments on homes bought in 1950.

$582. The higher group spent more both for family homes and for housing away from home.

Although 42 per cent of the families reported expenditures between $500 and $1,000 for family homes, there was considerable variation above and below these sums. Thirteen families, or 8 per cent of the total, spent less than $250, and one-third had costs between $250 and $500. Eighty-three per cent of those with expenditures under $500 were full-year home owners, 45 per cent of whom had no mortgage on their homes. One-sixth of the sample spent $1,000 or more for family homes, up to a maximum of $2,491. No full-year renter spent more than $1,470 for a family home, and only 5 full-year owners had costs above that figure. The relatively high expenditures of the 13 families who were both renters and owners in 1950 were the result of sale and acquisition costs, repairs, or replacements in the homes which they purchased, or above-average rents while they were tenants.

TABLE 21

Expenditures for Housing, by Type of Housing

Type of housing	Mean	Median	Range
All housing	$711.21	$576.00	$128.25 to 2,640.15
Family home	675.58	551.66	47.75 to 2,490.65
Away from home			
All families	35.63	14.00	....
Families reporting	53.44	35.00	.50 to 270.00

The present study is primarily interested in the money expenditures of the families in the sample, but it would be unrealistic to discuss housing costs without giving some consideration to the imputed or net value of occupancy of owned homes (N.V.O.) As the U.S. Bureau of Labor Statistics has pointed out, the money expenses of home owners for taxes, insurance, interest, repairs, and so on, do not tell the whole story of current housing costs. If a family either owns its home outright or has a substantial equity in it, annual cash expenditures are often less than the cost of renting an equally good house. N.V.O. is the difference between the estimated rental value of the owned home (during the months it was occupied) and the cash outlay for current housing expenses. N.V.O. is not only income in kind from the housing investment but also a consumption item, "since the family has chosen to take the return on its investment in the form of housing."[2]

---

[2]U.S. Department of Labor, Bureau of Labor Statistics, Money Disbursements of Wage Earners and Clerical Workers, 1934-36, Bulletin 638, Washington, D.C., 1941, p. 86.

TABLE 22

Expenditures for Housing, by Income Class, Tenure, and Type of Housing

Income class	All housing				Family home				Away from home	
	All families	Full-year owner	Full-year renter	Part-year own and rent	All families	Full-year owner	Full-year renter	Part-year own and rent	All families	Families reporting expenditures
Families reporting expenditures										
Families reporting, total..	159	109	37	13	159	109	37	13	...	106
Under $6,000........	76	52	19	5	76	52	19	5	...	50
$6,000 and over........	83	57	18	8	83	57	18	8	...	56
Average expenditures										
All families reporting.....	$711.21	$608.96	$802.20	$1,309.48	$675.58	$568.47	$774.04	$1,293.40	$35.63	$53.44
Under $6,000........	582.21	512.13	688.05	908.86	552.88	482.81	652.95	901.46	29.33	44.58
$6,000 and over........	829.32	697.30	922.68	1,559.87	787.92	646.62	901.87	1,538.37	41.40	61.35

TABLE 23

Expenditures for Family Home, All Families, by Tenure

Expenditure class	All families		Full-year owners		Full-year renters		Part-year own and rent	
	Number	Per cent	Number	Per cent	Number	Per cent	Number	Per cent

Families reporting expenditures

Expenditure class	Number	Per cent	Number	Per cent	Number	Per cent	Number	Per cent
All families	159	100.0	109	100.0	37	100.0	13	100.0
Under $250..............	13	8.2	13	11.9	0	.0	0	.0
$250 to $499..........	53	33.3	42	38.5	10	27.0	1	7.7
$500 to $749..........	45	28.3	36	33.0	8	21.6	1	7.7
$750 to $999..........	22	13.8	8	7.3	12	32.4	2	15.4
$1,000 to $1,499......	17	10.7	5	4.6	7	18.9	5	38.5
$1,500 to $1,999......	6	3.8	4	3.7	0	.0	2	15.4
$2,000 and over......	3	1.9	1	.9	0	.0	2	15.4

Average expenditures and ranges

Mean..................	$675.58		$568.47		$774.04		$1,293.40	
Median................	551.66		491.80		764.63		1,212.72	
Range.................	$47.75 to 2,490.65		$47.75 to 2,490.65		$264.90 to 1,470.00		$463.25 to 2,447.00	

The full cost of home ownership, in terms of money expenditures plus
N.V.O., not only gives a more complete picture of the total consumption
pattern of home owners, but also provides cost figures for home ownership
comparable with the expenses of families who rent their homes.

TABLE 24

Purchase Price of Homes Owned December 31, 1950, by Date of Purchase

	All homes		Homes purchased 1946-1950		Homes purchased before 1946	

Families reporting purchases

Price class	Number	Per cent	Number	Per cent	Number	Per cent
All home owners..........	119[a]	100.0	72	100.0	47	100.0
Under $5,000............	7	5.9	0	.0	7	14.9
$5,000 to $7,499........	29	24.4	3	4.2	26	55.3
$7,500 to $9,999........	18	15.1	7	9.7	11	23.4
$10,000 to $12,499.......	22	18.5	21	29.2	1	2.1
$12,000 to $14,999.......	19	16.0	17	23.6	2	4.3
$15,000 to $17,499.......	10	8.4	10	13.9	0	.0
$17,500 to $19,999.......	7	5.9	7	9.7	0	.0
$20,000 to $22,499.......	4	3.4	4	5.6	0	.0
$22,500 to $24,999.......	3	2.5	3	4.2	0	.0

Average purchase prices and ranges

	All homes	Homes purchased 1946-1950	Homes purchased before 1946
Mean	$10,941	$13,707	$6,704
Median	10,500	12,525	6,250
Range	2,144 to 24,100	5,000 to 24,000	2,144 to 12,750

[a]Omits one home which was received as a gift.

In this study the average N.V.O. for all families who occupied owned
homes at any time during 1950 was $687; for the full-year owners alone, it
was $769. If the N.V.O. for both full- and part-year owners is averaged in
with the money expenditures for housing of the entire sample, the total
housing cost is increased from $711 to $1,238. When this expense in kind
for full-year owners is added to their cash outlay, it raises the full-year
owner's average total housing costs from $609 to $1,378. The cash expenditures of full-year home owners were considerably lower than similar expenses of full-year renters, but their total housing cost, including N.V.O.,
was 72 per cent above the renters. It is perhaps worth noting that for this
added cost the average home owner lived in a house with more rooms and
baths than were found in the average renter's home.

When money costs alone are considered, the proportion of total consumption expenditures going to housing was 10.7 per cent for families with incomes less than $6,000, and 12.9 for the higher income group. Here again
it is important to note the significance of N.V.O. If N.V.O. plus housing re-

ceived without cost[3] is treated as nonmoney income and added to money income after taxes, the average family income is raised from $6,077 to $6,604,
with almost exactly the same number of cases having money-plus-N.V.O.
incomes under $6,500 as have cash incomes under $6,000. If, in addition,
N.V.O. and free housing are added to money expenditures, and the families
are classified by money-plus-N.V.O. income, the proportion of total consumption expenditures going for housing is 19.1 per cent for all families,
18.6 per cent for those with incomes less than $6,500, and 19.5 per cent
for the high income group. In other words, when N.V.O. is added both to
income and expenditures, the difference in the proportions spent for housing by the lower and upper income groups is narrowed.[4]

EXPENDITURES OF HOME OWNERS

Sixty-nine per cent of the sample owned homes during all of 1950, and
another 7 per cent became owners by the end of the year. In this study, the
proportion of families owning their own homes showed little or no increase
with the rise in the income level. Full-year owners constituted slightly
more than two-thirds of both the group with incomes less than $6,000 and
that with incomes more than $6,000; owners at the end of the year had in-
creased to approximately three-quarters of both income levels. This is in
contrast to B.L.S. studies, which show home ownership increasing as in-

---

[3]In this study only 1 family received any housing without cost, and the
value of that housing was only $160.

[4]The U.S. Bureau of Labor Statistics, analyzing housing expenditures
in selected cities in 1935-1936, stated "as the higher income levels are
reached, expenditures for housing become a progressively smaller proportion of the cost of maintaining a family." However, B.L.S. was referring to
a far wider range of incomes than are represented in the Heller Committee
study. Among salaried business and professional families in the income
groups of $4,000 and over, the B.L.S. showed very small changes in the pro-
proportions spent for housing, with some up and others down. (U.S. Department of Labor, Bureau of Labor Statistics, Family Expenditures in Selected
Cities, 1935-36, Vol. I, Housing, Bulletin No. 648, Washington, D.C., 1941,
pp. 3, 354-355.) When the National Resources Committee reported on the
1935-1936 B.L.S. data, it stated ". . . the per cent of current consumption
going to housing remains fairly constant—approximating 18 per cent at all
income levels." (Consumer Expenditures in the United States, Estimates
for 1935-36, Washington, D.C., 1939, p. 24.) The B.L.S. and the N.R.C.
included N.V.O. and free housing both in expenditures and as a part of income. Income was defined as net money income before taxes plus N.V.O.
and free housing. The Heller Committee data in the text above are for net
money income after taxes plus N.V.O. and free housing. However, a re-
classification of these data by the B.L.S. and N.R.C. income definition
yields essentially the same results: the 79 cases in the lower half of the income range spent 18.5 per cent of all consumption expenditures for housing,
whereas the remaining 80 cases in the upper half of the range spent 19.6
per cent.

come goes up; the present findings on this point probably reflect the relatively narrow range of incomes in the Heller Committee study.[5]

Characteristics of owned homes.—With the exception of one semidetached dwelling, all owners at the end of 1950 lived in separate houses. The number of rooms in these houses varied from four to thirteen, but 82 per cent had five to seven rooms, with the average for all houses being 6.3. Fifty-eight per cent of the homes had one bathroom and no additional plumbing facilities, and one-quarter had two complete baths. Finally, three-quarters of the houses had central heating (piped from a central source), and the rest had other types of installed heating.

Seventy-one per cent of the homes owned at the end of 1950 were built before 1942, and slightly more than half of these before 1930. Five houses were constructed during the war years, and the remaining quarter were built after 1946. The average price paid for all homes was $10,941; 50 per cent cost between $7,500 and $15,000. Seven of the homes, all purchased in 1939 or earlier, cost less than $5,000; a like number purchased after the war cost between $20,000 and $25,000 (two of the latter group were built before 1940; the other five were put up in the postwar period). The average cost of the houses bought before and during the war was $6,704. In contrast, those purchased after 1945 cost on the average $13,707, a figure nearly $1,000 above the price of any home purchased in the prewar or war years.

Mortgage indebtedness.—Almost three-fourths of the home owners were still paying off mortgages on their homes at the end of 1950. Of those families for whom information was available, 5 per cent had mortgages with five or less years to run, and the rest were divided about equally into two groups, with six to fifteen, or sixteen to twenty-five years to run. The amount of mortgage debt outstanding ranged from $686 to $13,800, and the average for all families having such obligations was $6,801. Forty per cent of those with mortgage debt had unpaid balances of less than $6,000, and about the same proportion owed between $6,000 and $10,000. To summarize the mortgage picture from a slightly different angle: as of the end of 1950, 27 per cent of all the home owners owed nothing on their homes, 4 per cent owed less than one-fifth of the purchase price, slightly more than one-third owed between 20 and 60 per cent, and approximately the same proportion owed 60 per cent or more. The mortgages carried were almost equally

[5]U.S. Department of Labor, Bureau of Labor Statistics, Family Expenditures in Selected Cities, 1935-36, Vol. I, Housing, Bulletin No. 648, Washington, D.C., 1941, p. 17. Also Family Spending and Saving in Wartime, Bulletin No. 822, Washington, D.C., 1945, p. 123. In the latter bulletin, where combined figures were reported for all cities, the increase in home owners between the $3,000-$5,000 income group and the $5,000-$10,000 group was relatively small; the large increases appeared in the income classes below $3,000 and the class of $10,000 and over.

TABLE 25

Home Owners' Mortgage Indebtedness and Years Mortgage to Run, December 31, 1950

	Number of owners	Per cent of owners
All home owners........................	120	100.0
No mortgage debt	32	26.7
Mortgage debt outstanding	88	73.3

Amount of mortgage debt

	Number of owners	Per cent of owners
Total with mortgage debt.............	88	100.0
Under $2,000......................	6	6.8
$2,000 to $3,999	15	17.0
$4,000 to $5,999	14	15.9
$6,000 to $7,999	18	20.5
$8,000 to $9,999	19	21.6
$10,000 to $11,999	13	14.8
$12,000 to $13,999	3	3.4

Years mortgage to run

	Number of owners	Per cent of owners
Total with mortgage debt.............	88	....
Years not reported	4	....
Years reported, total	84	100.0
0.1 to 5........................	4	4.8
5.1 to 10.......................	18	21.4
10.1 to 15......................	23	27.4
15.1 to 20......................	25	29.8
20.1 to 25.....................	14	16.7

Average mortgage debt outstanding and range, December 31, 1950

All home owners	
Mean ··	$4,987.51
Median ···	4,889.94
Owners with mortgages	
Mean ··	6,801.15
Median ···	6,992.94
Range ··	$686 to $13,800

divided between government insured or guaranteed loans and conventional
types. Half of the government group were insured by the Veterans Administration; about a third by the Federal Housing Administration; the remainder
were combined V.A. and F.H.A. loans.

Total housing expenditures—full-year owners.—Full-year home owners
made an average cash·expenditure of $609 for all their housing requirements;
$568 of this went for the family home and $40 for housing away from home,
chiefly while on vacation. Those families with incomes over $6,000 spent
$164 a year more for a family home and $21 more for housing away from
home than did the group with incomes less than $6,000. Full-year owners,
both as a whole and by income size, spent proportionately less of their
total cash consumption expenditures on housing than did the full-year renters: all full-year owners spent 10.2 per cent, whereas the renters spent

TABLE 26

Expenditures for Owned Homes, Full-Year Home Owners, by Type of Expenditure

Full-year owners reporting expenditures

Expenditure class	Total Number	Total Per cent	Interest Number	Interest Per cent	Taxes Number	Taxes Per cent	Repairs and replacements Number	Repairs and replacements Per cent	Insurance Number	Insurance Per cent	All other Number	All other Per cent
Full-year owners reporting, total...	109	100.0	78	100.0	109	100.0	90	100.0	65	100.0	15	100.0
Under $100...	1	.9	6	7.7	22	20.2	53	58.9	62	95.4	10	66.7
$100 to $199...	7	6.4	19	24.4	61	56.0	16	17.8	3	4.6	3	20.0
$200 to $299...	14	12.8	16	20.5	19	17.4	7	7.8	0	.0	0	.0
$300 to $399...	19	17.4	27	34.6	6	5.5	2	2.2	0	.0	0	.0
$400 to $499...	14	12.8	4	5.1	1	.9	3	3.3	0	.0	1	6.7
$500 to $599...	17	15.6	4	5.1	0	.0	2	2.2	0	.0	0	.0
$600 to $699...	14	12.8	1	1.3	0	.0	0	.0	0	.0	0	.0
$700 and over...	23	21.1	1	1.3	0	.0	7	7.8	0	.0	1	6.7

Average expenditures, ranges, and per cent reporting expenditures

	Total	Interest	Taxes	Repairs and replacements	Insurance	All other
All full-year owners						
Mean	$568.47	$202.65	$164.38	$157.76	$23.31	$20.37
Median	491.80	190.20	160.00	47.00	18.48	...
Full-year owners reporting						
Mean.............	568.47	283.20	164.38	191.07	39.08	148.00
Median...........	491.80	283.74	160.00	67.09	30.00	38.78
Range............	47.75 to 2,490.65	16.50 to 706.55	17.36 to 403.32	1.00 to 2,343.87	8.25 to 156.96	8.07 to 1,071.25
Per cent of full-year owners reporting ...	100.0	71.6	100.0	82.6	59.6	13.8

14.3 per cent. Owners with incomes less than $6,000 spent 9.2 per cent, and those with incomes more than $6,000 spent 11 per cent; in contrast, the renters in the lower income group spent 13.9 per cent, but those in the higher income group spent 14.6 per cent.

Expenditures for owned homes[6]—full-year owners.—Full-year home owners spent an average of $206 less on their family homes than did full-year renters—the cash expenditures for the two groups being $568 and $774 respectively. This difference is in part accounted for by the fact that 28 per cent of the full-year owners had no mortgage debt, and their average expenditure was $438 in contrast to $620 for those full-year owners who were still paying on their mortgages. Fifty-nine per cent of the full-year owners reported expenditures between $300 and $700. Twenty-two, or one-fifth, of the owners spent less than $300 for housing; 82 per cent of this group owned their homes outright. Twenty-three spent more than $700, with 10 having expenses of $1,000 or more. Only 4 of these 23 families had no mortgage payments, but they, as well as 7 others in this group, had relatively high expenditures for repairs and replacements.

The average expenditure for all full-year home owners included $203 for interest on a mortgage; taxes at $164; repairs and replacements costing $158; insurance at $23; and $20 for miscellaneous expenses. Each of the four main components of expense for family homes contained a wide range · of expenditures, although the bulk of such costs were within relatively narrow limits. Seventy-two per cent of the full-year owners made interest payments on mortgages, and their payments averaged $283. Nearly one-third of such payments were less than $200, and 55 per cent were between $200 and $400. All owners had tax payments, which averaged $164; 56 per cent paid between $100 and $200, and a fifth less than $100. The average insurance payment for the 60 per cent of the families reporting such expense was $39; here the range was narrower than in other items, with the lowest payments apparently representing one-year premiums, whereas the majority of families paid premiums for three years. Seventy-eight per cent of the families paying premiums spent less than $50, and only 5 per cent spent more than $100. Finally, 83 per cent of the families made repairs or replacements in their homes. They spent an average of $191, but individual expenditures ran from $1.00 to $2,344. Fifty-nine per cent of those spending reported outlays under $100, and 77 per cent spent less than $200. The fact that the remaining families spent all the way from $200 to $2,344 makes

---

[6]As used in this study, current expenditures for owned homes do not include down payments on homes bought in 1950, principal payments on mortgages, special assessments, or the cost of home improvements, all of which are considered to be home investments. The main items of current housing expense are interest on mortgages, taxes, insurance, and repairs and replacements.

TABLE 27

Average Expenditures for Rented Homes, Full-Year Renters,
by Income Class and Type of Expenditure

Income class	Number of families	Total cost rented home	Rent	Repairs and special fees			
				All families	Families reporting expenditures		
					Number	Per cent of all renters	Amount
All full-year renters	37	$774.04	$754.02	$20.02	15	40.5	$49.39
Under $6,000 ..	19	652.95	628.14	24.81	8	42.1	58.92
$6,000 and over	18	901.87	886.90	14.97	7	38.9	38.50

TABLE 28

Monthly Rentals, December 31, 1950, by Type of Dwelling Unit

	All dwelling units		Houses		Apartments	

Dwelling units, by size of rent

Monthly rental December 31, 1950	Number	Per cent	Number	Per cent	Number	Per cent
All dwelling units	39	100.0	24	100.0	15	100.0
$20 to $39	3	7.7	1	4.2	2	13.3
$40 to $59	12	30.8	7	29.2	5	33.3
$60 to $79	13	33.3	9	37.5	4	26.7
$80 to $99	5	12.8	5	20.8	0	.0
$100 and over	6	15.4	2	8.3	4	26.7

Average monthly rentals and ranges

Mean	$67.68	$67.73	$67.62
Median	65.00	65.00	69.00
Range	20.70 to 132.50	20.70 to 132.50	25.00 to 115.00

the mean of $191 somewhat misleading, since half of the families making
repairs or replacements spent $67 or less.

As already noted, full-year owners with incomes over $6,000 did spend,
on the average, more cash for current family home expenses than was spent
by the owners with incomes under $6,000; those in the lower income group
spent $483 and the remainder of the owners $647. This difference is chiefly
the result of higher expenditures for repairs and replacements by the upper
income group, since there was very little difference in the cash expenditures
for interest, taxes, or insurance. For repairs and replacements all full-
year owners in the upper income group had a mean expenditure of $216
(median $89); among the lower income owners the mean was $94 and the
median $22.

TABLE 29

Facilities Included in the Rent, December 31, 1950, by Type of Dwelling Unit

	All dwelling units		Houses		Apartments	
	Number	Per cent of all units	Number	Per cent of all houses	Number	Per cent of all apartments
All dwelling units	39	....	24	....	15	....
Garage	25	64.1	16	66.7	9	60.0
Water	20	51.3	7	29.2	13	86.7
Hot water	13	33.3	6	25.0	7	46.7
Garbage disposal	15	38.5	6	25.0	9	60.0
Heat...................	6	15.4	0	.0	6	40.0
Electricity	5	12.8	0	.0	5	33.3
Gas	4	10.3	0	.0	4	26.7
Stove	18	46.2	9	37.5	9	60.0
Refrigerator	14	35.9	7	29.2	7	46.7
Washing machine	1	2.6	0	.0	1	6.7
Basic furniture	4	10.3	3	12.5	1	6.7
All furnishings	1	2.6	0	0	1	6.7

EXPENDITURES OF HOME RENTERS

Characteristics of rented homes.—Thirty-seven families rented homes
all year and 2 others became renters during the year, bringing the proportion
of renters to 24 per cent of the total sample. Twenty-four, or 62 per cent
of all the renters, rented houses, and the rest lived in apartments or flats.
These rented dwelling units typically contained four or five rooms; a few
of the houses had as many as eight, but no apartment had more than six
rooms. All the apartments and seventeen of the houses had one bathroom
and no additional plumbing facilities; only one house had two complete baths.
Eleven houses and nine apartments had central heating; the remaining had
some other form of installed heating equipment.

Expenditures for rented homes—full-year renters.—The total housing
costs of full-year renters averaged $802, of which $774 was for a family
home. The expenditures for a home were primarily for the rent, which
averaged $754 a year or almost $63 per month, with very little difference
between the rents for houses and apartments. Rents varied widely both for
families with incomes below $6,000 and for families with incomes above
$6,000, but the higher group spent an average of $74 per month, whereas
the lower group spent $52 a month. Forty per cent of all full-year renters
had some other expenses for their family homes—usually repairs which
were not taken care of by the landlord. These additional expenditures were
generally small, averaging $20 for the entire group and $49 for those having
such expenses.

It is also of interest to consider the monthly rentals paid at the end of the
year. These figures reflect any changes in rents for full-year renters, and
they include the rents paid by 2 families who had lived in owned homes for

part of the year but were renting at the end of 1950.[7] The average monthly rental
at the end of the year was $68 for both houses and apartments; 31 per cent of
the rents were between $40 and $60, and one-third were between $60 and $80.

There are two factors of importance in connection with the amount of rent
paid—the size of the dwelling unit, and the facilities (including furnishings)
included in the rent. The number of renters in this study is too small to
permit an analysis of rentals by dwelling size and by specific facilities provided. However, a general description can be given of the types of facilities
included in the rent.

Thirty-six of the thirty-nine dwellings which were rented at the end of
the year had some facility included in the rent. In almost two-thirds of the
cases the rent included a garage; in just over half, it included water; in 46
per cent, a stove. From 33 to 38 per cent of the cases had one or more of
the following: hot water, garbage disposal, refrigerator; from 10 to 15 per
cent reported heat, gas, electricity, and/or some furniture.

As would be expected, fewer facilities were included in house rents than
in the rent for apartments. The three dwellings for which no facilities were
included in the rent were all houses, and just over three-quarters of the
other houses had only a garage. There were, however, six attached houses
in a single large real estate development, for which the rent covered water,
hot water, garbage disposal, refrigerator, and stove. These were four- or
five-room units with rents from $77 to $89 per month, sums considerably
higher than the rentals for other houses of similar size. In three houses the
landlord provided basic furniture, but the rents did not differ from others
with the same number of rooms. All the apartments had some facility included in the rent. In 87 per cent water was provided. Sixty per cent had
garage, stove, and/or garbage disposal; from 27 to 47 per cent had one or
more of the following: heat, hot water, gas, electricity, refrigerator.
There was one partly, and one completely furnished apartment; only for the
completely furnished apartment was the rent relatively high for apartments
of the same size.

It is impossible to determine the specific effect of size and facilities on
the amount of rent paid. Apartments were slightly smaller than houses, yet
the average rents were the same for both. The fact that house rents in general included fewer facilities than did those for apartments indicates that
house renters usually had some household expenses which were not incurred
by those living in apartments; if rents exclusive of facilities could be compared, it would probably be found that the houses had higher rentals than the
apartments.

[7] These 2 families lived in rented dwellings ten and eleven months and
their rents were $132.50 and $115.00. These were two of the highest rents
paid by any of the families studied.

Chapter VI
EXPENDITURES FOR
HOUSEHOLD OPERATION

TOTAL HOUSEHOLD OPERATION

As used in this study, household operation includes fuel, light, refrigeration, and water, as well as many widely divergent items ranging from telephones to postage stamps. The entire group of families spent an average of $459 for all the items in this section, an amount equal to 7.7 per cent of total consumption expenditures. This average cost was about two-thirds the size of the expense for all housing, and a few dollars higher than the sum spent for housefurnishings. Families with incomes less than $6,000 spent an average of $391, and those with higher incomes spent $521. The higher-income families also spent about 1 per cent more of their total consumption costs for household operation than did those with lower incomes; since fuel, light, refrigeration, and water took almost identical proportions in both groups, this difference is largely attributable to all other expenses in this category.

Expenditures for total household operation varied from $213 to $1,623; only 15 per cent of the families spent $600 or more. Fifty-five per cent spent between $200 and $400, with nearly two-thirds of this group spending between $300 and $400. Because household operation covers such a heterogeneous collection of items, it is difficult to single out specific reasons for the wide differences in the sums spent. However, included in the 30 families whose expenses were between $200 and $300 was 1 who had no expense for fuel, light, refrigeration, and water, and 7 who spent less than $100 for these items. The group with low expenses also included the only 2 families who spent less than $100 for all household operation exclusive of fuel, light, refrigeration, and water. At the other end of the expenditure range, 3 families spent more than $1,000 for household operation; all 3 reported

TABLE 30

Expenditures for Household Operation, by Type of Expenditure

	Total household operation		Fuel, light, refrigeration, water		Miscellaneous	

Families reporting expenditures

Expenditure class	Number	Per cent	Number	Per cent	Number	Per cent
Families reporting, total ...	159	100.0	157	100.0	159	100.0
Under $100	0	.0	26	16.6	2	1.3
$100 to $199	0	.0	121	77.1	45	28.3
$200 to $299	30	18.9	10	6.4	49	30.8
$300 to $399	57	35.8	0	.0	24	15.1
$400 to $499	22	13.8	0	.0	16	10.1
$500 to $599	26	16.4	0	.0	7	4.4
$600 and over..........	24	15.1	0	.0	16	10.1

Average expenditures and ranges

Families reporting						
Mean	$459.09		$137.14[a]		$323.68	
Median	384.06		133.02[a]		251.62	
Range	212.64 to		5.00 to		93.64 to	
	1,623.36		293.64		1,449.68	

[a]The mean for the total sample (159 cases) for fuel, light, refrigeration, and water is $135.41; the median, $132.72

expenses of more than $1,000 exclusive of fuel, light, refrigeration, and water, and 2 of them were among the 10 families spending more than $200 for these utilities.

FUEL, LIGHT, REFRIGERATION, AND WATER

The average expenditure of all families for this group of items was $135 which was 2.3 per cent of total consumption expenditures and 30 per cent of the total cost of house operation. Since gas is used by most families for heating as well as cooking in the San Francisco Bay area, it accounted for 40 per cent of the cost of this group of utilities; electricity represented one-third, and water one-quarter of the total spent.

Two families had no expenses in this category, both being full-year apartment renters with the cost of all utilities and heat included in the rent. Except these 2, all families had some expense for gas and electricity, and 90 per cent had water costs. Twenty-nine per cent of the entire sample spent relatively small amounts for all other fuel (wood, prestologs, oil, and the like), or for ice or freezer rent.

Slightly more than three-quarters of all family expenditures were between $100 and $200. Most of the 26 families whose costs were less than $100 reported some special circumstance which accounted for their small expenditures: 11 had water included in the rent (including 1 family who also had

TABLE 31

Expenditures for Fuel, Light, Refrigeration, and Water,

By Income Class and Type of Expenditure

Income class	Total	Gas	Electricity	Water	All other[a]
Families reporting expenditures					
Families reporting, total	157	157	157	142	46
Under $6,000..............	76	76	76	68	18
$6,000 and over	81	81	81	74	28
Average expenditures and ranges					
All families	$135.41	$53.60	$45.39	$33.20	$3.22
Under $6,000..............	129.17	51.16	44.50	30.98	2.53
$6,000 and over	141.13	55.85	46.20	35.23	3.85
Families reporting, total	137.14	54.29	45.97	37.17	11.13
Under $6,000..............	129.17	51.15	44.50	34.63	10.70
$6,000 and over	144.61	57.23	47.34	39.51	11.41
Range.....................	5.00 to 293.64	2.73 to 125.00	2.27 to 129.60	8.00 to 92.00	.25 to 76.90
Per cent of families reporting expenditures					
Families reporting, total......	98.7	98.7	98.7	89.3	28.9
Under $6,000..............	100.0	100.0	100.0	89.5	23.7
$6,000 and over	97.6	97.6	97.6	89.2	33.7

[a]Miscellaneous fuel, ice, and freezer rent.

heat provided), 7 paid for one or more of these utilities for less than the full year, and 2 had discounts on their gas and electricity bills. Only 10 families spent more than $200 in this category and none as much as $300; 5 of this group lived in seven- or eight-room houses, which was undoubtedly a factor in raising their utility expenses.

Although the amount of money spent on fuel, light, refrigeration, and water did not change appreciably with income, one factor which did influence expenditures for gas and electricity was the size of the dwelling units. One hundred and six of the families in the study lived in the same dwelling units all year, were not away from home for more than one month during the year, and paid the full costs[1] of both gas and electricity. For this selected group, both these costs rose as the number of rooms in the dwelling units increased. Obviously, other factors could also have affected the size of family expenditures for these utilities—factors such as local utility rates, the number and age of persons in the family, the number and types

[1]A few families reported part of these costs as business expenses, or, as employees of a utility company, received gas and electricity at a discounted rate.

TABLE 32

Expenditures for Gas and Electricity, Selected Families, by Size of House

Size of house	Number of families	Average expenditure	
		Gas	Electricity
All families...............	106	$56.21	$47.31
3 and 4 rooms...........	12	46.74	38.75
5 and 6 rooms...........	60	55.02	46.56
7 or more rooms	34	61.64	51.64

of household appliances used, or the fuel used for heating, cooking, refrigeration, and so on. Forty-one of the 106 families had one or more of the following household appliances: ironers, dryers, dishwashers, garbage disposal, or deep-freeze units. The gas and electric bills of these families were examined to see if their expenditures differed from those of families with fewer appliances. Although it was true that the bills of this group were slightly higher, the difference was not significant. It therefore appears that size of house was the main factor in determining expenditures for gas and electricity.

MISCELLANEOUS EXPENDITURES
FOR HOUSEHOLD OPERATION

Seventy per cent of the average cost of all household operation went for a varied assortment of items, with an average expense for all families of $324, or 5.4 per cent of total consumption expenditures. Although there was great variability in these expenditures, only a few families spent very small or very large sums. Fifty-nine per cent spent between $100 and $300, and one-quarter between $300 and $500. Only 2 families spent less than $100, and only 3 had expenses exceeding $800, running from $1,020 to $1,450. The 2 lowest expenditures, which in each case were between $90 and $100, had no wages for domestic help or baby sitters and very low telephone costs. The 3 families with the highest costs reported the largest expenditures for wages—between $670 and $810, and 2 of them also had large telephone and telegraph bills.

The largest expenditures in this group were for telephone and telegraph service and wages. For all families the average expenditure for these items was $71 and $68 respectively, and each accounted for slightly more than one-fifth of the total expenditures in this section of household operation. All families reported telephone costs, but only 58 per cent employed household help or sitters. The average amount paid for wages by those families reporting such expenditures was $118.

Laundry sent out plus laundry and cleaning supplies accounted for almost one-quarter of all miscellaneous expenditures, whereas 28 per cent was

TABLE 33

Miscellaneous Expenditures for Household Operation, by Income Class and Type of Expenditure

Income class	Total	Telephone and telegraph	Wages	Laundry out	Laundry supplies	Garbage disposal	Insurance	All other
Families reporting expenditures								
Families reporting, total	159	159	92	119	159	146	57	159
Under $6,000............	76	76	40	54	76	69	25	76
$6,000 and over	83	83	52	65	83	77	32	83
Average expenditures and ranges								
All families	$323.68	$70.92	$68.03	$43.17	$34.94	$9.02	$7.75	$89.85
Under $6,000.........	262.21	63.79	33.16	37.69	34.64	8.88	6.23	77.82
$6,000 and over	379.96	77.44	99.96	48.19	35.21	9.15	9.15	100.86
Families reporting, total	323.68	70.92	117.58	57.68	34.94	9.82	22.02	89.84
Under $6,000····	262.21	63.79	63.01	53.04	34.64	9.78	19.72	77.82
$6,000 and over ·····	379.96	77.44	159.55	61.54	35.20	9.86	23.74	100.86
Range........	93.64 to 1,449.68	29.68 to 180.00	2.00 to 810.00	1.25 to 239.07	6.08 to 121.52	.75 to 32.40	5.00 to 135.46	20.91 to 457.39
Per cent of families reporting expenditures								
Families reporting, total	100.0	100.0	57.9	74.8	100.0	91.8	35.8	100.0
Under $6,000.....	100.0	100.0	52.6	71.1	100.0	90.8	32.9	100.0
$6,000 and over	100.0	100.0	62.7	78.3	100.0	92.8	38.6	100.0

spent for a diverse category containing such items as matches and moving costs. Most family expenditures in this last group were small, but there were 10 who spent between $113 and $370 for moving expenses, repair and servicing of appliances, or reupholstering.

Expenditures for these miscellaneous categories of household operation increased as income went up: families with incomes less than $6,000 spent an average of $262 but those with incomes of $6,000 or more spent $380. This situation was true not only for the total of such expenditures, but for each subsection as well, although in some cases differences were negligible. The greatest variation between the two income groups appeared in their expenditures for wages: all families with incomes of less than $6,000 spent an average of $33, but the cost for the higher income group was three times this amount. Sixty-three per cent of those with higher incomes had expenditures for wages, in contrast with 53 per cent of those in the lower income group. The average expenditure of the lower income families who paid wages was $63; the higher income group spent two and one-half times as much.

Chapter VII
EXPENDITURES FOR
HOUSEFURNISHINGS

Housefurnishings probably include the most heterogeneous assortment of
purchases to be found in any of the main categories of family expenditures.
Not only is a large variety of items included, but item by item there is
obviously great variation in quality and/or size, and consequently in the
price paid. Nor are these the only reasons why it is difficult—if not impossible—to describe the "typical" housefurnishings purchases of any group of
families. A report limited to a given year, as is this one, shows tremen-
dous variations between families in the amounts spent for housefurnishings.
One reason for this, as pointed out by the U.S. Bureau of Labor Statistics,
is that, "Since the majority of the items which come under this heading are
at least semidurable in nature, families are usually able to adjust the level
of their spending to the current family situation. . . . A family . . . may
do without any new additions to its stock of goods in a year when its income
is reduced or other demands are particularly urgent."[1] On the other hand,
because the Heller Committee study was made in 1950, it is likely that some
families made purchases of consumer durables in advance of the time they
might otherwise have made them, in order to avoid anticipated shortages
arising from the Korean War. Considering all these potentials for variation
in the size and nature of housefurnishings expenditures, it is evident that
the present sample was far too small to allow any generalizations from the
housefurnishings expenditure data. It is only possible to report in broad
terms how 159 families spent their housefurnishings dollars in 1950.

Expenditures for housefurnishings represented 7.5 per cent of all the
money the average family spent for current consumption. The average cash

---

[1]U.S. Department of Labor, Bureau of Labor Statistics, Money Disbursements of Wage Earners and Clerical Workers, 1934-36, Bulletin No.
638, Washington, D.C., 1941, p. 115.

TABLE 34

Expenditures for Housefurnishings, by Type of Furnishing

Expenditure class	Total furnishings		Kitchen, cleaning, laundry equipment		Furniture		Textiles		Floor covering		China, glass, etc.		Miscellaneous	
	No.	Per cent	No.	Per cent	No.	Per cent	No.	Per cent	No.	Per cent	No.	Per cent	No.	Per cent
Families reporting expenditures														
Families reporting, total	159	100.0	145	100.0	115	100.0	148	100.0	63	100.0	122	100.0	158	100.0
Under $100, total	22	13.8	88	60.7	56	48.7	126	85.1	36	57.1	120	98.4	132	83.5
Under $25	5	3.1	54	37.2	28	24.3	57	38.5	26	41.3	95	77.9	61	38.6
$25 to $49	3	1.9	21	14.5	12	10.4	42	28.4	5	7.9	18	14.8	35	22.2
$50 to $74	7	4.4	7	4.8	10	8.7	21	14.2	3	4.8	5	4.1	19	12.0
$75 to $99	7	4.4	6	4.1	6	5.2	6	4.1	2	3.2	2	1.6	17	10.8
$100 to $199	30	18.9	9	6.2	23	20.0	16	10.8	12	19.0	2	1.6	15	9.5
$200 to $299	21	13.2	15	10.3	18	15.7	3	2.0	4	6.3	0	.0	8	5.1
$300 to $399	17	10.7	18	12.4	8	7.0	3	2.0	5	7.9	0	.0	1	.6
$400 to $499	18	11.3	4	2.8	6	5.2	0	.0	0	.0	0	.0	2	1.3
$500 to $999	37	23.3	10	6.9	3	2.6	0	.0	6	9.5	0	.0	0	.0
$1,000 and over	14	8.8	1	.7	1	.9	0	.0	0	.0	0	.0	0	.0
Average expenditures, ranges, and per cent reporting expenditures														
All families														
Mean	$444.85		$145.72		$115.38		$49.69		$57.40		$13.95		$62.71	
Families reporting														
Mean	444.85		159.79		159.52		53.39		144.86		18.18		63.11	
Median	348.69		45.51		103.93		36.20		51.75		10.00		36.48	
Range	8.54 to 1,880.56		.99 to 1,093.02		2.50 to 1,225.59		1.04 to 350.00		1.00 to 879.75		.45 to 199.55		.62 to 481.53	
Per cent reporting	100.0		91.2		72.3		93.1		39.6		76.7		99.4	

outlay for all families was $445; families with incomes less than $6,000
spent $385 and the higher income group $500. The proportion of total current consumption expenditures going for this category was 7.1 per cent
for those with the lower incomes, and 7.8 per cent for the families whose
incomes were $6,000 or more.

The range in family expenditures was very wide; for total housefurnishings families spent anywhere from $9 to $1,881, and there was a similarly
wide range in most of the subsections. Only 22 families, or 14 per cent of
the sample, spent less than $100 for all housefurnishings; nearly one-third
spent between $100 and $300; 22 per cent spent from $300 to $500, and 23
per cent spent from $500 to $1,000. Fourteen families, or nearly one-tenth
of the sample, spent $1,000 or more.

Families who owned or rented their homes all year spent an average of
$397 and $395 respectively for housefurnishings. Considerably larger sums
were spent by most of the 13 families that lived in both rented and owned
homes during the year, and their average expenditure was $984.

Although the average costs of full-year owners were about the same as
those of full-year renters, the fact that 19 of the 37 renters had refrigerators, stoves, or some other housefurnishings included in the rent might
have been expected to reduce the expenditures of this particular group.
Actually, families who did have any of these items included in the rent had
a higher average expenditure for total housefurnishings than the remaining
full-year renters; families with these facilities in the rent spent $466,
whereas the others averaged only $320. Several of the families that had
stoves or refrigerators included in their rent reported 1950 purchases of
these items. Specific reasons for such expenditures are lacking, but possibly the items provided in the rent were of poor quality or old, or, in
some cases, families may have made purchases as a part of long-range
plans for owning their own homes.

MAJOR ITEMS OF EXPENDITURE

Kitchen, cleaning, and laundry equipment.—This category includes not
only pots, pans, and dishmops, but such major household appliances as
refrigerators, stoves, and washing machines. Although only a relatively
small number of major appliances were bought in 1950, most families
owned stoves, refrigerators, vacuum cleaners, and washing machines, and
a few also owned other large equipment.

Kitchen, cleaning, or laundry equipment as a group accounted for one-
third of the total cost of housefurnishings. Ninety-one per cent of all families reported expenditures for this combined category. They spent an average of $160, but the size of individual family expenditures varied from $1 to
$1,093. Sixty-one per cent of the families spent less than $100; about half as

TABLE 35

Families Owning Selected Household Appliances, December 31, 1950

Type of household appliance	All families		Owners		Renters	
	Number	Per cent	Number	Per cent	Number	Per cent
All families	159	....	120	....	39[a]	....
Stove	148	93.1	120	100.0	28[a]	71.8
Refrigerator	150[b]	94.3	120[b]	100.0	30[c]	76.9
Vacuum cleaner	150	94.3	116	96.7	34	87.2
Washing machine	143	89.9	119	99.2	24	61.5
Ironing machine	35	22.0	31	25.8	4	10.3
Mechanical dryer	10	6.3	9	7.5	1	2.6
Deep-freeze unit	8	5.0	8	6.7	0	.0
Dishwashing machine	7	4.4	7	5.8	0	.0

[a]Remainder of the renters had stoves included in the rent.
[b]Includes one ice refrigerator.
[c]Remainder of the renters had refrigerators included in the rent.

many spent between $100 and $400; and 10 per cent spent $400 or more.

The largest expenditures were for kitchen and laundry equipment, which averaged $115 and $126 respectively. Although there were many small purchases in both these categories, one-quarter of the sums spent for kitchen equipment and 36 per cent of those for laundry equipment were $200 or more, with 7 families spending between $500 and $846. Among the larger items purchased were refrigerators, stoves, deep-freeze units, washing machines, and dryers, with several families buying more than one of these appliances. ·

Expenditures for cleaning equipment were much smaller, averaging $24 per family spending. Ninety-four per cent were less than $100, and none was as much as $200. The purchase of vacuum cleaners was the chief reason for the few relatively high expenditures in this category. Of the 21 families who spent $50 or more for cleaning equipment, all but 1 bought a vacuum cleaner.

Furniture.—Furniture accounted for just over one-fourth of all the money spent for housefurnishings, with 72 per cent of the families making some purchases. The average amount spent by these families was $160, but since this classification includes everything from kitchen chairs to expensive living or dining room furniture, there was of course great variability in the expenditures. Nearly half of the sums spent were less than $100; 20 per cent were between $100 and $200; 23 per cent ranged from $200 to $400; and 9 per cent were larger sums up to $1,226.

Twenty per cent of the furniture dollar went for beds, springs, mattresses, and the like, and 18 per cent for dining room and dinette sets. The average expenditures by those families purchasing items in these two groups were $85 and $194 respectively. Chairs accounted for 17 per cent of the furniture costs, with an average expenditure per family spending of $142 for up-

TABLE 36

Expenditures for Kitchen, Cleaning, and Laundry Equipment, by Type of Equipment

	Kitchen		Cleaning		Laundry	

Families reporting expenditures

Expenditure class	Number	Per cent	Number	Per cent	Number	Per cent
Families reporting, total ..	105	100.0	109	100.0	67	100.0
Under $100, total	76	72.4	102	93.6	41	61.2
Under $25	58	55.2	79	72.5	36	53.7
$25 to $49	14	13.3	9	8.3	3	4.5
$50 to $74	3	2.9	2	1.8	2	3.0
$75 to $99	1	1.0	12	11.0	0	.0
$100 to $199	3	2.9	7	6.4	2	3.0
$200 to $299	7	6.7	0	.0	15	22.4
$300 to $399	9	8.6	0	.0	5	7.5
$400 to $499	6	5.7	0	.0	1	1.5
$500 and over..........	4	3.8	0	.0	3	4.5

Average expenditures, ranges, and per cent reporting expenditures

All families			
Mean	$76.04	$16.50	$53.19
Families reporting			
Mean	115.14	24.06	126.23
Median...............	21.01	5.90	19.63
Range	1.02 to 846.07	.35 to 136.39	.50 to 600.04
Per cent reporting	66.0	68.6	42.1

holstered chairs and $26 for all other types. Twelve per cent of the furniture dollar was spent for sofas, sofa beds, and studio couches, and the average family outlay for those who made such purchases was $164. Many other kinds of furniture were bought, but no other category accounted for more than 8 per cent of the money spent for furniture, and the sums involved were usually small.

Floor coverings and textiles.—Only 40 per cent of the families reported expenditures for rugs or other floor coverings, whereas 93 per cent had some expense for household textiles. These two categories represented 13 and 11 per cent respectively of all housefurnishings expenditures. Again, both included a wide variety of items—all the way from cotton scatter rugs to wall-to-wall wool carpeting, and from dish towels to draperies. The result was great variability in expenditures for both types of items. The average amount spent by those families that made purchases was $145 for floor coverings and $53 for textiles. There were many very small expenditures in each of these categories; on the other hand, 15 families spent sums ranging from $200 to $880 for rugs and carpets, and a half-dozen families spent from $219 to $350 for various household textiles. In all but one case, the large expenditures for textiles included the purchase of curtains and draperies for $200 or more.

China, glass, silverware, wooden and plastic ware.—Seventy-seven per cent of the families bought something in this group, but the vast majority of their expenditures were small, and the total cost represented only 3 per cent of all housefurnishings expenditures. No family can be said to have spent extravagantly for any of these items. Seventy-eight per cent of those who reported expenditures in this category spent less than $25. Only 2 families spent more than $100; 1 bought a set of silver-plate flatware for $111, and the other bought a set of dishes for $97 and two place settings of sterling silver flatware for $65. Since nothing is known about what the families studied already owned in the way of china, glass, or flatware, it is impossible to analyze current purchases in terms of replacements or additions to stock; only one thing seems very clear—this was one of the places where the strictest economy was being practiced.

Miscellaneous housefurnishings.—All but 1 family bought some miscellaneous furnishings, and the average total expenditure for the countless things included in this group was $63, which represented 14 per cent of all the money spent for housefurnishings. Eighty-four per cent of these expenditures were less than $100 per family; only 3 families spent $300 or more, and none as much as $500. The largest single expense in this category was for new sewing machines which were purchased by 9 families at prices ranging from $150 to $314.

METHOD OF PURCHASING
HOUSEFURNISHINGS

The majority of the families included in this study bought their housefurnishings for cash, but 46 families, or 29 per cent of the sample, made one or more installment purchase. The total cost of these purchases, including carrying and any other charges, was $14,511.[2] This represents an average installment expenditure of $315 per family, or half the average of $635 spent by the 46 families for all housefurnishings. Those families that made no installment purchases had an average expenditure of $367 for total housefurnishings.

Only 5 of the 46 families spent less than $100 on installment purchases; almost three-fourths of the group spent between $100 and $400; and 7 families spent larger amounts, up to a maximum of $1,444. The 2 families with

---

[2]This amount includes the full purchase price of goods purchased on installment during 1950. Balances due on these goods at the end of 1950 were classified as increases in liabilities, and payments made in 1950 on goods bought on installment in prior years were classified as decreases in liabilities. (See chap. xvi, pp. 166 ff.)

the largest installment expenditures became home owners during the year;
1 had installment purchases of $972 for a bedroom set, refrigerator, sew-
ing machine, and $350 worth of draperies; the other spent $1,444 on installment for a refrigerator, stove, washing machine, carpeting, chairs, and
a bed.

Twenty-six, or 56 per cent of those families buying any housefurnishings
on installment, purchased only one item (or set, in the case of five furniture
purchases). Four of these families spent less than $100 each for the purchase
of vacuum cleaners; 21 spent between $100 and $400 on a wide variety of
items; and the remaining family spent $828 for wool rugs. All told, fifteen
appliances, nine items of furniture; and two wool rugs or carpeting were
purchased.

Twenty families bought two or more items on installment. Fourteen of
this group spent less than $400 each on their total time purchases, and the
other 6 spent between $511 and $1,444. Ten families bought seventeen appliances; 11 families bought furniture; 9, rugs or carpeting; 1, draperies; and
4, miscellaneous items of minor importance.

Although only 30 per cent of those making purchases bought housefurnishings on installment, there is some evidence that a few other families probably borrowed money to pay for some, if not all, of their major housefurnishings purchases. Unfortunately, information was not specifically requested
on the purposes of all loans made to these families. In 2 cases, however,
data were available that indicated that the families borrowed $300 and $410
each in order to buy housefurnishings. In addition to this specific information, 2 of the families that bought only one item on installment (costing $163
and $309) had total housefurnishings expenditures of $573 and $1,605 and
loans outstanding at the end of the year of $1,200 and $1,957. Finally, 9
families made no installment purchases but did buy one or more relatively
large housefurnishing items and had sizable debts outstanding at the end of
the year. These 9 families spent all the way from $339 to $1,612 for housefurnishings, and their loan debts at the end of 1950 ranged from $400 to
$3,260, with 6 being $1,000 or more. It seems reasonable to assume that
11 families probably paid for at least some of their housefurnishings by
borrowing money,[3] and therefore, though they bought for cash, they went
into debt to satisfy their housefurnishings needs.

[3]None of these 11 families bought a car in 1950, and therefore, at least
some part of their unidentified loan debts were all the more likely to have
resulted from housefurnishings purchases.

Chapter VIII

EXPENDITURES
FOR CLOTHING

TOTAL CLOTHING EXPENDITURES

The families included in this study had an average income before taxes of
$6,637—an amount larger than the incomes of roughly 80 per cent of the
families in the San Francisco-Oakland urbanized area.[1] Since it is generally true that families with higher incomes not only spend more dollars for
clothing, but also allocate a higher proportion of their total consumption
expenditures for this item, it would be expected that the families in this
study spent quite sizable amounts for their wardrobes. Actually their clothing expenditures were very moderate.

Expenditures for clothing and clothing services by all families averaged
$623, or 10.5 per cent of the average total expenditures for current con-
sumption. The 1950 Bureau of Labor Statistics income and expenditure
study included all income and occupational groups, and the average family
expenditure for all current consumption items was $4,477 in the San Fran-
cisco-Oakland Bay area. The average clothing expenditure of these Bay
area families was $494, or 11 per cent of all their current consumption
expenditures.[2] It might have been expected that the salaried workers in
the Heller Committee study would spend a larger proportion of their income
for clothing than the families in the B.L.S. study because their incomes
were higher, and they also belonged to a socioeconomic group usually thought
of as wearing a high quality of clothing—a quality which probably could not
be found at the prices most of them actually paid. Since 1950 was a year of

---

[1]U.S. Bureau of the Census. U.S. Census of Population, 1950. Vol. II,
Characteristics of the Population, Part 5, California, chap. B., U.S. Government Printing Office. Washington, D.C., 1952, p. 128.

[2]U.S. Department of Labor, Bureau of Labor Statistics, Family Income,
Expenditures, and Savings in 1950, Bulletin 1097, pp. 18 and 20.

TABLE 37

Expenditures for Clothing, All Families, by Type of Expenditure

Expenditure class	Total clothing		Clothing purchases		Clothing services	
	Number	Per cent	Number	Per cent	Number	Per cent
All families	159	100.0	159	100.0	159	100.0
Under $100	1	.6	2	1.3	126	79.2
$100 to $199	5	3.1	8	5.0	31	19.5
$200 to $399	28	17.6	40	25.2	2	1.3
$400 to $599	48	30.2	50	31.4	0	.0
$600 to $799	36	22.6	36	22.6	0	.0
$800 to $999	28	17.6	15	9.4	0	.0
$1,000 and over	13	8.2	8	5.0	0	.0

Average expenditures and ranges

Mean ···················	$622.98	$548.71	$74.27
Median ················	574.61	520.95	64.32
Range ················	70.55 to	19.50 to	12.07 to
	1,600.85	1,499.75	251.67

high prices, possibly these families found that the difference between their incomes and the prices they had to pay necessitated at least a temporary shift in their spending habits. As a result they may have tried to stretch their dollars by buying cheaper clothing. On the other hand, if we could compare these families with a group at the same socioeconomic level (in terms of jobs and real income) a decade earlier, it might be found that the families studied in 1950 spent proportionately less on clothing and more for other things because of long range basic changes in their spending patterns.[3]

Although the dollar sums spent per family for clothing and clothing services varied widely, there was considerable concentration within relatively narrow limits. Fifty-three per cent of the families spent between $400 and $800. Only 6 families reported expenditures of less than $200, including 1 that received large gifts of clothing and spent less than $100. Very large expenditures occurred infrequently, but there were 13 families that spent $1,000 or more. Similarly, the proportion of total consumption costs spent for clothing and clothing services varied greatly—from 1.1 to 23.5 per cent— but 40 per cent of these expenditures were between 5 and 10 per cent, and 45 per cent from 10 to 15 per cent of total consumption costs.

Clothing expenditures would be expected to vary with income and size of family, and in general the higher income families in this study did have larger cash outlays for clothing. Families with incomes of less than $6,000

---

[3]Such a change in standards of wage earner families occurred between 1917-1919 and 1934-1936. U.S. Department of Labor, Bureau of Labor Statistics, Money Disbursements of Wage Earners and Clerical Workers, 1934-36, Bulletin 638, pp. 40-41.

TABLE 38

Expenditures for Clothing, All Families, by Income Class and Type of Expenditure

Income class	Total expenditures		Purchases		Services	
	Mean	Median	Mean	Median	Mean	Median
All families · · · · · · · · · · · · · ·	$622.98	$574.61	$548.71	$520.95	$74.27	$64.32
Under $5,000 · · · · · · · · · · ·	491.69	439.10	406.78	383.30	84.91	82.68
$5,000 to $5,499· · · · · · · · ·	567.16	553.64	500.10	484.10	67.06	55.78
$5,500 to $5,999· · · · · · · · ·	553.15	527.32	481.66	457.62	71.49	68.35
$6,000 to $6,499· · · · · · · · ·	662.66	628.89	594.70	588.76	67.96	62.00
$6,500 to $6,999· · · · · · · · ·	692.82	685.23	610.87	585.63	81.95	66.00
$7,000 and over · · · · · · · · ·	755.20	707.19	677.55	648.86	77.65	66.91
Under $6,000 · · · · · · · · · · ·	542.14	521.87	468.75	454.37	73.39	65.98
$6,000 and over · · · · · · · · ·	697.00	669.71	621.92	593.69	75.08	64.32

TABLE 39

Clothing Purchases by Husbands and Wives

	Husbands	Wives

Persons reporting expenditures

Expenditure class	Number	Per cent	Number	Per cent
Persons reporting, total · · · · · ·	158	100.0	158	100.0
Under $25 · · · · · · · · · · · · · · ·	6	3.8	4	2.5
$25 to $49 · · · · · · · · · · · · · ·	7	4.4	5	3.2
$50 to $74 · · · · · · · · · · · · · ·	15	9.5	5	3.2
$75 to $99 · · · · · · · · · · · · · ·	16	10.1	19	12.0
$100 to $124 · · · · · · · · · · · ·	19	12.0	15	9.5
$125 to $149 · · · · · · · · · · · ·	15	9.5	20	12.7
$150 to $174 · · · · · · · · · · · ·	17	10.8	17	10.8
$175 to $199 · · · · · · · · · · · ·	16	10.1	12	7.6
$200 to $224 · · · · · · · · · · · ·	12	7.6	12	7.6
$225 to $249 · · · · · · · · · · · ·	10	6.3	9	5.7
$250 to $274 · · · · · · · · · · · ·	8	5.1	8	5.1
$275 to $299 · · · · · · · · · · · ·	4	2.5	3	1.9
$300 and over · · · · · · · · · · · ·	13	8.2	29	18.4

Average expenditures, ranges, and per cent reporting expenditures

All persons		
Mean · · · · · · · · · · · · · · · · · · ·	$162.05	$193.67
Median · · · · · · · · · · · · · · · · · ·	152.95	167.97
Persons reporting · · · · · · · · · · ·		
Mean · · · · · · · · · · · · · · · · · · ·	163.08	194.89
Median · · · · · · · · · · · · · · · · · ·	153.01	169.94
Range · · · · · · · · · · · · · · · · · · ·	3.68 to 555.11	13.32 to 740.49
Per cent reporting · · · · · · · · · ·	99.4	99.4

spent an average of $542, whereas $697 was spent by families with incomes of $6,000 or more. Although within both groups there were families with small and large expenditures, 10 of the 13 families that spent more than $1,000 were in the higher income class.

TABLE 40

Clothing Purchases for All Full-Year Boys and Girls Age 2 and Over, by Age Groups

Expenditure class	Total		2 to 5 years		6 to 11 years		12 to 15 years		16 years and over	
	Boys	Girls	Boys	Girls	Boys	Girls	Boys	Girls	Boys	Girls
					Number					
All boys and girls	141	126	50	43	60	53	17	20	14	10
Under $25	11	8	9	4	2	4	0	0	0	0
$25 to $49	29	18	18	10	8	8	1	0	2	0
$50 to $74	28	25	12	17	11	8	5	0	0	0
$75 to $99	27	15	5	3	20	11	1	1	1	0
$100 to $124	15	18	2	5	9	11	2	2	2	0
$125 to $149	11	11	1	1	5	6	2	3	3	1
$150 to $174	9	5	2	2	3	1	3	1	1	1
$175 to $199	6	6	1	0	1	0	1	5	3	1
$200 and over	5	20	0	1	1	4	2	8	2	7
					Per cent					
All boys and girls	100.0	100.0	100.0	100.0	100.0	100.0	100.0	100.0	100.0	100.0
Under $25	7.8	6.3	18.0	9.3	3.3	7.5	.0	.0	.0	.0
$25 to $49	20.6	14.3	36.0	23.3	13.3	15.1	5.9	.0	14.3	.0
$50 to $74	19.9	19.8	24.0	39.5	18.3	15.1	29.4	.0	.0	.0
$75 to $99	19.1	11.9	10.0	7.0	33.3	20.8	5.9	5.0	7.1	.0
$100 to $124	10.6	14.3	4.0	11.6	15.0	20.8	11.8	10.0	14.3	.0
$125 to $149	7.8	8.7	2.0	2.3	8.3	11.3	11.8	15.0	21.4	10.0
$150 to $174	6.4	4.0	4.0	4.7	5.0	1.9	17.6	5.0	7.1	10.0
$175 to $199	4.3	4.8	2.0	.0	1.7	.0	5.9	25.0	21.4	10.0
$200 and over	3.5	15.9	.0	2.3	1.7	7.5	11.8	40.0	14.3	70.0

Average expenditures and ranges

	Total		2 to 5 years		6 to 11 years		12 to 15 years		16 years and over	
	Boys	Girls	Boys	Girls	Boys	Girls	Boys	Girls	Boys	Girls
All boys and girls										
Mean	$88.76	$117.30	$56.68	$70.69	$89.76	$93.57	$126.14	$208.24	$153.66	$261.64
Median	76.04	97.08	45.81	59.20	86.20	86.02	117.17	195.39	141.46	252.20
Range	4.04 to 327.13	7.54 to 417.45	4.04 to 180.71	10.77 to 293.76	18.63 to 204.23	7.54 to 297.24	33.32 to 297.19	97.55 to 417.45	26.34 to 327.13	129.01 to 381.05

TABLE 41

Per Capita and Family Clothing Purchases for Infants under Two, by Age Groups

	Total under 2 years	Under 1 year	1 to 2 years
Infants under 2			
Total in sample	36	12	24
Expenditures reported	34	10	24
Average expenditure per infant			
Mean	$46.82	$28.78	$54.34
Median	26.48	19.70	40.26
Range of expenditures per infant	6.21 to 133.55	8.18 to 77.92	6.21 to 133.55
Families with infants under 2			
Number with infants	32	12	22
Expenditures reported	31	10	22
Average expenditure per family			
Mean	$51.35	$28.78	$59.28
Median	24.85	19.70	47.62
Range of expenditures per family	7.91 to 246.61	8.18 to 77.92	6.21 to 246.61
Mean expenditures, all families in sample	10.01	1.81	8.20

Clothing expenditures varied somewhat with the number of persons in the household, but the differences were small. Expenditures were influenced more by the age and sex of the children than by their number. Although there was a slight tendency for expenditures of more than $1,000 to occur more frequently among the larger families, they seemed more directly related to family income than to family size.

CLOTHING PURCHASES

The average cost of family clothing purchases for all families (including both full- and part-year family members) was $549. Women and girls together spent an average of $296 per family; the family average for men and boys was $243, and clothing for children under two averaged $10 per family. Although these figures indicate the total which the average family spent for clothing, a more significant analysis can be made in terms of the purchases of full-year family members by sex, and also by age of the children.

Men's clothing purchases.—The heads of all families spent an average of $162 for their clothing. Sixty per cent spent between $75 and $225, and the top 8 per cent had expenditures ranging between $300 and $555. The largest amounts were generally in families in which the wives also spent considerable money on clothing. In contrast, 1 man reported no expendi-

TABLE 42A

Clothing Purchases of Husbands, by Type of Clothing

Type of clothing	Number reporting expenditures	Per cent of all husbands	Total expenditures, those reporting		
			Mean	Median	Range[a]
Husbands reporting, total ····	158	99.4	$163.08	$153.01	$3.68 to 555.11
Coats and jackets, total ··	49	30.8	31.75	27.43	1.34 to 140.71
Topcoats, overcoats ··	20	12.6	55.61	51.37	30.89 to 103.50
Other coats and outdoor jackets ····	34	21.4	13.05	10.36	1.34 to 39.73
Suits, total ·············	115	72.3	86.57	71.42	15.00 to 310.51
Business ···········	115	72.3	86.03	67.28	15.00 to 279.45
Dress ···············	1	.6	62.10	...	62.10
Other ···············	0	.0	...	...	...
Separate sport jackets ···	25	15.7	27.94	20.70	5.18 to 77.63
Separate trousers and slacks ···············	89	56.0	16.87	16.56	3.04 to 45.03
Jeans, etc. ··············	16	10.1	5.89	4.89	3.00 to 10.24
Shirts, total ·············	138	86.8	22.54	18.92	3.11 to 68.26
Business ············	123	77.4	17.90	15.14	3.11 to 56.92
Sport ···············	90	56.6	9.40	8.23	1.55 to 23.29
Other ···············	14	8.8	4.45	4.12	.31 to 10.25
Sweaters ···············	17	10.7	8.08	8.70	1.91 to 20.65
Underwear and nightwear·	132	83.0	11.09	9.99	1.43 to 38.30
Robes ··················	6	3.8	12.58	12.91	6.19 to 20.70
Socks ··················	132	83.0	7.63	6.09	.72 to 27.00
Shoes ··················	123	77.4	20.56	18.63	4.09 to 61.99
Overshoes ·············	14	8.8	2.83	2.86	2.02 to 4.04
House slippers ···········	29	18.2	5.30	5.12	2.07 to 9.26
Hats ··················	83	52.2	11.78	10.35	.81 to 37.26
Accessories, total ······	138	86.8	16.54	9.56	1.00 to 117.49
Ties ···············	126	79.2	9.63	6.54	1.09 to 46.56
Other[b] ··············	79	49.7	13.52	5.97	.78 to 98.86
All other clothing ·······	35	22.0	5.29	4.14	1.14 to 15.53

[a]A few of the unusually small expenditures were for second-hand (often rummage sale) items.
[b]Including jewelry and watches.

tures, 3 spent under $10, and 13 less than $50. The man who spent nothing received gifts of clothing valued at $300; a few others reported much smaller gifts; and some apparently were able to get along with clothing purchased in previous years, except for the purchase of a few socks, ties, shirts, or shoes. When the husband spent less than $50, total family clothing purchases were also below the average for the group as a whole; in other words, although the man's clothing expenditure was the lowest in these particular families, other family members also spent relatively little for their wardrobes.

Although many different prices were paid for each type of clothing, typically these men paid $60 for wool suits, $12 for shoes, $10 for hats, $3.65 for shirts, 60 cents for cotton socks, and $1.50 for ties.

Women's clothing purchases.—The average clothing expenditure of the wives was $194—20 per cent more than their husbands spent. Sixty per cent of the women spent between $75 and $225, and slightly less than a fifth had

TABLE 42B

Clothing Purchases of Wives, by Type of Clothing

Type of clothing	Number reporting expenditures	Per cent of all wives	Total expenditures, those reporting		
			Mean	Median	Range[a]
Wives reporting, total	158	99.4	$194.89	$169.94	$13.32 to 740.49
Coats and jackets, total..	...	...	...	...	...
Wool coats	72	45.3	44.44	36.23	9.32 to 191.48
Fur coats	2	1.3	139.38	...	123.50 to 155.25
Other coats and jackets	37	23.3	11.56	7.25	1.34 to 62.10
Suits	60	37.7	41.45	33.64	.25 to 134.39
Separate skirts	86	54.1	11.25	9.29	.50 to 38.30
Dresses, total.........	150	94.3	38.82	32.02	2.07 to 155.25
House	97	61.0	12.99	10.26	1.50 to 93.15
Street	115	72.3	26.33	15.53	2.03 to 92.89
Semiformal	49	30.8	22.97	17.60	2.07 to 82.80
Formal	16	10.1	24.45	23.03	3.11 to 87.98
Other (including jumpers)	2	1.3	9.00	...	5.00 to 13.00
Slacks, jeans, etc.	80	50.3	7.04	5.15	.84 to 44.19
Blouses	111	69.8	10.08	8.28	.25 to 36.07
Sweaters	60	37.7	9.76	6.20	1.04 to 28.77
Underwear and nightwear	150	94.3	28.18	23.89	2.66 to 103.51
Robes	49	30.8	11.88	9.26	1.00 to 38.81
Stockings	146	91.8	12.60	10.87	1.00 to 55.89
Socks	63	39.6	1.80	1.48	.30 to 6.24
Shoes	148	93.1	23.48	20.06	3.05 to 123.05
Overshoes	26	16.4	2.84	2.34	1.44 to 6.18
House slippers	68	42.8	4.36	4.09	1.03 to 10.88
Hats	118	74.2	13.33	9.32	1.04 to 98.23
Accessories, total	124	78.0	20.88	13.49	.75 to 126.89
Purses	93	58.5	11.41	9.82	1.24 to 45.70
Other[b]	107	67.3	14.29	8.40	.50 to 89.22
All other clothing	68	42.8	8.60	7.20	.52 to 61.75

[a]A few of the unusually small expenditures were for second-hand (often rummage sale) items.
[b]Including jewelry and watches.

costs between $300 and a high of $740. Thus more than twice as many women as men spent $300 or more for their clothing, but only half as many spent less than $75. In most cases the women with high expenditures were in families in which total clothing purchases were far above the average for the entire sample, and the husbands also spent relatively large amounts. However, in the family in which the wife spent $740, the husband bought only $137 worth of clothing. Nine women spent less than $50, including 4 with expenditures under $25, and 1 reported no expenditures at all. Six of this group of 10 received gifts of clothing, but such gifts were usually small, four being valued at less than $25, and only one at as much as $100. As was true with the men, with 1 exception the women with the lowest expenses were members of families whose total clothing purchases were small.

The prices paid for women's clothes varied, of course, but they typically bought winter coats for $45 and summer coats for $25. They spent $15 for wool dresses, $9 for dress shoes, $5 for felt hats, and $1.50 for nylon stockings. Although some purchased a considerable amount of clothing, including a few quite expensive things, the vast majority bought few clothes and what they did buy were moderate in price.

Children's clothing purchases.—Expenditures for the 24 children, from one to two years old, averaged $54 for both sexes.[4] Among the children over two, however, there were important differences in the expenditures for boys and girls. The average spent for all boys two and older was $89, in contrast to $117 for the girls. Although 25 per cent of all children two and older spent less than $50, proportionately more boys than girls were in this expenditure group. At the other end of the scale, one-quarter of the girls but only 14 per cent of the boys spent $150 or more, and four times as many girls as boys had expenditures of $200 or more.

The average expenditure for all boys two to five was $57, and for the girls, $71. Sums under $50 were reported spent for 54 per cent of the boys, but for slightly less than a third of the girls in this age group. The average amounts spent for boys and girls six to eleven were very similar—$90 and $94. For 68 per cent of the boys and 58 per cent of the girls expenditures were under $100.

Obviously the girls from twelve to fifteen were becoming more clothes conscious, and they were much more expensive to dress than boys of the same ages. The average amount spent for the girls was $208 in contrast to only $126 for the boys. None of the girls spent less than $75, whereas 35 per cent of the boys spent sums below this figure. Seventy per cent of the girls spent more than $150, in contrast to 35 per cent of the boys. Finally, expenditures of $200 or more were reported for 40 per cent of the girls and only 12 per cent of the boys. Not only did the average mother spend less for herself than for her daughters in the age brackets above eleven, but practically all who had daughters twelve to fifteen, and a third with older girls, spent less than the average for the entire group of mothers. Eleven of the 15 who had these older girls spent more for their daughters' clothes than for their own.

Among the children sixteen and older, the average expenditure for the boys was $154, and for the girls $262. Thirty-six per cent of the boys but none of the girls spent less than $125. Seventy per cent of the girls spent $200 or more, but only 14 per cent of the boys spent as much as this.

The foregoing discussion serves to point up another fact about the children's clothing purchases: There were consistent differences in the money spent for children of different ages—the older the child, the more his wardrobe cost. For the boys, the greatest proportionate increase came for those six to eleven; their clothes cost more than half again as much as was spent

---

[4]For expenditures for all infants under two years of age, see table 41, p. 82.

TABLE 42C

Clothing Purchases of Full-Year Boys Age Two and Over, by Type of Clothing and Age Group

Type of clothing	Number reporting expenditures	Per cent of all full-year boys	Total full-year boys — Total expenditures, those reporting			Full-year boys by age groups — Number reporting and total expenditures							
			Mean	Median	Range[a]	2 to 5 years Number	Mean	6 to 11 years Number	Mean	12 to 15 years Number	Mean	16 years and over Number	Mean
Full-year boys reporting													
Total.............	141	100.0	$88.76	$76.04	$4.04 to 327.13	50	$56.68	60	$89.76	17	$126.14	14	$153.66
Coats and jackets...													
Total........	97	68.8	13.56	10.20	1.03 to 85.65	25	8.84	48	12.33	14	16.18	10	27.62
Topcoats, overcoats	16	11.3	14.10	12.94	3.11 to 30.79	10	10.47	4	16.04	0	...	2	28.34
Other coats and outdoor jackets..	91	65.5	11.98	9.32	1.03 to 54.86	19	6.12	48	10.99	14	16.18	10	21.96
Suits, total	27	19.1	19.13	10.25	1.00 to 119.03	16	7.83	5	15.97	1	36.23	5	55.01
General purpose..	14	9.9	30.29	25.34	2.95 to 119.03	4	10.01	4	18.16	1	36.23	5	55.01
Dress	0	.0	...	...	...	0	...	0	...	0	...	0	...
Other.........	13	9.2	7.11	7.19	1.00 to 15.42	12	7.11	1	7.19	0	...	0	...
Separate sport jackets	21	14.9	11.63	12.94	1.02 to 25.88	3	2.70	10	11.83	4	14.19	4	15.26
Separate trousers and slacks	90	63.8	13.65	11.30	1.04 to 47.51	20	6.94	43	13.52	13	16.94	14	20.62
Jeans, etc......	96	68.1	9.80	8.26	.30 to 30.99	36	7.61	46	10.62	9	15.19	5	8.34
Shirts, total.....	110	78.0	12.91	8.68	1.55 to 93.61	28	6.00	53	11.79	16	19.40	13	24.38
General purpose.	23	16.3	5.01	4.14	.82 to 12.26	2	1.44	5	4.59	5	3.45	8	7.29
Sport........	107	75.9	11.90	8.73	1.55 to 89.99	26	6.17	52	11.25	16	17.94	13	18.49
Other........	7	5.0	4.60	4.60	4.04 to 8.18	1	4.66	1	3.08	2	3.10	3	6.09
Sweaters........	63	44.7	6.56	5.12	.10 to 31.05	17	4.36	28	5.89	8	9.03	10	10.20
Underwear and nightwear......	123	87.2	8.53	7.86	1.34 to 31.61	40	8.90	54	7.32	15	10.50	14	9.99
Robes	19	13.5	7.56	7.19	2.33 to 15.53	6	4.77	8	7.28	3	11.73	2	10.84
Socks.........	131	92.9	4.34	3.62	1.00 to 23.55	45	2.59	56	4.32	17	5.97	13	8.29
Shoes.........	137	97.2	25.40	22.41	3.62 to 95.69	49	20.78	58	26.67	17	28.62	13	32.88
Overshoes	44	31.2	3.76	4.09	1.04 to 7.76	14	3.88	24	3.84	4	3.72	2	2.07
House slippers ...	51	36.2	3.31	3.11	1.04 to 8.28	21	3.04	25	3.36	4	4.63	1	2.58
Hats.........	60	42.6	1.87	1.59	.15 to 6.47	25	1.88	26	2.07	6	1.22	3	1.38
All other clothing...	87	61.7	8.62	5.13	.21 to 60.22	21	6.65	42	6.29	16	16.49	8	10.26

[a] A few of the unusually small expenditures were for second-hand (often rummage sale) items.
[b] Including jewelry and watches.

TABLE 42D

Clothing Purchases of Full-Year Girls Age Two and Over, by Type of Clothing and Age Groups

Type of clothing	Total full-year girls					Full-year girls by age group — Number reporting and total expenditures							
	Number reporting all expenditures	Per cent all full-year girls	Total expenditures, those reporting			2 to 5 years		6 to 11 years		12 to 15 years		16 years and over	
			Mean	Median	Range[a]	Number	Mean	Number	Mean	Number	Mean	Number	Mean
Full-year girls reporting, total	126	100.0	$117.30	$97.08	$7.54 to 417.45	43	$70.69	53	$93.57	20	$208.24	10	$261.64
Coats and jackets, total	81	64.3	20.40	18.61	2.05 to 66.19	24	14.12	30	18.47	19	25.70	8	33.87
Wool coats	52	41.3	19.90	18.26	5.64 to 51.75	14	13.28	24	16.62	8	32.21	6	32.07
All other coats	41	32.5	6.84	3.36	1.81 to 23.75	12	5.44	18	4.96	9	13.54	2	2.04
Jackets	28	22.2	12.02	9.29	1.55 to 53.82	10	8.76	6	10.97	9	12.09	3	24.82
Suits	29	23.0	22.06	23.29	3.05 to 67.28	3	13.03	8	13.66	9	27.50	9	27.04
Separate skirts	75	59.5	11.16	6.22	.93 to 63.07	15	3.10	31	5.90	19	19.46	10	23.77
Dresses, total	109	86.5	21.06	13.95	1.81 to 134.57	34	12.43	46	18.06	19	25.70	10	55.43
School	101	80.2	17.66	12.42	1.81 to 93.16	32	11.97	45	16.81	15	22.62	9	33.88
Semi-formal	22	17.5	12.80	10.35	2.44 to 36.23	4	6.56	5	9.69	6	11.90	7	19.36
Formal	8	6.3	20.04	23.29	5.18 to 31.00	0	...	0	...	4	17.58	4	22.50
Other (incl. jumpers)	13	10.3	5.40	4.14	2.06 to 15.53	4	3.32	5	5.18	2	3.62	2	11.90
Slacks, jeans, etc.	95	75.4	7.67	5.70	1.04 to 43.16	33	7.22	40	7.24	16	9.71	6	7.63
Blouses	77	61.1	7.48	4.66	.05 to 29.46	20	4.69	28	4.11	20	11.98	9	14.16
Sweaters	85	67.5	12.41	7.93	1.02 to 59.57	20	5.93	36	7.18	19	23.06	10	23.93
Underwear and nightwear	118	93.7	12.61	10.14	1.03 to 44.98	39	8.50	49	10.14	20	20.00	10	26.00
Robes	43	34.1	5.73	5.00	1.04 to 14.49	15	5.18	18	5.20	6	7.56	4	7.38
Stockings	21	16.7	4.00	3.42	1.04 to 8.62	0	...	2	1.60	12	3.70	7	5.20
Socks	118[b]	93.7	3.76[b]	3.23[b]	.62 to 13.20[b]	41[b]	3.34[b]	53	3.54	17	5.50	7	3.59
Shoes	124	98.4	22.14	20.88	2.59 to 92.52	43	19.54	51	22.41	20	26.51	10	23.18
Overshoes	58	46.0	3.56	3.56	.73 to 7.25	21	3.12	29	3.83	6	4.51	2	2.04
House slippers	66	52.4	3.37	3.08	1.02 to 8.28	25	3.24	24	3.36	10	3.98	7	3.02
Headwear	53	42.1	4.37	3.08	.88 to 20.56	19	3.32	18	3.78	13	4.87	3	12.42
Accessories	92	73.0	8.19	4.68	.26 to 54.33	26	3.73	38	5.89	18	15.46	10	15.42
All other clothing[c]	72	57.1	8.01	5.25	.52 to 58.75	16	3.28	29	7.28	18	11.95	9	10.91

[a] A few of the unusually small expenditures were for second-hand (often rummage sale) items.

[b] 118 girls reported the purchase of socks, but 1 girl in the two to five age group did not report the amount spent. Therefore the mean, median, and range for all girls are based on 117 cases, and the mean for the two to five group on 40 cases.

[c] Including jewelry and watches.

TABLE 43

Expenditures for Clothing Services, by Type of Service

Families reporting expenditures

Expenditure class	Total services		Cleaning and pressing		Shoe repair		All other services	
	Number	Per cent	Number	Per cent	Number	Per cent	Number	Per cent
Families reporting, total....	159	100.0	158	100.0	153	100.0	155	100.0
Under $25	8	5.0	32	20.3	136	88.9	134	86.5
$25 to $49	42	26.4	67	42.4	12	7.8	16	10.3
$50 to $74	44	27.7	37	23.4	5	3.3	4	2.6
$70 to $75	32	20.1	13	8.2	0	.0	0	.0
$100 to $149	22	13.8	6	3.8	0	.0	1	.6
$150 to $199	9	5.7	3	1.9	0	.0	0	.0
$200 to $299	2	1.3	0	.0	0	.0	0	.0

Average expenditures, ranges, and per cent reporting expenditures

	Total services		Cleaning and pressing		Shoe repair		All other services	
All families								
Mean	$74.27		$47.75		$12.36		$14.16	
Median	64.32		40.10		9.05		11.00	
Families reporting								
Mean	74.27		48.05		12.84		14.53	
Median	64.32		40.48		9.75		11.10	
Range	12.07 to 251.67		3.75 to 181.90		1.00 to 74.80		.20 to 103.00	
Per cent reporting	100.0		99.4		96.2		97.5	

for the boys two to five. The rise in the boys' expenditures continued for the older age groups, but at a decreasing rate. In contrast, clothing costs for the six to eleven girls increased by slightly less than a third over the younger girls, but the cost for girls twelve to fifteen was 122 per cent greater than that of the six to eleven group. The increase for children over sixteen was much the same for boys and girls: 22 and 26 per cent above those age twelve to fifteen.

A few typical prices will give some idea of the quality of clothes which these children wore. For boys ten to fifteen years old, outdoor wool jackets cost $8.95, separate wool trousers $8.50, jeans $3.25, cotton sport shirts $2.50, shoes $7.95, and socks 50 cents. Average prices paid for clothing for girls six to eleven included wool coats at $16.50, wool skirts $5, cotton school dresses $3.98, jeans $1.98, wool sweaters $3.95, shoes $6.50, and socks 39 cents.

In summary, although the number of children did affect the amount a family spent for clothing, the age and sex of the children were even more important factors. For example, a family with 2 children twelve or older was likely to spend more for clothing than one with 2 younger children, and a family with 2 very young children probably spent less than 1 with 1 girl in her teens.

The clothing expenditures of the families in this study indicate, both by the quantity and quality of the items purchased, that the group in general was clothed with considerable attention to economy. A few spent generously and perhaps may be said to have indulged in some luxury items. However, even the 2 women who bought fur jackets paid only $125 and $155 for them, and these sums could not have purchased very luxurious garments. On the other hand, those with very low expenditures did not necessarily have shabby clothing, since they may have very well made larger purchases the year before.

CLOTHING SERVICES

Every family spent something for clothing repair and upkeep in addition to their purchases, and they reported an average expenditure of $74. There seemed to be no consistent relationship between income and expenditures for total clothing services. Families with incomes of less than $6,000 spent practically the same amount for all clothing services as did those with higher incomes. The same situation was true in the various components of clothing services: expenditures did not vary directly with income. Family expenditures for total services covered a wide range, but 79 per cent were less than $100, and slightly less than half were between $50 and $100. Only 2 families spent $200 or more.

The largest average expenditure was for cleaning and pressing, amounting to $48 for those reporting such expenses. One family reported no expenditures for such services; one-fifth of the families spent less than $25; 63 per cent, less than $50; and 94 per cent reported expenditures of less than $100. The cost of shoe repairs averaged $12 for all families in the sample; only 5 families had costs between $50 and $75, and the vast majority spent less than $25. Small sums were also spent for all other types of clothing services including alterations and repairs, dyeing, and watch and jewelry repair. The average of these combined expenditures was only $14; 86 per cent of the families spent less than $25, and the highest expense was $103.

It is clear that most families spent moderately for the upkeep of their clothing. Only about one-fifth of the sample had costs of $100 or more for all clothing services, and there were very few large expenditures for the specific service categories. The average sum of $48 spent for cleaning would have allowed the family to send three or four coats, suits, or dresses to the cleaner each month, and the $12 average for shoe repairs would have been sufficient to have about four pairs of shoes half-soled and heeled each year.

Chapter IX
EXPENDITURES FOR TRANSPORTATION

TOTAL TRANSPORTATION

Transportation was an important item of expenditure for these families, ranking second only to food. Every family spent something; all but 8 owned an automobile at some time during 1950, and all but 11 had other transportation expenses. The average expenditure for total transportation was $924, or 15.5 per cent of all consumption expenditures, and automobile expenditures accounted for 89 per cent of all transportation costs.[1] Expenditures for total transportation varied widely: 1 family that did not own a car spent less than $100; 40 per cent of all families spent between $200 and $500; and 27 per cent, made up almost entirely of families that had purchased cars in 1950, spent $1,000 or more.[2]

The amounts spent for total transportation showed an unexpected variation by income groups. When the 159 families were divided into six income groups, the highest average expenditure for total transportation was in the lowest income group, and average expenditures declined in each of the next three groups. The two highest groups did not follow this pattern, but even they were lower than the group with incomes under $5,000. All families with incomes under $6,000 spent 9 per cent more for total transportation than those with higher incomes, and the difference was largely due to automobile expenses, since the two income groups spent $102 and $101 respectively for nonautomobile expenses.

---

[1]All automobile expenditures were adjusted to exclude expenses for the business use of a car. Such costs, reported by 21 families, were classified as occupational expenses and subtracted from income.

[2]The total net cost, after any trade-in allowance, of an item purchased in 1950 was classified as a 1950 expenditure, even if not completely paid for within the year.

TABLE 44

Expenditure for Transportation, by Type of Transportation

Families reporting expenditures

Expenditure class	Total transportation		Automobile						All other transportation	
			Total		Purchase		Operation			
	Number	Per cent	Number	Per cent	Number	Per cent	Number	Per cent	Number	Per cent
Families reporting, total...	159	100.0	151	100.0	55	100.0	151	100.0	148	100.0
Under $100, total...	1	.6	0	.0	5	9.1	0	.0	76	51.4
Under $25...	0	.0	0	.0	0	.0	0	.0	27	18.2
$25 to $49...	1	.6	0	.0	1	1.8	0	.0	20	13.5
$50 to $74...	0	.0	0	.0	3	5.5	0	.0	21	14.2
$75 to $99...	0	.0	0	.0	1	1.8	0	.0	8	5.4
$100 to $199...	5	3.1	5	3.3	2	3.6	7	4.6	58	39.2
$200 to $299...	13	8.2	25	16.6	1	1.8	30	19.9	11	7.4
$300 to $399...	22	13.8	34	22.5	4	7.3	57	37.7	1	.7
$400 to $499...	28	17.6	23	15.2	1	1.8	34	22.5	0	.0
$500 to $999...	47	29.6	23	15.2	5	9.1	23	15.2	2	1.4
$1,000 to $1,999...	15	9.4	15	9.9	26	47.3	0	.0	0	.0
$2,000 and over...	28	17.6	26	17.2	11	20.0	0	.0	0	.0

Average expenditures, ranges, and per cent reporting expenditures

	Total transportation	Automobile Total	Purchase	Operation	All other transportation
All families					
Mean...	$923.52	$822.04	$457.64	$364.40	$101.48
Median...	541.66	438.25	...	350.91	76.10
Families reporting					
Mean...	923.52	865.59	1,323.00	383.71	109.03
Median...	541.66	453.25	1,500.00	361.43	87.38
Range...	45.50 to 3,224.25	151.97 to 3,060.98	45.00 to 2,685.00	114.64 to 985.18	.60 to 875.00
Per cent reporting...	100.0	95.0	34.6	95.0	93.1

TABLE 45

Expenditures for Transportation, by Income Class and Type of Transportation

Income class	Mean expenditure					Median expenditure				
	Total transportation	Automobile			All other transportation	Total transportation	Automobile			All other transportation
		Total	Purchase	Operation			Total	Purchase	Operation	
All families	$923.52	$822.04	$457.64	$364.40	$101.48	$541.66	$438.25	....	$350.91	$76.10
Under $5,000	1,118.83	1,049.59	688.88	360.71	69.24	630.62	583.72	....	347.28	60.60
$5,000 to $5,499	927.70	828.52	533.35	295.17	99.18	460.76	417.34	....	307.10	81.16
$5,500 to $5,999	887.33	769.14	407.85	361.29	128.19	511.14	420.52	....	358.62	95.55
$6,000 to $6,499	759.99	659.73	268.20	391.53	100.26	534.77	420.38	....	370.22	96.50
$6,500 to $6,999	992.15	897.52	516.07	381.45	94.63	548.03	489.75	....	359.46	81.76
$7,000 and over	942.50	832.47	435.51	396.96	110.03	535.14	451.30	....	355.35	53.35
Under $6,000	966.81	864.82	528.04	336.78	101.99	534.28	429.26	....	340.54	75.62
$6,000 and over	883.89	782.87	393.18	389.69	101.02	543.11	447.20	....	359.80	76.10
Families reporting, total ...	923.52	865.59	1,323.00	383.71	109.03	541.66	453.25	$1,500.00	361.43	87.38
Under $5,000	1,118.83	1,049.59	1,377.76	360.71	72.88	630.62	583.72	1,699.00	347.28	61.20
$5,000 to $5,499	927.70	966.61	1,244.47	344.37	102.86	460.76	475.12	1,566.20	354.60	85.52
$5,500 to $5,999	897.33	797.63	1,141.97	374.68	132.94	511.14	422.89	1,025.28	372.59	104.35
$6,000 to $6,499	759.99	659.73	1,519.77	391.53	100.26	534.77	420.38	1,668.82	370.22	96.50
$6,500 to $6,999	992.15	1,009.71	1,266.73	429.13	111.09	548.03	522.73	1,344.62	403.80	122.80
$7,000 and over	942.50	832.47	1,596.88	396.96	138.48	535.14	451.30	1,692.46	355.35	93.90
Under $6,000	966.81	925.72	1,254.09	360.50	106.18	534.28	469.70	1,490.92	352.75	83.82
$6,000 and over	883.89	812.23	1,418.86	404.30	111.80	543.11	452.72	1,500.00	370.22	105.00

TABLE 46

Number of Automobiles Owned, by Date of Manufacture and Income of Owners

Date of manufacture	Number of automobiles owned					
	January 1, 1950			December 31, 1950		
	Income of owners					
	All incomes	Under $6,000	$6,000 and over	All incomes	Under $6,000	$6,000 and over
Total cars	153	69	84	163	75	88
Postwar—1946 or later ..	67	22	45	102	42	60
Prewar—1942 or earlier .	86	47	39	61	33	28
Ratio of postwar to prewar cars............	.8	.5	1.2	1.7	1.3	2.1

AUTOMOBILE PURCHASE AND UPKEEP

The average expenditure for the purchase and upkeep of cars was $822.
Families with incomes less than $6,000 spent an average of $865, and the
higher income group $783. The larger car expense for the lower income
group was related to car purchase rather than operation; the group spent an
average of $337 for operation and upkeep of an automobile, whereas those
with higher incomes spent $390. On the other hand, those with incomes
under $6,000 spent an average of $528 for car purchase, as against $393
spent by the higher income group. The fact that families with lower incomes
spent more for the purchase of cars than those in the higher income brackets
was not the result of buying more expensive cars. Actually those with incomes of $6,000 or more bought cars with an average net cost 12 per cent
greater than the average cost of the cars bought by the lower income group.
However, 42 per cent of the families in the lower group bought cars, but
only 28 per cent of the upper income group made such purchases. This was
probably because the cars owned by the lower income group were older and
in greater need of replacement. At the beginning of 1950 more than two-
thirds of the cars owned by the lower income families had been manufactured
in 1942 or earlier; in contrast, less than half the cars owned by the upper
income group were that old. During 1950 families in the lower income bracket increased the proportion of postwar to prewar cars which they owned from
.5 to 1.3, or 120 per cent. In the same period families with higher incomes
raised their proportion of postwar cars from 1.2 to 2.1, or only 75 per cent.

Car ownership.—Nearly all families owned a car at some time in 1950.
In the main, these were one-car families, although at the end of 1950, 12
were two-car families. Sixty-three per cent of the cars owned at the end of
1950 by all the families were manufactured in 1946 or later years. Even
with the larger amount spent in 1950 for car purchases by the lower income
group, and the resulting greater relative decrease in the age of the cars

which they owned, the cars owned by the higher income group were on the whole considerably newer than those owned by families in the lower bracket. Fifty-six per cent of the cars owned by the lower income families and slightly more than two-thirds of those owned by the upper bracket were postwar models.

Forty-seven per cent of the one hundred and sixty-three cars owned at the end of 1950 were in the lowest price group, made up of Fords, Chevrolets, and Plymouths.[3] Almost the same number of cars were among the eleven which made up the next two price groups. Only eleven cars were in a higher price bracket, and no family owned a Cadillac or similar expensive car. Sixty-one per cent of all the cars were purchased new, and the make of the car owned showed a relationship to whether it was purchased new or used—the higher the price range of the car, the less apt the family was to have bought it new. Only slightly more than one-fourth of the cars in the highest price class, 56 per cent of the cars in the next lower class, and nearly two-thirds of the cars in the two lowest price classes, were bought new. Both income groups showed this general pattern, although in all but one of the price fields those with higher incomes bought a higher proportion of new cars than did the lower income group.

Fifty-five families in the sample purchased fifty-six cars during 1950, twenty-nine of which were new, and twenty-seven secondhand. However, 73 per cent of the total money spent for the purchase of automobiles went for the new cars. The average price of all cars purchased, including any financing charges and extras bought at the time of purchase, was $1,660, but after trade-in allowances and adjustments for the business use of cars,[4] the average expenditure was $1,299. The price of new cars averaged $2,347, but with the trade-in allowance and the adjustment for business use, the average cost was $1,839. Although the prices of new cars varied from

---

[3]Cars currently being manufactured were grouped by the purchase prices of 4-door sedans as reported in Consumer Reports (Consumers Union), May, 1953. If various models of the car appeared in more than one group, the car was classified here in the cheapest of the groups in which it was listed. Using this as a general guide, all cars owned by 1 or more families were classified into the following groups:
Group 1. Ford, Chevrolet, Plymouth
Group 2. Dodge, Hudson, Hillman, Nash, Pontiac, Studebaker, Willys
Group 3. Buick, DeSoto, Mercury, Oldsmobile
Group 4. Chrysler, Kaiser, Lincoln, LaSalle, Packard

[4]A percentage of the total price equal to the proportion of miles driven for business was subtracted from the total price paid in the case of 4 families who bought cars. The average amount subtracted was $29.10 for all car buyers, and $407.40 for the 4 car-buying families that reported business use.

TABLE 47

Characteristics of Automobiles Owned December 31, 1950, by Income Class of Owners

| | All owners | | Income class of owners | | | |
| | | | Under $6,000 | | $6,000 and over | |
	Number	Per cent	Number	Per cent	Number	Per cent
All cars	163	100.0	75	100.0	88	100.0
Year model						
Prewar (1942 and prior)	61	37.4	33	44.0	28	31.8
Postwar (1946 to 1951)	102	62.6	42	56.0	60	68.2
Purchased new or used						
Purchased new	100	61.3	42	56.0	58	65.9
Purchased used	63	38.7	33	44.0	30	34.1
Price group[a]						
Group 1	77	47.2	37	49.3	40	45.5
Purchased new	51	66.2	22	59.5	29	72.5
Purchased used	26	33.8	15	40.5	11	27.5
Group 2	43	26.4	19	25.3	24	27.3
Purchased new	28	65.1	13	68.4	15	62.5
Purchased used	15	34.9	6	31.6	9	37.5
Group 3	32	19.6	14	18.7	18	20.5
Purchased new	18	56.2	6	42.9	12	66.7
Purchased used	14	43.8	8	57.1	6	33.3
Group 4	11	6.7	5	6.7	6	6.8
Purchased new	3	27.3	1	20.0	2	33.3
Purchased used	8	72.7	4	80.0	4	66.7

[a] See footnote 3, p. 95.

TABLE 48

Purchase Prices of Automobiles Purchased in 1950, by Income Class of Buyers and Type of Car Bought

Price class[a]	All cars			New cars			Used cars		
	All buyers	Income class		All buyers	Income class		All buyers	Income class	
		Under $6,000	$6,000 and over		Under $6,000	$6,000 and over		Under $6,000	$6,000 and over
Number									
All cars	56[b]	33	23	29	16	13	27	17	10
Under $500	10	6	4	0	0	0	10	6	4
$500 to $999	5	5	0	0	0	0	5	5	0
$1,000 to $1,499	4	2	2	0	0	0	4	2	2
$1,500 to $1,999	13	9	4	6	5	1	7	4	3
$2,000 to $2,499	13	7	6	12	7	5	1	0	1
$2,500 to $2,999	11	4	7	11	4	7	0	0	0
Per cent									
All cars	100.0	100.0	100.0	100.0	100.0	100.0	100.0	100.0	100.0
Under $500	17.9	18.2	17.4	.0	.0	.0	37.0	35.3	40.0
$500 to $999	8.9	15.2	.0	.0	.0	.0	18.5	29.4	.0
$1,000 to $1,499	7.1	6.1	8.7	.0	.0	.0	14.8	11.8	20.0
$1,500 to $1,999	23.2	27.3	17.4	20.7	31.2	7.7	25.9	23.5	30.0
$2,000 to $2,499	23.2	21.2	26.1	41.4	25.0	38.5	3.7	.0	10.0
$2,500 to $2,999	19.6	12.1	30.4	37.9	43.8	53.8	.0	.0	.0
Average prices and ranges									
Mean	$1,659.91	$1,519.03	$1,862.06	$2,346.69	$2,248.22	$2,467.89	$922.26	$832.73	$1,074.48
Median	1,901.20	1,831.00	2,098.62	2,312.92	2,276.25	2,562.00	800.00	555.92	1,364.70
Range	30.00 to 2,947.59	30.00 to 2,947.59	175.00 to 2,947.33	1,560.37 to 2,947.59	1,560.37 to 2,947.59	1,797.30 to 2,947.33	30.00 to 2,000.00	30.00 to 1,962.32	175.00 to 2,000.00

[a]The purchase price is the price before any trade-in allowance; it includes any installment or credit charges, plus the price of all extra equipment bought at the time of purchase.

[b]One family bought 2 cars in 1950. Thus, 55 families bought 56 cars.

TABLE 49

Purchase Price, Trade-In, Adjustment for Business Use, and Net Cost of Cars Bought in 1950, by Income Class of Buyers, and Type of Cars Bought

	All cars			New cars			Used cars		
	All buyers	Income class		All buyers	Income class		All buyers	Income class	
		Under $6,000	$6,000 and over		Under $6,000	$6,000 and over		Under $6,000	$6,000 and over
Cars purchased, total	56	33	23	29	16	13	27	17	10
Purchase price[a]	$1,659.91	$1,519.03	$1,862.06	$2,346.69	$2,248.22	$2,467.89	$922.26	$832.73	$1,074.48
Trade-in	331.44	281.84	402.62	488.13	433.48	555.39	163.14	139.12	204.00
Adjustment for business use[b]	29.10	21.10	40.58	19.82	35.93	.00	39.07	7.14	93.34
Net cost[a] after trade-in and adjustment for business use	1,299.37	1,216.09	1,418.86	1,838.74	1,778.81	1,912.50	720.05	686.47	777.14

[a] The purchase price and net cost after deductions include any financing charges and extras bought at the time of purchase.

[b] Expenses for the business use of a car were reported by four automobile purchasers; such costs were classified as occupational expenses and were deducted from income and not classified as expenditures, in accordance with B. L. S. procedure.

TABLE 50

Method of Purchase of New and Used Cars

Method of purchase	All cars		New cars		Used cars	
	Number of families	Per cent	Number of families	Per cent	Number of families	Per cent
Families purchasing, total..	55[a]	100.0	29	100.0	26[a]	100.0
Purchased for cash......	26	47.3	14	48.3	12	46.2
Purchased by installment or other borrowing, total	29	52.7	15	51.7	14	53.8
Installment	12	21.8	7	24.1	5	19.2
Other borrowing, total	17	30.9	8	27.6	9	34.6
Specified for car...	10	18.2	4	13.8	6	23.1
Not specified......	7	12.7	4	13.8	3	11.5

[a]One family bought two used cars. Thus, 55 families bought a total of fifty-six cars, and 26 families bought twenty-seven used cars.

$1,560 to $2,948, most were in the neighborhood of $2,000. Since the lower income group purchased somewhat more cars in the lowest price group, the average price of their new cars was $2,248, in comparison with $2,468 for the upper income families. However, the actual amounts spent by these two income groups averaged $1,779 and $1,912 after trade-in allowances and adjustments for business use.

The average price of the twenty-seven used cars purchased in 1950 was $922, and with the trade-in allowance and adjustment for business use it was $720. There was naturally much greater variability in the cost of used cars: three cost less than $100 and were obviously old jalopies; 56 per cent cost less than $1,000; and 44 per cent ranged from $1,000 to a high of $2,000. Families with incomes below $6,000 bought used cars with an average price of $833, in contrast to $1,074 for those with higher incomes. However, when trade-in allowances and adjustments for business use were taken into account, the expenditures of the two groups were much closer—$686 and $777. As already noted, in spite of the fact that families with incomes less than $6,000 purchased lower priced cars (whether new or used), the total amount they spent to buy cars was somewhat higher than the upper income group because proportionately more of them bought cars.

Method of financing auto purchases.—Several methods of financing auto purchases were used by the families in this study. Forty-seven per cent paid cash, another 22 per cent purchased their cars on installment, and 18 per cent borrowed specifically to buy a car. Thirteen per cent of those who bought cars borrowed money but did not report the specific purpose for which the debt was incurred. However, it seems probable considering the size of the loans, that the money involved was used to pay for their cars. Therefore it seems safe to assume that a little more than half the families

TABLE 51

Expenditures for Operation of Automobile, by Type of Expenditure

Type of expenditure	Mean expenditures		Per cent of total operating costs	Families reporting expenditures				
	All families	All car owners		Number	Per cent of all owners	Expenditures		
						Mean	Median	Range
Operation costs, total	$364.40	$383.71	100.0	151	100.0	$383.71	$361.43	$114.64 to 985.18
Gas and oil, total	147.46	155.27	40.5	151	100.0	155.27	149.42	25.08 to 449.40
Gas	135.04	142.19	37.1	151	100.0	142.19	135.24	23.75 to 413.40
Oil	12.42	13.08	3.4	150	99.3	13.17	12.00	1.33 to 45.92
Insurance, total	74.07	78.00	20.3	150	99.3	78.52	73.99	23.33 to 170.72
Fire and theft[a]	...	...	...	129	85.4	...	...	5.25 to 32.00
Public liability[a]	...	...	...	150	99.3	...	...	27.30 to 134.10
Collision[a]	...	...	...	96	63.6	...[b]	...	15.00 to 89.00
Repairs	53.36[b]	56.21[b]	14.6	128	84.8	66.39[b]	45.01[b]	2.04 to 350.91
Tires and tubes	22.19	23.36	6.1	85	56.3	41.50	37.26	3.09 to 190.67
Registration, fees, and licenses ...	19.55[b]	20.59[b]	5.3	151	100.0	20.59[b]	18.00[b]	3.38 to 63.00
Lubrication	13.38[b]	14.09[b]	3.6	139	92.1	15.32[b]	11.62[b]	2.00 to 79.52
Battery	6.63	6.98	1.8	64	42.4	16.47	16.02	5.18 to 32.57
Accessories	4.56	4.80	1.3	45	29.8	16.10	15.91	.68 to 63.97
Miscellaneous[c]	23.75	25.01	6.5	146	96.7	25.86	17.00	1.00 to 135.00

[a]Since the majority of families reporting expenditures for car insurance were unable to give an accurate cost breakdown for each type of insurance carried, the average costs for the three specific coverages are omitted.

[b]The average is based on 1 less case than the total reporting, because 1 family was unable to report the specific amount spent.

[c]Includes parking fees, tolls, fines, and so on.

TABLE 52

Expenditures for Transportation Other Than Owned Automobile,
By Type of Transportation

	Type of transportation				
	Total		Local[a]		All other[b]

Families reporting expenditures

Expenditure class	Number	Per cent	Number	Per cent	Number	Per cent
Families reporting, total ···	148	100.0	147	100.0	60	100.0
Under $100, total ········	76	51.4	83	56.5	51	85.0
Under 50 ············	47	31.8	57	38.8	48	80.0
$50 to $99 ············	29	19.6	26	17.7	3	5.0
$100 to $199 ············	58	39.2	60	40.8	4	6.7
$200 to $299 ············	11	7.4	4	2.7	2	3.3
$300 and over ··········	3	2.0	0	.0	3	5.0

Average expenditures, ranges, and per cent reporting expenditures

	Total	Local[a]	All other[b]
All families			
Mean ·················	$101.48	$76.82	$24.66
Median ···············	76.10	63.60	...
Families reporting			
Mean ·················	109.03	83.09	65.35
Median ···············	87.38	67.00	25.75
Range ···············	.60 to 875.00	.50 to 253.50	1.55 to 718.00
Per cent reporting ········	93.1	92.5	37.7

[a]Local transportation includes street cars, busses, trains, taxis, and shared cars or
car pools (when car not owned by respondent). Such transportation is used to go to work,
or to school, or for shopping, etc.

[b]All other transportation includes trips outside the Bay Area for pleasure or personal
business, plus miscellaneous forms of transportation such as the purchase, upkeep, or
rental of a motorcycle, boat, or trailer; rental of an automobile; or drivers' licenses for
non-car owning family.

used some type of credit in the purchase of their cars. The proportion of
credit purchases was almost the same for both new and used cars. All types
of credit were reported by purchasers in both income brackets, but only 44
per cent of the higher income buyers used any credit, in contrast with 59
per cent of the buyers in the lower income group.

Car operation and upkeep.—For all families in the sample the cost of
operating cars averaged $364, or 6.1 per cent of total consumption expendi-
tures. If the 8 families that did not own cars are omitted, the average expenditure was $384. Car owners with incomes of less than $6,000 spent an
average of $360 and those with higher incomes $404, or 12 per cent more
than the lower bracket.

There was a considerable degree of concentration in the car operation
and upkeep expenditures: 38 per cent spent between $300 and $400, and 80
per cent between $200 and $500. However, individual expenditures ranged
from $115 to $985. The family that spent only $115 owned a Hillman car for

TABLE 53

Expenditure for Local Transportation, by Type and Place of Residence

All families

Type of transportation	Total area		San Francisco		Elsewhere	
	Average expenditure	Per cent of total	Average expenditure	Per cent of total	Average expenditure	Per cent of total
Local transportation, total .	$76.82	100.0	$56.74	100.0	$85.25	100.0
Street car, bus, train ..	67.39	87.7	50.60	89.2	74.43	87.3
Man to work	53.21	69.3	25.68	45.3	64.77	76.0
All other	14.17	18.5	24.92	43.9	9.66	11.3
Taxi, shared car	9.43	12.3	6.14	10.8	10.82	12.7

Families reporting

Type of transportation	Total area			San Francisco			Elsewhere		
	Average expenditure	Number of families	Per cent of all families	Average expenditure	Number of families	Per cent of all families	Average expenditure	Number of families	Per cent of all families
Local transportation, total .	$83.09	147	92.5	$57.97	46	97.9	$94.54	101	90.2
Street car, bus, train ..	75.99	141	88.7	52.85	45	95.7	86.84	96	85.7
Man to work	86.33	98	61.6	43.10	28	59.6	103.63	70	62.5
All other	20.68	109	68.6	29.28	40	85.1	15.69	69	61.6
Taxi, shared car	30.62	49	30.8	19.23	15	31.9	35.64	34	30.4

six months of the year and drove only about 3,000 miles, whereas the family with the highest expense owned two cars all year and drove a total of 13,600 miles. The smallest and largest amounts spent by families that owned one car all year were $150 and $750; these 2 families drove 3,000 and 13,000 miles, respectively, during the year.

The average operation cost of $384 was made up of a variety of items, the largest of which was gas and oil combined, at an average cost of $155, or 40 per cent of all automobile operation expenditures. Expenditures for gas varied greatly, from $24 to $413, but 69 per cent of the families spent between $100 and $200 and only 11 per cent spent larger sums. The average expenditure for oil was $13; 35 per cent of these expenditures were less than $10, and no family spent more than $46.

All but 1 car owner carried some form of insurance at an average cost of $79. Fifty-seven per cent spent between $50 and $100, and only 5 families spent more than $150, up to a maximum of $171. The size of these expenditures was, of course, related to the kinds and amounts of insurance carried. The most common type of insurance was public liability, and this protection was carried by all but 1 car owner; 85 per cent of the owners had fire and theft coverage, and 64 per cent carried collision insurance.

Twenty-three car-owning families reported no repair bills. Eighteen of this group bought new cars in 1949 or 1950, and 3 others bought used cars in 1950. The remaining 85 per cent of the car owners spent an average of $66 for repairs. As would be expected, these expenditures varied widely from $2 to as much as $351; however, half were $45 or less, and only 17 per cent were $100 or more. The 2 families with repair bills of more than $300 both owned 1941 cars which required major repairs in 1950.

All the car owners had some other expenses in connection with operation of their cars, and the average expenditure for all the remaining items by all car-owning families was $95. All owners had registration and license costs; 97 per cent spent something for miscellaneous items; 92 per cent had expenses for lubrication; 56 per cent reported buying tires and tubes, and smaller numbers had other types of operating expenses.

TRANSPORTATION OTHER THAN OWNED AUTOMOBILE

Families as a whole spent an average of $101 or 1.7 per cent of total consumption expenditures for nonautomobile transportation. Eleven families had no such expenditures; they were all car owners and in most cases the husband drove to work either in a company car or his own car. The average amount spent by families reporting an expenditure for nonautomobile transportation was $109. There was great variability in these transportation costs: 32 per cent of the families spent less than $50 and 51 per cent less than $100. Most of the remaining families spent between $100 and $200, but

9 per cent reported larger sums, with 3 families spending from $363 to $875.

About three-quarters of all nonautomobile transportation expenses represented local transportation within the Bay area. The 147 families who used local transportation had an average expenditure of $83: 56 per cent of these families spent less than $100, 41 per cent spent from $100 to $200, and the four highest expenditures ranged between $200 and $254.

The total sample included 47 families who lived in San Francisco and 112 who lived in Alameda, Contra Costa, Marin, or San Mateo counties. The San Francisco families who used local transportation spent an average of $58, and those who lived in the surrounding areas spent $95. The major reason for this difference was the cost of transportation to work. Sixty-nine per cent of the total cost of local transportation within the Bay area was spent by the husband to get to his job. San Francisco men who used such transportation spent an average of $43, whereas most of those who lived in the other areas commuted to San Francisco and their expenditures averaged $104.

Only 60 families, or 38 per cent of the entire group, reported any other transportation expenditures. For the group of families as a whole such expenditures averaged $25, but for those who reported expenses the average sum spent was $65. Forty-seven per cent of these expenditures were less than $25, and 85 per cent were less than $100. Three families, however, spent sums of $300, $600, and $718, mainly for vacation travel expenses.

In summary, all transportation costs for the 159 families in the study averaged $924. Eighty-nine per cent of this figure represented automobile costs: an average of $458 was used to purchase cars, and $364 went for car operation. Local transportation, chiefly the husbands' costs for travel to work, represented about three-fourths of all other transportation costs. The remainder was largely spent for vacation travel.

Chapter X
EXPENDITURES FOR MEDICAL
AND DENTAL CARE

TOTAL FAMILY EXPENDITURES FOR

MEDICAL AND DENTAL CARE

During 1950 the 159 families included in this study spent $59,567, or $375 per family, for all types of medical and dental care and for premiums for prepayment plans. The average bill for medical care was $272 and for dentistry $110.[1]

Expenditures for all health care were 6.3 per cent of total consumption expenditures, with 4.6 per cent for medical care, and 1.7 per cent for dental care.[2] There were wide differences among the families in the sums spent for health care. Every family reported some expenditure, including a few very small sums, but only 4 per cent spent less than $100. Eighteen per cent spent from $100 to $200, 54 per cent $300 or more, with nearly one-fifth reporting costs of more than $500. Four of the five largest expenditures were between $1,056 and $1,245, and the highest family bill was $3,349. Similarly, total medical expenses expressed as a per cent of consumption expenditures varied greatly, from .1 per cent to 48.6 per cent. Nine per cent of the families spent less than 2.5 per cent; 49 per cent from 5 to 10 per cent; and 1 in 10 spent 10 per cent or more. The unequal incidence of medical bills, which has always shown up in studies of expenditures for these services, again was evident in this study. Furthermore, there did not appear to be any consistent relationship between the size of bills for

---

[1]One family reported a small sum which could not be allocated between medical care and dentistry.

[2]For comparison with data from other sources based on income before taxes: the proportion of income before taxes which was spent for health care was 5.6 per cent, of which 4.1 per cent was for medical, and 1.5 per cent for dental care.

TABLE 54

Family Expenditures for Medical and Dental Care, by Income Class

(including premiums for prepayment plans)

	All families			Income class					
				Under $6,000			$6,000 and over		
	Total	Medical[a]	Dental[a]	Total	Medical	Dental	Total	Medical[a]	Dental[a]
All families······									
Mean ········	$374.63	$270.41	$101.43	$338.87	$252.90	$85.97	$407.38	$286.44	$115.59
Median ·······	326.25	205.70	59.00	262.78	189.19	50.65	355.37	222.84	71.00
Families reporting									
Mean ········	374.63	272.12	109.71	338.87	252.90	92.02	407.38	289.93	126.24
Median ·······	326.25	205.70	69.50	262.78	189.19	51.50	355.37	222.84	84.75
Range ········	5.00 to 3,348.60	5.00 to 3,293.60	5.00 to 710.00	6.25 to 1,238.86	6.25 to 1,209.36	5.00 to 613.50	5.00 to 3,348.60	5.00 to 3,293.60	6.00 to 710.00

[a] Averages exclude the 1 family that could not allocate its costs between medical and dental care. The total expenditure of this family was $443.80, or an average of $2.79 for 159 families.

health care and the income of the family. Although families with incomes of less than $6,000 spent an average of $339 and those with higher incomes $407, small bills were reported by families in both income groups, and some families in each group had bills of more than $1,000.

TABLE 55

Family Expenditures for Medical and Dental Care
(including premiums for prepayment plans)

Expenditure class	Total medical and dental		Medical		Dental	
	Number	Per cent	Number	Per cent	Number	Per cent
Families reporting, total ...	159	...	159	...	148	...
Size of expenditures unknown	0	...	1[a]	...	1[a]	...
Families with known expenditures, total	159	100.0	158	100.0	147	100.0
Under $100, total........	6	3.8	20	12.7	93	63.3
Under $50	4	2.5	4	2.5	59	40.1
$50 to $99	2	1.3	16	10.1	34	23.1
$100 to $199, total.......	29	18.2	55	34.8	30	20.4
$100 to $149.........	11	6.9	25	15.8	21	14.3
$150 to $199.........	18	11.3	30	19.0	9	6.1
$200 to $299	38	23.9	37	23.4	12	8.2
$300 to $399	27	17.0	22	13.9	8	5.4
$400 to $499	29	18.2	14	8.9	1	.7
$500 to $599	16	10.1	3	1.9	1	.7
$600 and over	14	8.8	7	4.4	2	1.4

[a]One family was unable to allocate its expenditures between medical and dental care.

MEDICAL CARE EXPENDITURES

Every family reported some expenditure for one or more of the services classified as medical care. The average spent was $272,[3] of which $199 went for direct payment for these services and another $73 for various types of prepaid insurance plans. Again the sums spent varied widely. Twenty, or 13 per cent of the families, reported bills of less than $100, but only four of these bills were under $50. Twenty-three per cent of the families spent between $200 and $300; 29 per cent more than $300; and 10 families, or 1 in 16, had bills of $500 or more, with the four largest sums ranging from $1,087 to $3,294. As was true for total health care, there was no consistent relationship between medical expenditures and size of income; some large expenditures were reported at every income level.

It would be expected that medical expenditures would vary directly with size of family. The average expenditures were larger by $58 for 4-person

[3]Excludes 1 family that could not allocate its expenses between medical and dental bills.

TABLE 56

Expenditures for Medical Care, by Family Size
(including premiums for prepayment plans)

Expenditure class	All families		Family size					
			Under 3.49		3.50 to 4.49		4.50 and over	
	Number	Per cent	Number	Per cent	Number	Per cent	Number	Per cent
All families	159	...	49	...	71	...	39	...
Size of expenditure unknown	1	...	0	...	0	...	1	...
Families with known expenditures, total.	158	100.0	49	100.0	71	100.0	38	100.0
Under $100, total	20	12.7	8	16.3	7	9.9	5	13.2
Under $50	4	2.5	1	2.0	2	2.8	1	2.6
$50 to $99	16	10.1	7	14.3	5	7.0	4	10.5
$100 to $199, total	55	34.8	16	32.7	28	39.4	11	28.9
$100 to $149	25	15.8	9	18.4	13	18.3	3	7.9
$150 to $199	30	19.0	7	14.3	15	21.1	8	21.1
$200 to $299	37	23.4	10	20.4	18	25.4	9	23.7
$300 to $399	22	13.9	10	20.4	3	4.2	9	23.7
$400 to $499	14	8.9	3	6.1	10	14.1	1	2.6
$500 and over	10	6.3	2	4.1	5	7.0	3	7.9

Average family expenditures and ranges

Families with known expenditures								
Mean	$272.12		$234.64		$293.26		$280.96	
Median	205.70		200.00		200.36		218.49	
Range	5.00 to 3,293.60		5.00 to 833.86		6.25 to 3,293.60		16.50 to 1,209.36	

Average per capita expenditures

Families with known expenditures	$69.15		$78.12		$73.97		$55.30	

than for 3-person families, but families of 5 or more members reported slightly smaller expenditures than did those with 4. Since these averages may have been affected by a few unusual cases, the proportions of families of different sizes who spent less than $150 is more significant. Thirty-five per cent of the families of 3, 28 per cent of the 4-person families, and 21 per cent of the larger families reported expenditures of less than $150. Thus, although even in a small family a serious illness may have resulted in large bills for a physician, hospital, or other services, there was some tendency for lower expenditures to be reported somewhat more frequently by the smaller families. The influence of family size can also be seen in per capita expenditures. Because the medical bills of the wives in these families were generally higher than the expenses of other family members, large families were apt to spend less per capita than small families. Again it should be recognized that the specific dollar differences may have been somewhat affected by a few unusual cases.

TABLE 57

Aggregate Family Expenditures for Medical Care, by Type of Care
(excluding premiums for prepayment plans)

Type of care	Aggregate expenditures	
	Amount	Per cent
Medical care, total[a]	$31,465.59[a]	. . .
Unallocated care[b]	1,828.82[b]	. . .
Allocated medical care, total	29,636.77	100.0
Physicians	16,340.85	55.1
Drugs and supplies	7,584.60	25.6
Laboratory tests, X rays, appliances	2,016.58	6.8
Oculists and glasses	1,685.70	5.7
Hospital room	1,255.54	4.2
Nursing services	558.00	1.9
Other practitioners	195.50	.7

[a]Excludes 1 family that could not allocate expenses between medical and dental care.
[b]Twelve families reported combined bills including two or more types of medical care. Eleven of these families had a hospital room included in the combined expenses; 7 had physicians included; 7 had laboratory tests, X rays, etc; 5 had nursing services.

TYPES OF MEDICAL SERVICE

The families in this study spent an average of $199 (excluding the cost of prepayment plans) for the services of physicians, hospitals, drugs, and all other kinds of medical care. In analyzing expenditures for medical care in terms of the types of services for which these sums were spent, the costs of prepayment plans were omitted because they could not be allocated to various types of services and to different family members.

TABLE 58

Family Expenditures for Medical Care, by Type of Care
(excluding premiums for prepayment plans)

Expenditure class	Total medical	Physicians	Drugs and supplies	Laboratory tests, X rays, appliances	Oculists and glasses	Hospital room	Nursing services	Other practitioners
				Number				
Families receiving medical care, total[a]	158	155	154	92	66	47	13	14
Size of expenditures unknown, total	0	7	0	7	0	11	5	0
Families with known expenditures, total	158	148	154	85	66	36	8	14
No cost[b]	1	2	1	6	0	12	1	0
Under $25	8	43	58	50	40	11	1	12
$25 to $49	18	22	39	20	18	7	2	2
$50 to $74	19	20	26	5	6	1	2	0
$75 to $99	19	13	9	2	2	1	0	0
$100 to $149	20	21	14	0	0	1	1	0
$150 to $199	23	9	5	1	0	2	0	0
$200 to $249	14	7	0	1	0	0	1	0
$250 and over	36	11	2	0	0	1	0	0

	Per cent							
Families with known expenditures, total	100.0	100.0	100.0	100.0	100.0	100.0	100.0	100.0
No cost[b]	.6	1.4	.6	7.1	.0	33.3	12.5	.0
Under $25	5.1	29.1	37.7	58.8	60.6	30.6	12.5	85.7
$25 to $49	11.4	14.9	25.3	23.5	27.3	19.4	25.0	14.3
$50 to $74	12.0	13.5	16.9	5.9	9.1	2.8	25.0	.0
$75 to $99	12.0	8.8	5.8	2.4	3.0	2.8	.0	.0
$100 to $149	12.7	14.2	9.1	.0	.0	2.8	12.5	.0
$150 to $199	14.6	6.1	3.2	1.2	.0	5.6	.0	.0
$200 to $249	8.9	4.7	.0	1.2	.0	.0	12.5	.0
$250 and over	22.6	7.4	1.3	.0	.0	2.8	.0	.0

Average expenditures, ranges, and per cent receiving care

Families with known expenditures								
Mean	$199.15	$110.41	$49.25	$23.72	$25.54	$34.88	$69.75	$13.96
Median	134.94	58.50	36.00	14.75	20.00	11.32	47.50	10.00
Range	.00 to 3,251.00	.00 to 2,981.00	.00 to 284.94	.00 to 207.50	.75 to 97.50	.00 to 260.39	.00 to 245.00	4.00 to 45.00
Per cent receiving care	100.0	98.1	97.5	58.2	41.8	29.7	8.2	8.9
Per cent receiving care with some cost	99.4	98.7	99.4	93.5	100.0	74.5	92.3	100.0

[a] One family is excluded because it could not allocate all its expenses between medical and dental care.
[b] Care at no cost was received through prepayment plans, the services of friends and relatives, or from the Veterans' Administration or State Workmen's Compensation.

TABLE 59

Family Members Receiving Medical Care and Average Expenditures
(excluding premiums for prepayment plans)

	Total family members		Heads	Wives	Children under 18	All other family members
	Number	Average expenditure				
Total persons in sample	639	...	159	159	292	29
Care unallocated by family members	4[a]	...	1	1	2	0
Care allocated by family members	635	$50.10[a]	158	158	290	29
No care	40	.00	12	11	12	5
Total receiving care ...	595	53.51[b]	146	147	278	24
Cost unallocated	236	33.92[b]	56	57	112	11
Cost allocated	359	66.01	90	90	166	13
Per cent of family members receiving care	93.7	...	92.4	93.0	95.9	82.8

[a]One family which included 4 persons is omitted because information was not given as to which family members received care. This family received all medical care free from a relative who was a physician.

[b]Excludes 7 persons who were in one family that could not allocate expenditures between medical and dental care; therefore the average expenditures are based on 588 and 229 cases respectively.

Almost every family consulted a physician, and the bills for these services amounted to 55 per cent of those medical bills which could be broken down by types of expenditures. Expenditures for drugs were also reported by practically every family, and accounted for one-fourth of the total. Fifty-eight per cent of the families had some expenditures for laboratory tests and X rays, and 42 per cent reported some eye care; these two items accounted for 7 and 6 per cent of the total. Other services were used only by a few families, and the expenditures were small when distributed over all families.

There were 12 families who could not allocate their expenditures to specific types of services; however, their total costs were generally small, although a few were between $100 and $351. The total unallocated sum spent by the 12 families was $1,829; practically all these expenditures were for care while hospitalized, including in some instances the physician's bill. As a result, the sums allocated to hospital care and physicians are somewhat understated, but this does not invalidate the general picture of the amount spent for the various types of services.

Physicians.—All but 3 families received some service from a physician, and the 148 cases for which these expenditures could be definitely determined spent an average of $110.[4] Forty-nine per cent of the bills were less

---

[4]There were 7 families who could not segregate expenditures as between physician and some other type of medical care, and they were therefore excluded from the computation of this average.

than $60, and 30 per cent less than $25. There were, however, a considerable number of large bills, and 12 per cent of the families (about 1 in 8) reported expenditures from $200 to much larger amounts. Two families in this highest group spent $513 and $543, another $890, and a fourth $2,981. In all these families it was an illness of the wife which required most of the expenditure: physicians' bills of $425 for care of the wife at childbirth and for another illness as well, $300 for maternity care, $800 for "deficiency shots," and $2,915 for psychotherapy, were included in the above expenditures. At the other end of the scale, 2 families received care from a physician at no cost; in 1 case the service was provided by a prepayment plan, and in the other by a company doctor.

Drugs.—Expenditures for drugs were also reported by almost all families, and the average amount spent was $49, or 45 per cent of the sum spent for physicians' services. Although 48 per cent of the drug expenditures were less than $35, 14 per cent of the families spent $100 or more. There were two large bills amounting to $285; one represented almost entirely the wife's purchases, and in the other case the wife spent $109 and the husband and 2 children $59 each.

Hospital care (room, board, general nursing).—There were 47 families, or 30 per cent of the total group, in which some member was hospitalized during the year. Only 36 of these families were able to segregate their expenses for room, board, and general nursing.[5] Twelve of the 36 families made no direct payments for this care—prepayment plans paid all the costs for 11 families, and in the other case, care was provided by Workmen's Compensation. The average expenditure for hospital care for all 36 families that were able to segregate this item was $35 per family, but for the 17 families that paid part of their own bills and the 7 who bore the full cost themselves the average was $52. Eleven of the 36 families paid sums of less than $25, and only 4 had expenses of more than $100, with 1 family reporting a hospital bill of $260. Only 7 families paid all their own hospital costs; in 4 of these families the persons hospitalized were not members of prepayment plans, and in the other 3, although the persons were members of plans, the illnesses for which they were hospitalized were not covered by those plans.

It is impossible to estimate what the hospital bills of families with memberships in prepayment plans would have been without such memberships; however, it is quite clear that the savings were very substantial. Most of

---

[5]There were 7 families with expenditures that could not give separate costs for physician, hospital, and tests and X rays, and an additional 4 families did not report what types of services they received while hospitalized. These 11 cases were therefore excluded from the computation of these averages.

TABLE 60

Expenditures for Medical Care, by Family Members

Expenditure class	Total family members		Heads		Wives		Children under 18		All other family members	
	Number	Per cent	Number	Per cent	Number	Per cent	Number	Per cent	Number	Per cent
Members receiving care with										
known cost, total	359	100.0	90	100.0	90	100.0	166	100.0	13	100.0
No cost	2	.6	2	2.2	0	.0	0	.0	0	.0
Under $100, total	313	87.2	82	91.1	69	76.7	151	91.0	11	84.6
Under $25	162	45.1	45	50.0	36	40.0	74	44.6	7	53.8
$25 to $49	67	18.7	21	23.3	14	15.6	30	18.1	2	15.4
$50 to $74	50	13.9	10	11.1	13	14.4	25	15.1	2	15.4
$75 to $99	34	9.5	6	6.7	6	6.7	22	13.3	0	.0
$100 to $199	24	6.7	2	2.2	9	10.0	13	7.8	0	.0
$200 to $299	9	2.5	1	1.1	5	5.6	2	1.2	1	7.7
$300 and over	11	3.1	3	3.3	7	7.8	0	.0	1	7.7

Average expenditures and ranges

	Total family members		Heads		Wives		Children under 18		All other family members	
Members receiving care with known cost										
Mean	$66.01		$45.63		$124.04[a]		$45.24		$70.58	
Median	29.30		20.41		36.64		29.65		18.00	
Range	.00 to 2,987.50		.00 to 590.00		.26 to 2,987.50		.50 to 260.00		.47 to 447.50	

[a]If the 8 women to whom a child was born in 1950 were excluded, the mean would be $99.17. These women had an average expenditure of $378.89.

the families who had some expense in addition to the care received without cost through a prepaid plan reported small expenditures. Only 1 such family had a bill over $60, because the wife was hospitalized for twenty-eight days, and although she had hospital insurance, she incurred an additional bill of $260. The number of instances in which the family paid all their own hospital costs is too small to compare their expenditures with the expenditures of those who received hospital care through a prepayment plan. It is, however, not surprising to find that 4 of the 7 families who paid all their own hospital costs had bills from $90 to $192, but only 1 of the families that received benefits from prepayment coverage had a hospital bill of more than $60.

Laboratory tests, X rays, and appliances.—Expenditures for laboratory tests, X rays, orthopedic appliances, and hearing aids were reported by 58 per cent of these families, and for those whose expenditures were known the average cost was $24. There were 5 families in which all the services in this category were furnished by a prepayment plan, and 1 in which the Veterans Administration provided a hearing aid. Nearly two-thirds of the families (including these 6) had expenditures of less than $25, and in only 2 were the sums spent more than $100. One of these spent $165, chiefly for a hearing aid, and the second spent $208, almost entirely for X-ray treatments for an elderly mother-in-law who had cancer.

Oculist and glasses.—Forty-two per cent of the families used the services of an oculist or purchased glasses. The average expenditure was $26; 88 per cent spent less than $50, and the two largest bills were $90 and $98, paid by families in which more than 1 person purchased glasses.

Other services.—There were 13 families, or 8 per cent of the sample, that reported expenditures for nursing services. Five of these families were unable to separate the sum spent for nursing from other medical expenses. One of the remaining 8 families received free nursing care, apparently by a friend or relative, and of the others only 2 spent more than $75. These 2 had expenditures of $100 and $245 for nursing care after the birth of a child. Fourteen families used the services of other practitioners, such as osteopaths, chiropractors, or faith healers, and none of their expenditures was more than $45.

Although for each category of medical expenditure many families spent small sums, there were, almost without exception, some large bills for every type of service. Furthermore, it must be recognized that even relatively small bills for several kinds of medical care may result in a large total medical bill.

MEDICAL CARE
EXPENDITURES
OF INDIVIDUALS

Ninety-four per cent of the individuals included in this study reported some kind of medical care. In some instances this care was limited to the purchase of medicine for some minor ailment, whereas in others it involved visits to a physician or hospital at considerable expense. There were many cases in which family medical expenditures could not be allocated among the individual members, and therefore, though some care was reported for 595 persons, specific expenditures were available for only 359 individuals.

The average medical expenditure of the 359 persons whose expenses could be allocated to specific individuals was $66—considerably higher than the average of $54 for all 595 persons who received care. The average expense of those persons whose expenditures could not be allocated to specific individuals was $34; this lower per capita expenditure appears to be related to the fact that 25 per cent of this group reported that their only medical expense was for drugs and supplies. In sharp contrast, only 12 per cent of those with allocated expenditures reported that their only costs were for these items. This indicates that the average expenditure of those with allocated expenses is biased upward, and the lower per capita figure of $54 based on 595 persons expresses the average level of expenditure more accurately. However, the upward bias among those with allocated expenses appeared to be about the same for the husbands, wives, and children, although somewhat larger for other family members. Thus, with the possible exception of this last group, there is no reason to suppose that if it had been possible to allocate the costs to all individuals, there would have been any drastic change in the relationships between the expenditures of the various family members.

There were considerable differences in the average allocatable sums spent by the various members of these families. The husbands' expenditures averaged $46, but their wives spent $124, and the children under eighteen years, $45. The incidence of the costs for each family member was, as might be expected, very unequal. Fifty-two per cent of the husbands spent less than $25, 41 per cent between $25 and $100, and 4 per cent had bills of $200 or more, with a maximum of $590. The wives' expenditures were as a whole much larger than those of their husbands, but nevertheless, 40 per cent spent less than $25, and 37 per cent between $25 and $100. Thirteen per cent, however, spent $200 or more, with 4 spending amounts varying from $768 to $2,988. The birth of a child is often important in determining the size of medical expenditures, and in this group of 90 women, whose medical bills could be separated from those of other family members, there were 8 to whom a child was born during the year. When the costs for these

TABLE 61

Number of Families and Individuals with Memberships
in Prepaid Medical Care Plans in 1950

	Total	No membership	Full-year or part-year membership	Full-year membership
Families or individuals[a]				
All families	159	11	148	121[b]
All individuals	639	83	556	523
Husbands	159	12	147	143
Wives.....................	159	20	139	131
Children under 18	292	37	255	239
All other	29	14	15	10
Per cent of all families or individuals				
All families	100.0	6.9	93.1	76.1
All individuals	100.0	13.0	87.0	81.8
Husbands	100.0	7.5	92.5	89.9
Wives	100.0	12.6	87.4	82.4
Children under 18	100.0	12.7	87.3	81.8
All other	100.0	48.3	51.7	34.5

[a]The classification by individuals is not based on the family unit. For example, some of the 82 individuals with no coverage were members of families in which some person was covered by a prepaid medical care plan.
[b]Families were classified as having full-year membership only if all members of the family were covered for 12 months. However, since most family policies excluded children under one month of age and persons eighteen years of age and over, if these persons were not covered it was assumed that they were ineligible. Families in which such persons were not covered were classified as having full-year membership if all other persons were covered for twelve months (or less, in the case of babies under one year old).

women were excluded,[6] the average medical expense of the wives was $99, considerably less than for the group of women as a whole, but still more than twice the sum spent by their husbands.

The expenditures for children varied within narrower limits than did those of their parents. Forty-five per cent were less than $25, and about the same proportion between $25 and $100. The largest sums spent for individual children were $260 and $205. Similarly, the two highest medical bills for relatives living with the family were $448 and $228.

PREPAID MEDICAL CARE
Prepaid medical care plans in this study included all insurance-type arrangements for hospital, surgical, and medical care which provided benefits in the form of services or cash reimbursement for all or part of this care.

---

[6]This procedure gives only a rough approximation of expenditures without childbirth costs. It would have been desirable to include the expenditures of all women for illnesses other than childbirth, but expenditures by type of illness were not available, and thus all the expenditures of women who had children in 1950 had to be omitted.

TABLE 62

Family Expenditures for Memberships in Prepayment Plans

Expenditure class	All families reporting expenditures		Families with full-year memberships[a]	
	Number	Per cent	Number	Per cent
Families reporting, total.......	148	...	121	...
Size of expenditure unknown ..	1[b]	...	0	...
Families with known expenditures, total	147	100.0	121	100.0
Under $25	2	1.4	0	.0
$25 to $49	33	22.4	27	23.2
$50 to $74	26	17.7	25	20.7
$75 to $99	73	49.7	65	53.7
$100 and over	13	8.8	4	3.3

Average family expenditures and ranges

All families[c]		
Mean	$73.54	...
Median	76.80	...
Families reporting[c]		
Mean	79.05[d]	$77.08
Median	80.40[d]	76.80
Range	6.25 to 180.00	42.60 to 180.00

[a]All eligible family members covered all year (or less than a year in the case of babies under one year old).

[b]One family had 1 person covered part of the year in a student plan at an unavailable cost. No other member of the family was covered.

[c]Excludes one case with cost not reported.

[d]Includes eleven polio and four other policies covering special conditions. If these plans at a total cost of $213.70 had been excluded, the mean and median for 147 cases would be $77.59 and $77.84 respectively.

TABLE 63

Number of Memberships in Prepaid Medical Care Plans, by Type of Insurer

Type of insurer	Number[a]	Per cent
Total	215	100.0
Nonprofit...................................	117	54.4
Blue Cross	61	28.4
Kaiser Foundation	22	10.2
California Physicians' Service	14	6.2
Health Service System of San Francisco	10	4.7
Miscellaneous[b]	10	4.7
Commercial	98	45.6
Group plans through employer	79	36.7
Individual plans	4	1.9
Miscellaneous (special conditions)[c]	15	7.0

[a]Memberships covering 1 or more family members for the whole, or any part of the calendar year.

[b]Seven of these plans were in educational institutions which provided some health care for enrolled students.

[c]These policies covered special conditions only (for example, eleven were polio policies) in contrast to the other commercial policies which were not restricted to one specific condition.

Membership in some kind of prepaid medical care plan was very common among this group of families; 148, or 93 per cent, reported that some family member belonged to a prepayment plan at some time during the year, and 82 per cent of the memberships covered the entire family for the full year. This high proportion of membership is probably related to the method of selecting the sample, which resulted in the inclusion of a large number of employees of large companies. These companies were perhaps more likely to offer group membership in prepayment plans than were small firms.

There were 639 individuals in the study; 87 per cent of these persons were members of prepayment plans at some time during the year, and 94 per cent of their memberships were for the entire year. There were not very great differences in the proportions of husbands, wives, and children who had prepaid coverage, although memberships were somewhat more frequent among the husbands. Twenty-nine other persons eighteen years of age and older were members of these families, but only about half belonged to prepayment plans. The people in this last group who were not covered were in the main elderly parents of the husband or wife and not eligible to belong to the family plans; in addition, they were not employed and may have found it difficult to secure individual memberships in prepayment plans.

Premiums.—Since premiums for prepayment plans are ordinarily on a family basis, these expenditures must be analyzed in terms of families rather than individuals. The average premium paid by the total group of 159 families was $74, or 27 per cent of their average medical care expenditures. The average premium paid by families with some membership during the year was $79; 22 per cent spent between $25 and $50, and half between $75 and $100. Only 2 families reported premiums under $25, 1 because of a membership of only one month, and the other because only 1 person was covered. Thirteen families, or 9 per cent of those who reported memberships, spent sums from $100 to $180. In some cases these families were members of relatively high premium plans for the entire year; in others, the addition of polio policies raised the total premiums above $100. This group also included a few families that for some unspecified reason belonged to two plans with similar coverage.

Types of plans.—Several types of plans were represented by the memberships reported by these families. Because in some families some persons were members of one plan and some of another, or a person was covered by more than one type of plan (e.g., polio and some other), memberships in two hundred and fifteen plans were reported by the 148 families. Fifty-four per cent of the memberships were in nonprofit prepayment plans: 28 per cent in Blue Cross, 10 per cent in Kaiser Foundation, 6 per cent in California Physicians' Service, 5 per cent in the Health Service System of San Francisco, and 5 per cent in miscellaneous plans. Thirty-seven per

TABLE 64

Number of Families with Full-Year Memberships in Prepayment Plans, by Type of Insurer and Coverage

Type of insurer	Total families[a]		Type of coverage								
			Number					Per cent			
			Hospital only	Hospital and surgical[b]	Hospital, surgical, medical			Total	Hospital only	Hospital and surgical	Hospital, surgical, medical, total
	Number	Per cent			Total	Families fully covered	Dependents, hospital and surgical only[c]				
All insurers	121	100.0	2	29	90	40	50	100.0	1.7	24.0	74.4
Blue Cross	19	15.7	2	3	14	14	0	100.0	10.5	15.8	73.7
Kaiser Foundation	16	13.2	0	0	16	16	0	100.0	.0	.0	100.0
California Physicians Service	11	9.1	0	1	10	0	10	100.0	.0	9.1	90.9
Health Service System of San Francisco	2	1.7	0	0	2	2	0	100.0	.0	.0	100.0
Miscellaneous nonprofit	1	.8	0	0	1	1	0	100.0	.0	.0	100.0
Commercial arranged by employer	40	33.1	0	25	15	3	12	100.0	.0	62.5	37.5
Full-year coverage through use of two plans	32[d]	26.4	0	0	32	4	28	100.0	.0	.0	100.0

[a] All eligible family members covered all year (or less than one year in the case of babies under one year) classified by the policy with the broadest coverage for any one member of the family.

[b] In the 29 families reporting, all family members had hospital and surgical coverage.

[c] In the 50 families reporting, the subscribers all had hospital, surgical, and medical coverage, but in all but 1 of these families, the dependents had hospital and surgical coverage only (in 1 family the dependents had only hospital coverage).

[d] Twenty-nine of these families were covered by a group commercial insurance policy arranged by their employer for part of the year, and changed to a group Blue Cross contract for the remainder of the year.

cent of the memberships were in group plans arranged by employers through private commercial insurance companies; 2 per cent were in commercial plans carried individually; and finally 7 per cent were in miscellaneous commercial plans which provided coverage for special conditions such as polio or accidents, and which were always carried together with some other type of medical care insurance.

FAMILIES WITH FULL-YEAR
COVERAGE FOR ALL MEMBERS

One hundred and twenty-one families reported full-year family coverage— that is, both parents and all children over one month but less than eighteen years old were members of a prepayment plan for twelve months.[7] Eighty- five of these families were members of a single plan all year. Twenty-nine families transferred from one plan to another in the middle of the year, and there were 3 in which some members belonged to one plan, and some to another (in the latter cases the cost of family coverage included more than one plan). Finally, there were 4 families that reported full-year coverage for all family members in two plans; in these cases only data on the plan with the broadest coverage were considered.

Premiums.— The average cost of full-year family coverage as defined above was $77, as against the $79 expenditure of all families who were members of prepaid plans at any time during the year. Only 3 per cent of the full- year premiums were $100 or more, in contrast with 9 per cent of the total premiums paid by families with any membership during the year. This dif- ference resulted from the fact that most of these high-cost premiums were reported by families that had memberships in more than one plan, whereas the above analysis of the cost of full-year coverage includes only one plan per family—that with broadest coverage.

Kinds of protection provided.—Seventy-four per cent of the 121 families with full-year coverage belonged to plans which provided hospital, surgical, and medical care; 24 per cent had coverage for hospital and surgical care; and 2 per cent subscribed to plans providing only hospital care. Blue Cross was the one plan with some contracts which provided hospital care only, but 74 per cent of the Blue Cross memberships included hospital, surgical, and medical benefits. All the members of the Kaiser Foundation plan had this type of protection, as did 91 per cent of the members of California Physi-

----

[7]Since most family policies exclude children less than one month old and eighteen years of age or older, if these persons were not covered it was assumed that they were ineligible and the family was classified as having 12-month coverage for all members. Polio policies were omitted, as were four other policies which covered such special conditions as acci- dents rather than the general types of illnesses included in most prepay- ment policies.

TABLE 65

Average Annual Family Premiums for Full-Year Memberships in Prepayment Plans, by Type of Insurer and Coverage

Type of insurer	Total plans		Type of coverage					
			Hospital only		Hospital and surgical		Hospital, surgical, and medical	
	Number	Average premium	Number	Average premium	Number	Average premium	Number	Average premium
Total	93[a]	$70.53	4	$48.44	30	$52.60	58	$81.93
Blue Cross	22	70.15	4	48.44	4	73.69	14	75.35
Kaiser Foundation	16	69.15	0	...	0	...	16	69.15
California Physicians' Service	11	94.75	0	...	1	113.20[b]	10	92.90
Health Service System of San Francisco	2	121.30	0	...	0	...	2	121.30
Miscellaneous nonprofit	1	180.00	0	...	0	...	1	180.00
Private commercial arranged by employer	40	60.22	0	...	25	46.80	15	82.60
Commercial—individually carried[c]	1	36.00	0	...	0	...	0	...

[a]Of the 121 families in table 64, 32 had full-year coverage through part-year coverage in two plans. Of the remaining 89 families, 4 had full-year coverage for all family members in two plans (2 families carried full-year memberships in both Blue Cross and Kaiser Foundation; the third had both Blue Cross and California Physicians' Service; and the fourth was covered by both Blue Cross and a commercial insurance company policy carried individually). Thus ninety-three plans carried by 89 families may be discussed in terms of premiums for a full year of coverage for the entire family.

[b]Individually carried (not a group subscription).

[c]Type of protection is unknown.

cians' Service. Sixty-two per cent of the plans of commercial insurance companies provided hospital and surgical benefits, and the rest included medical benefits as well.

In order to analyze the cost of full-year family coverage by the types of plans involved, it was necessary to omit those families that shifted their memberships from one plan to another during the year, as well as those in which full-year family coverage was secured only through a combination of two or more plans. This discussion is therefore limited to 89 families in which ninety-three full-year memberships were reported. Forty-three per cent of these memberships were in plans set up by the employer through commercial insurance companies, and the average premium was $60. Most of the remaining memberships were in three nonprofit organizations, and the average premiums paid were $95 for California Physicians' Service, $70 for Blue Cross, and $69 for Kaiser Foundation.

There were also differences in cost which were related to the types of coverage. The 4 families who had only hospital coverage paid an average premium of $48, whereas for those plans providing hospital and surgical benefits, the average premium was $53. There were wide differences in the premiums for the latter coverage: most of the families with this type of protection were members of one commercial plan offered by an insurance company to its employees at a cost of $47 per year; a few were members of a Blue Cross plan with a premium of $74; and 1 had a California Physicians' Service policy which cost $113. The premiums paid for plans which covered hospital, surgical, and medical care also varied considerably. The Kaiser Foundation's premium averaged $69; Blue Cross averaged $75; commercial insurance plans were $83; and California Physicians' Service was $93.

These expenditures for prepayment premiums must be interpreted with caution. In the case of at least 10 families (belonging to a plan with hospital, surgical, and medical coverage) the employer paid part of the cost of membership, and thus the full cost was higher than the amount spent by the families themselves. Twenty-five families belonged to a plan with hospital and surgical coverage for which the premium was undoubtedly low because the insurance company for which the heads of these families worked made the plan available at an unusually low cost. There may have been a few other companies that paid part of the premiums, but in most other cases the sums paid by the employee appeared to cover the full premium.

Another important aspect of the expenditures for prepayment plans was the great differences in the amount of care provided by policies in any one of the classifications. Although within the limits of this study it was not possible to make a detailed analysis of the exact provisions of each plan, enough evidence was available to indicate a wide degree of variability. For

TABLE 66

Full-Year Family Members Receiving Medical Care, by Length of Memberships in Prepayment Plans

| | Total persons | | Memberships in prepayment plans | | | | | |
| | | | Full- and part-year | | Full-year | | Part-year | None |
	Number	Per cent	Number	Per cent	Number	Per cent	Number	Number
All family members	639	...	556	...	523	...	33	83
Part-year family members	24	...	14	...	9	...	5	10
Care unallocated by family members..	4	...	4	...	0	...	4	0
No care received	38	...	29	...	28	...	1	9
Received only drugs and supplies.....	98	...	80	...	74	...	6	18
Full-year family members receiving care other than drugs and supplies, total...	475	100.0	429	100.0	412	100.0	17	46
Some care through prepaid plan, total..	163	34.3	163	38.0	159	38.6	4	...
No cost except premium	12	2.5	12	2.8	12	2.9	0	...
Additional cost	151	31.8	151	35.2	147	35.7	4	...
No care through prepaid plan, total ...	312	65.7	266	62.0	253	61.4	13	46
Without cost................	3	.6	3	.7	3	.7	0	0
With cost	309	65.1	263	61.3	250	60.7	13	46

example, some of the plans classified as providing hospital, surgical, and medical care provided medical care only while hospitalized, whereas others provided some care for nonhospitalized illnesses, either for the employee alone or for both the employee and his dependents. Furthermore, some plans provided service benefits; others operated on a reimbursement basis, paying specified sums for hospital, surgical, or medical care—sums which might, or might not, cover the full cost.

INDIVIDUALS RECEIVING SERVICES
FROM PREPAID PLANS

In analyzing the extent to which individuals who were members of prepaid medical plans received services from the plans, and in comparing the expenditures of those who were members of plans with the costs of nonmembers, certain persons have been omitted. The following individuals were omitted: those who received no care, persons who were in the family only part of the year, part-year plan members, and those who reported expenditures for drugs and supplies and no other form of medical care. Prepayment plans seldom covered the costs of drugs and supplies, and therefore the inclusion of persons who reported these items as the only type of medical care received would have exaggerated the proportion of individuals who received no care through their plan. Furthermore, it was impossible to allocate expenditures for the family medicine cabinet to specific family members.

The following analysis is limited to 475 persons who received some medical care in addition to drugs and supplies. Eighty-seven per cent, or 412 persons were full-year members of prepayment plans. Thirty-nine per cent of these full-year members, or 159 individuals, received some care through their prepayment plans, and all but 12, or 7 per cent, had some cost in addition to the premium. This study did not include detailed questions as to why 253 full-year members received no services from their plans, but it is probable that many of these people who had no hospitalized illness were members of plans which covered only hospitalized illnesses. Others may have required only an occasional visit to a physician and their prepayment plans may not have covered the first few visits to a doctor, or they may have had illnesses which were excluded from coverage. For example, 1 person received expensive medical care which was not covered by the prepayment plan, and 5 persons were hospitalized but had no part of their costs paid by the plans to which they belonged. Those 5 included three childbirth cases and one miscarriage which were not covered by prepayment plans, and one work injury which was covered by Workmen's Compensation insurance.

Those full-year plan members who received some care through a prepayment plan spent an average of $56, whereas full-year members, plus

TABLE 67

Expenditures of Individuals for Medical Care, Full-Year Plan Members and Nonmembers, by Sources of Care
(excluding drugs and supplies and premiums for prepayment plans)

Expenditure class	Total full-year and nonmembers[a]		Full-year plan members				No plan memberships		Total with no care through plans	
			Some care through plans		No care through plans					
	Number	Per cent	Number	Per cent	Number	Per cent	Number	Per cent	Number	Per cent
Full-year family members receiving medical care, total	458	...	159	...	253	...	46	...	299	...
Size of expenditure unknown	4	...	2	...	2	...	0	...	2	...
Persons with known expenditures, total	454	100.0	157	100.0	251	100.0	46	100.0	297	100.0
No cost	15	3.3	12	7.6	3	1.2	0	.0	3	1.0
Under $100, total	403	88.8	126	80.3	238	94.8	39	84.7	277	93.3
Under $25	253	55.7	78	49.7	155	61.8	20	43.5	175	58.9
.$25 to $49	85	18.7	28	17.8	44	17.5	13	28.2	57	19.2
$50 to $74	46	10.1	8	5.1	32	12.7	6	13.0	38	12.8
$75 to $99	19	4.2	12	7.6	7	2.8	0	.0	7	2.4
$100 to $199	18	4.0	10	6.4	4	1.6	4	8.7	8	2.7
$200 to $299	7	1.5	3	1.9	3	1.2	1	2.2	4	1.3
$300 to $399	5	1.1	2	1.3	2	.8	1	2.2	3	1.0
$400 and over	6	1.3	4	2.5	1	.4	1	2.2	2	.7

Average expenditures and ranges

Persons with known expenditures	Total full-year and nonmembers[a]		Some care through plans		No care through plans		No plan memberships		Total with no care through plans	
Mean	$49.53		$56.12		$43.90		$57.76		$46.05	
Median	18.75		16.50		18.64		30.00		20.00	
Range	.00 to 2,950.00		.00 to 850.00		.00 to 2,950.00		3.00 to 320.00		.00 to 2,950.00	

[a] Excludes 17 persons who were members of prepayment plans for only part of the year.

nonmembers who received no care through a plan, spent an average of $46. Although the information obtained in this study provided no basis for explaining why the group that had some care through their prepayment plans spent more than those whose care was without such assistance, it is possible that some of the group used medical services more often because at least some of the costs of the services would be paid by the prepayment plans.[8]

Assistance from a prepayment plan in paying medical bills occurred most frequently when the illness required hospitalization. There were 60 individuals who were hospitalized at some time during 1950. Fifty-three of these persons were full-year members of prepayment plans, and 48 of these members had all or part of their hospital bills paid by the plans.[9] Thus 90 per cent of those who were hospitalized and had full-year coverage and 80 per cent of all who were hospitalized had some part of their hospital bills paid by a plan. With one exception, the prepayment plans paid for some surgical or medical care in addition to at least part of the cost of the hospital room. There were only 5 members of prepayment plans who were hospitalized and had no part of the costs paid by plans. This was because the conditions for which they were hospitalized were not covered by the plans.

In 9 of the hospitalized cases with full-year coverage, prepaid plans paid the entire bill, but the others spent sums from a few dollars to $752. The average sum spent for hospitalized care in addition to prepayment premiums was $69, in contrast to the much larger sum of $151 which was spent by those who had no assistance from prepayment plans in paying bills for hospitalized illnesses. Although the numbers on which this analysis is based are small, and thus caution must be exercised in using the average expenditures, there is certainly evidence that most persons with full-year prepaid coverage who were hospitalized received substantial assistance in paying their hospital bills. However, it might well be noted that to the hospital bills of the 48 people who received some assistance from prepaid plans must be added their bills for nonhospitalized illnesses, and with this addition their total medical bills averaged $119.

---

[8] The National Family Survey of Medical Costs and Voluntary Health Insurance made by the Health Information Foundation in 1953 found that expenditures of families with insurance were higher than those without insurance. This study stated (p. 27): "This is in part due to greater utilization by those with insurance and possibly also utilization of a more expensive type of service, for example, a private room in a hospital instead of semi-private or ward." The study, however, does not include any detailed analysis of the reasons for the differences in expenditures as between insured and noninsured groups.

[9] Eight of the 48 persons also had some nonhospital care through prepayment plans.

TABLE 68

Expenditures of Individuals While Hospitalized, Full-Year Plan Members and Nonmembers

Expenditure class	Total full-year and nonmembers		Source of care			
			Received some care through plans		Received no care through plans	
	Number	Per cent	Number	Per cent	Number	Per cent
Full-year family members receiving care, total[a]....	60	100.0	48	100.0	12	100.0
No cost	10	16.7	9	18.7	1	8.3
Under $100, total........	34	56.7	32	66.7	2	16.7
Under $50	25	41.7	23	47.9	2	16.7
$50 to $99	9	15.0	9	18.7	0	.0
$100 to $199	7	11.7	3	6.2	4	33.3
$200 to $299	5	8.3	2	4.2	3	25.0
$300 and over	4	6.7	2	4.2	2	16.7

Average expenditures and ranges

Persons receiving care						
Mean	$85.34		$68.93		$150.98	
Median................	40.25		30.00		132.15	
Range	.00 to		.00 to		.00 to	
	752.39		752.39		330.00	

[a]It should be noted that the totals of this and the following table do not equal the totals on table 67. This difference is accounted for by the fact that 8 full-year plan members had both hospital and nonhospital care through prepayment plans; 34 full-year members had hospital care but no nonhospital care through a plan; and 1 full-year member had hospital care not through a plan and no nonhospital care. Finally, 7 persons not belonging to a plan had both hospital and nonhospital care.

There were 452 individuals who received some nonhospitalized care excluding drugs and supplies, and 406 of these persons were members of prepayment plans. Only 119 persons or 29 per cent of those with full-year prepayment coverage and 26 per cent of all persons with nonhospitalized care received some assistance from prepayment plans. Of the 119 receiving some assistance from plans, expenditures were known for 117;[10] in 10 of the 117 cases the prepaid plans paid the entire cost of nonhospitalized care, and only 5 cases had bills of $75 or more. The average sum spent for nonhospitalized care, all or part of which was paid by the prepayment plan, was $19, in contrast to $46 by those who had no nonhospital care through prepayment plans. Thus, unless it were assumed that most of these people who received care through prepayment plans had only very minor illnesses (and this is certainly not probable), it seems evident that these 117 people received considerable assistance in paying for this part of their medical costs. Again, however, it should be recognized that some of these people had hospitalized illnesses which were not covered by prepayment plans, and thus their total medical bills averaged $26.

[10]Eight of these persons received both hospital and nonhospital care from prepayment plans.

TABLE 69

Expenditures of Individuals for Nonhospitalized Care, Full-Year Plan Members and Nonmembers, by Source of Care

Expenditure class	Total full-year and nonmembers		Full-year plan members				Persons with no plan memberships		Total with no care through plans	
			Some care through plan		No care through plan					
	Number	Per cent	Number	Per cent	Number	Per cent	Number	Per cent	Number	Per cent
Full-year family members receiving care, total	452	...	119[a]	...	287	...	46	...	333	...
Size of expenditure unknown	4	...	2	...	2	...	0		2	...
Persons with known expenditures, total	448	100.0	117	100.0	285	100.0	46	100.0	331	100.0
No cost	12	2.7	10	8.5	2	.7	0	.0	2	.6
Under $100, total	415	92.6	105	89.7	268	94.0	42	91.3	310	93.7
Under $25	269	60.0	75	64.1	172	60.4	22	47.8	194	58.6
$25 to $49	87	19.4	21	17.9	51	17.9	15	32.6	66	19.9
$50 to $74	48	10.7	6	5.1	37	13.0	5	10.9	42	12.7
$75 to $99	11	2.5	3	2.6	8	2.8	0	.0	8	2.4
$100 to $199	11	2.5	1	.9	7	2.5	3	6.5	10	3.0
$200 to $299	6	1.3	1	.9	4	1.4	1	2.2	5	1.5
$300 and over	4	.9	0	.0	4	1.4	0	.0	4	1.2

Average expenditures and ranges

Persons with known expenditures										
Mean	$38.73		$19.06		$47.12		$36.75		$45.68	
Median	17.25		7.00		19.50		28.00		20.00	
Range	.00 to 2,950.00		.00 to 228.50		.00 to 2,950.00		3.00 to 220.00		.00 to 2,950.00	

[a]Includes 8 persons who received both hospital and nonhospital care through prepayment plans.

TABLE 70

Expenditures for Dental Care, by Family Size

| Expenditure class | All families | | Families by size | | | | | |
| | | | Under 3.49 | | 3.50 to 4.49 | | 4.50 and over | |
	Number	Per cent	Number	Per cent	Number	Per cent	Number	Per cent
All families	159	...	49	...	71	...	39	...
Families with no dental care	10	...	5	...	4	...	1	...
Families receiving dental care, total	149	...	44	...	67	...	38	...
Size of expenditure unknown	1	...	0	...	0	...	1	...
Families with known expenditures, total	148	100.0	44	100.0	67	100.0	37	100.0
No cost	1	.7	1	2.3	0	.0	0	.0
Under $100, total	93	62.8	31	70.5	42	62.7	20	54.1
Under $50, total	59	39.9	19	43.2	29	43.3	11	29.7
Under $25	19	12.8	3	6.8	13	19.4	3	8.1
$25 to $49	40	27.0	16	36.4	16	23.9	8	21.6
$50 to $99, total	34	23.0	12	27.3	13	19.4	9	24.3
$50 to $74	19	12.8	5	11.4	8	11.9	6	16.2
$75 to $99	15	10.1	7	15.9	5	7.5	3	8.1
$100 and over, total	54	36.5	12	27.3	25	37.3	17	45.9
$100 to $199	30	20.3	8	18.2	14	20.9	8	21.6
$200 to $299	12	8.1	3	6.8	3	4.5	6	16.2
$300 to $399	8	5.4	1	2.3	5	7.5	2	5.4
$400 to $499	1	.7	0	.0	1	1.5	0	.0
$500 and over	3	2.0	0	.0	2	3.0	1	2.7

Average expenditures and ranges

All families[a]								
Mean	$102.07		$73.19		$105.44		$133.03	
Median	59.00		48.00		53.50		82.50	
Families with known expenditures								
Mean	108.97		81.50		111.73		136.63	
Median	66.25		51.00		61.00		83.50	
Range	5.00 to 710.00		12.00 to 317.00		5.00 to 613.50		20.00 to 710.00	
Per capita expenditures[a]	25.69		24.37		26.59		26.18	

[a] Excluding the 1 family for whom the size of the expenditure was unknown.

In conclusion, in spite of the fact that 87 per cent of all the persons who received some hospital or nonhospital care in addition to drugs and supplies were members of prepayment plans thouoghout the entire year, only 39 per cent of these full-year members received any care through prepayment plans. Furthermore, though it might have been assumed that full-year plan members would spend less for medical care than nonmembers, in actuality they spent more than nonmembers, and if the individual costs of the premiums could be added, the difference in expenditures would be even greater.

The extent to which prepayment plans were of assistance varied greatly as between persons who were hospitalized and those who had nonhospitalized illnesses. Fifty-three of the 60 persons who were hospitalized were full-year members of prepayment plans, and since all but 5 received some assistance from their plans in paying their hospital bills, 80 per cent of the full-year plan members who were hospitalized had at least part of their bills paid by a plan. For those who were not hospitalized the situation was quite different. Of the 452 persons who had some care for nonhospitalized illnesses, 90 per cent were covered all year by prepayment plans, but only 29 per cent of the people with this protection had any care through their plans. This small number of people appears to have benefited considerably from their prepayment coverage, since their average bills were considerably lower than were those of the much larger group who, although they were members of plans, received no assistance in paying their bills for nonhospitalized illnesses. In summary, it can be stated that prepayment plans were of great assistance for those who had hospitalized illnesses, but most of the bills for nonhospitalized care were paid without any assistance from an insurance organization.

DENTAL CARE

There were 10 families who reported no dental care for any family members in 1950. The average expenditure of the entire group of families was $102, which was 1.7 per cent of all consumption expenditures, and 27 per cent of total medical and dental care costs. The average spent by those families that reported some dental care for at least 1 family member was $109. One family received all dental care free from a relative who was a dentist; 41 per cent of the family bills were less than $50; one-fifth were from $100 to $200; and 16 per cent were $200 or more. Half of these largest bills ranged from $300 to more than twice that amount. There was no consistent relationship between family income and dental expenditures; and there were both large and small bills at every income level. For example, a family with an income of $5,000 had a dental bill of $614, and the largest bill ($710) occurred in a family whose income was $6,100. However, there was a difference in the expenditures of families with incomes below and above $6,000; the

TABLE 71

Expenditures for Dental Care, by Family Members

Expenditure class	Total	Heads	Wives	Children 6 to 17	Children Under 6	All others
	Number					
Family members receiving dental care, total	406	104	123	129	33	17
Unallocated expenditures..	22	3	5	7	5	2
Total with allocated expenditures	384	101	118	122	28	15
No cost	7	3	2	1	1	0
Under $25, total	205	54	56	67	21	7
Less than $5	24	6	2	10	5	1
$5 to $9.99	55	14	13	19	8	1
$10 to $24.99	126	34	41	38	8	5
$25 to $49.99	84	17	29	30	3	5
$50 to $74.99	35	14	11	9	1	0
$75 to $99.99	10	3	2	2	2	1
$100 to $199.99	31	7	14	8	0	2
$200 and over	12	3	4	5	0	0
	Per cent					
Total with known expenditures	100.0	100.0	100.0	100.0	100.0	100.0
No cost	1.8	3.0	1.7	.8	3.6	.0
Under $25, total	53.4	53.5	47.5	54.9	75.0	46.7
Less than $5	6.2	5.9	1.7	8.2	17.9	6.7
$5 to $9.99	14.3	13.9	11.0	15.6	28.6	6.7
$10 to $24.99	32.8	33.7	34.7	31.1	28.6	33.3
$25 to $49.99	21.9	16.8	24.6	24.6	10.7	33.3
$50 to $74.99	9.1	13.9	9.3	7.4	3.6	.0
$75 to $99.99	2.6	3.0	1.7	1.6	7.1	6.7
$100 to $199.99	8.1	6.9	11.9	6.6	.0	13.3
$200 and over	3.1	3.0	3.4	4.1	.0	.0

Average expenditures, ranges, and per cent reporting

	Total	Heads	Wives	Children 6 to 17	Children Under 6	All others
All persons						
Mean	$25.51	$27.00	$35.61	$31.97	$4.12	$23.04
Median	7.00	9.88	15.00	12.00	...	5.00
Persons receiving dental care						
Mean	40.42	41.71	46.47	40.88	18.27	41.47
Median	20.00	20.00	25.00	19.25	9.00	25.00
Range..................	.00 to 515.00	.00 to 515.00	.00 to 457.00	.00 to 480.00	.00 to 90.00	4.00 to 168.00
Per cent reporting care	63.5	65.4	77.4	79.1	25.6	58.6

average dental expenditure of the lower group was $86, and for the higher bracket $116. Average dental bills also varied with size of family: families of 3 spent an average of $73, families of 4, $105, and larger families, $133. These expenditures increased with family size, and thus the average per capita expenditure for all individuals in the sample was about $25 for each size family.

Dental expenditures by individuals.—Visits to dentists were reported by 65 per cent of the husbands, 77 per cent of their wives, 79 per cent of the children 6 to 17, and approximately one-fourth of the younger children. The average amount spent by all individuals who had dental care was $40. About this sum was reported by the husbands and older children; the wives spent an average of $46; and the children under six only $18. Bills of less than $25 were reported by between 49 and 56 per cent of each of these groups except the very youngest children, 79 per cent of whom had dental bills less than $25. However, the range of expenditures was wide, and there were dental bills of more than $100 for 10 per cent of the husbands, 11 per cent of the older children, and 15 per cent of the wives.

Chapter XI

EXPENDITURES FOR PERSONAL CARE

TOTAL PERSONAL CARE

All families had some expenditures for personal care. The expenditures included services received largely at barber or beauty shops, and supplies such as cosmetics, shaving soap, shampoo, tooth paste, facial tissue, and a variety of miscellaneous items. The average family expenditure for total personal care was $118, or 1.9 per cent of all current consumption expenditures; for 80 per cent of the families this cost represented less than 2 1/2 per cent of each current consumption dollar. Slightly more than three-quarters of the sample spent between $50 and $150; only 4 per cent spent less than $50; and 5 per cent more than $200. Expenditures were almost equally divided between services and supplies.

There was no consistent variation of personal care expenditures by income level, and if family size is taken into account, per capita expenditures in families with incomes either over or under $6,000 were $28.

PERSONAL CARE SERVICES

All but 2 families had some expense for personal services; these 2 managed to spend nothing during 1950 by having home haircuts, shampoos, and other home services. The average family expenditure for personal services both for all families and those reporting expenditures was $55. Slightly more than two-thirds of the expenditures were between $25 and $75, but 12 per cent were less than $25, and 11 per cent more than $100. Husbands spent 45 per cent of all the money which went for personal services, and wives accounted for slightly less than one-third of the total; the children spent a little more than one-fifth, and all other family members 1 per cent of the personal service dollar.[1]

---

[1] The discussion of amounts spent for services by family members omits 1 family who spent a total of $31.10. The complete breakdown of this amount by family members was unavailable.

All but 3 husbands spent something for these services, and the average
expenditure was $25. Of those who reported expenditures, 93 per cent spent
between $10 and $40. With the exception of a total of $12.50 spent by 3 men
for miscellaneous services, all expenditures were for haircuts, for which 2
men spent the unusually high sum of about $75 each.

TABLE 72

Expenditures for Personal Care, by Type of Expenditure

	Total personal care		Personal services		Personal supplies	

Families reporting expenditures

Expenditure class	Number	Per cent	Number	Per cent	Number	Per cent
Families reporting, total...	159	100.0	157	100.0	159	100.0
Under $100, total	77	48.4	140	89.2	151	95.0
Under $25	1	.6	19	12.1	12	7.5
$25 to $49	6	3.8	58	36.9	63	39.6
$50 to $74	29	18.2	48	30.6	53	33.3
$75 to $99	41	25.8	15	9.6	23	14.5
$100 to $199, total	74	46.5	17	10.7	8	5.0
$100 to $124	32	20.1	12	7.6	4	2.5
$125 to $149	20	12.6	4	2.5	2	1.3
$150 to $174	13	8.2	1	.6	2	1.3
$175 to $199	9	5.7	0	.0	0	.0
$200 and over..........	8	5.0	0	.0	0	.0

Average expenditures by income class and ranges

All families						
Mean	$110.57		$55.31		$55.95	
Median	100.96		50.58		51.29	
Range	17.77 to		11.00 to		7.25 to	
	249.20		166.00		173.72	
Families with incomes under $6,000						
Mean	106.95		49.80		57.81	
Median	90.82		42.25		49.75	
Families with incomes $6,000 and over						
Mean	113.88		60.36		54.25	
Median	104.80		56.08		51.46	

It was surprising to find that all wives spent an average of $18, or 29 per
cent less than their husbands. Thirteen per cent of the women reported no
expenditures for personal services, and those with expenditures generally
spent small amounts—the average being $20. Sixty-nine per cent of the ex-
penditures were less than $20, but only 31 per cent of the men reported such
small expenses. Five women spent sums between $81 and $109—amounts
larger than those spent by any husband. These 5 women had relatively high
expenditures largely because of weekly or semimonthly trips to the beauty

TABLE 73

Expenditures per Family for Personal Services, by Family Member and Type of Service

Expenditure class	Husbands			Wives					Children	Other
	Total services	Haircuts	All other	Total services	Permanent at beauty shop	Supplies for home permanent	Waves and shampoos	All other	Total services	Total services
	Number of families reporting expenditures									
Families reporting, total	156	156	33	138	71	69	64	76	117	4
Size of expenditures unknown	1	1	0	1	1	0	0	1	1	0
Size of expenditures, total	155	155	3	137	70	69	64	76	116	4
Under $100, total	155	155	3	136	70	69	64	76	116	4
Under $50, total	152	152	3	121	68	69	60	76	115	4
Under $10	4	4	3	60	19	68	36	68	31	2
$10 to $19	44	44	0	35	31	1	6	5	47	0
$20 to $29	46	46	0	10	12	0	11	2	18	1
$30 to $39	55	56	0	10	6	0	4	1	17	0
$40 to $49	3	2	0	6	0	0	3	0	2	1
$50 to $99	3	3	0	15	2	0	4	0	1	0
$100 and over	0	0	0	1	0	0	0	0	0	0

Per cent of families reporting expenditures

Size of expenditures known,										
total	100.0	100.0	100.0	100.0	100.0	100.0	100.0	100.0	100.0	100.0
Under $100, total	100.0	100.0	100.0	100.0	100.0	100.0	100.0	100.0	100.0	100.0
Under $50, total	98.1	98.1	100.0	88.3	97.1	100.0	93.8	100.0	99.1	100.0
Under $10	2.6	2.6	100.0	43.8	27.1	98.6	56.2	89.5	26.7	50.0
$10 to $19	28.4	28.4	.0	25.5	44.3	1.4	9.4	6.6	40.5	.0
$20 to $29	29.7	29.7	.0	7.3	17.1	.0	17.2	2.6	15.5	25.0
$30 to $39	35.5	36.1	.0	7.3	8.6	.0	6.2	1.3	14.7	.0
$40 to $49	1.9	1.3	.0	4.4	.0	.0	4.7	.0	1.7	25.0
$50 to $99	.0	.0	.0	.7	.0	.0	.0	.0	.0	.0
$100 and over	.0	.0	.0	.7	.0	.0	.0	.0	.0	.0

Average expenditures, ranges, and per cent reporting expenditures

All families[a]										
Mean	$24.66	$24.58	$.08	$17.52	$6.91	$1.37	$6.53	$2.65	$12.11	$.47
Median	24.00	24.00	...	9.42	...	...	...	...	10.11	...
Families spending										
Mean	25.14	25.06	4.17	20.21	15.59	3.16	16.23	5.53	16.49	18.75
Median	24.00	24.00	4.50	11.50	11.75	2.78	6.00	4.50	15.00	15.87
Range	1.25 to 78.00	1.25 to 78.00	2.00 to 6.00	1.23 to 109.00	4.00 to 64.00	1.00 to 12.00	1.50 to 84.00	.40 to 30.00	1.00 to 60.00	1.25 to 42.00
Per cent reporting expenditures	98.1	98.1	1.9	86.8	44.7	43.4	40.3	47.8	73.6	2.5

[a] Excluding 1 family not reporting

parlor for waves and shampoos, professional permanent waves, or some combination of these items. Those women who reported expenditures spent an average of $16 for beauty shop permanents and $3 for home permanents; waves and shampoos cost those who reported them $16 a year; and $6 went for manicures, special treatments, and other miscellaneous services, combined.

Other adult family members (mostly parents of the husband or his wife) who reported personal service expenses spent an average of $19. Since there were only 4 persons reporting such expenses, the costs were not important for the families as a whole.

TABLE 74

Expenditures per Child for Personal Services, by Sex

Expenditure class	Total children .		Boys		Girls	
	Number	Per cent	Number	Per cent	Number	Per cent
Children in sample, total	311	100.0	167	100.0	144	100.0
No expenditures	131	42.1	46	27.5	85	59.0
Children with expenditures, total	180	57.9	121	72.5	59	41.0
Size of expenditure unknown	1	...	1	...	0	...
Children reporting size of expenditures, total	179	100.0	120	100.0	59	100.0
Under $10	81	45.3	36	30.0	45	76.3
$10 to $19	81	45.3	69	57.5	12	20.3
$20 to $29	10	5.6	9	7.5	1	1.7
$30 to $39	7	3.9	6	5.0	1	1.7

Average expenditures and ranges

All children			
Mean	$6.17	$9.43	$2.41
Median.................	2.50	10.00	...
Children reporting size of expenditures			
Median.................	10.69	13.04	5.89
Median.................	10.00	12.00	3.00
Range	1.00 to	1.00 to	1.00 to
	32.50	32.50	30.98

The average family expenditure for children's personal services was $12 for all families, and $16 for those families reporting expenditures. Eighty-two per cent of this was spent on the boys, who made up 54 per cent of all the children. For all the children in the sample, the average spent per child was $6; the average per boy was $9, and per girl $2. Seventy-two per cent of the boys spent something for personal care services, but only 41 per cent of the girls had any expense. The average per capita amount spent for the boys who had an expenditure was $13, and for the girls $6. Thus, not only did more boys than girls spend for services, but those boys who had

TABLE 75

Expenditures for Personal Supplies, by Type of Expenditure

Families reporting expenditures

Expenditure class	Total supplies		Soap		Cosmetics		All other	
	Number	Per cent	Number	Per cent	Number	Per cent	Number	Per cent
Families reporting, total	159	100.0	156	100.0	157	100.0	159	100.0
Under $100, total	151	95.0	156	100.0	157	100.0	157	98.7
Under $50, total	75	47.2	156	100.0	152	96.8	137	86.2
Under $10	1	.6	130	83.3	48	30.6	11	6.9
$10 to $19	6	3.8	24	15.4	57	36.3	25	15.7
$20 to $29	13	8.2	2	1.3	28	17.8	45	28.3
$30 to $39	25	15.7	0	.0	15	9.6	37	23.3
$40 to $49	30	18.9	0	.0	4	2.5	19	11.9
$50 to $99	76	47.8	0	.0	5	3.2	20	12.6
$100 and over	8	5.0	0	.0	0	.0	2	1.3

Average expenditures, ranges, and per cent reporting expenditures

Families reporting	Total supplies	Soap	Cosmetics	All other
Mean	$55.95	$6.18	$17.39	$32.71
Median	51.29	4.84	14.82	29.91
Range	7.25 to 173.72	.56 to 26.10	.24 to 74.10	3.40 to 109.42
Per cent reporting	100.0	98.1	98.7	100.0

expenditures spent more than twice as much as the girls who reported expenses. With the exception of $3 spent by 1 boy for shampoos, all of the boys' expenditures were for haircuts. The girls, on the other hand, had, varied expenditures—for haircuts, permanent waves, and a few waves and shampoos.

PERSONAL CARE SUPPLIES

All families had expenditures for personal care supplies, and the average amount spent was $56. Seventy-three per cent of these expenditures were between $25 and $75, but 12 families spent less than $25, and 8 spent more than $100.

These supplies were not classified by family members, because most of the items bought were of the type used by more than 1 person and often by the entire household. However, contrary to the situation found in personal services, it is probable that the women spent more for personal supplies than the men. This is suggested by the fact that the largest single item in personal supplies was cosmetics, for which the average family expenditure was $17, or slightly less than one-third of the total family expense for all supplies.

Certainly very few families spent extravagantly or even generously for the items inclued in the categories of personal care. The men ordinarily had about one haircut every two weeks and spent practically nothing for any other kind of personal service. Twenty-one women spent nothing for services, and only a few spent more than enough to have one beauty shop permanent or its equivalent in home permanents, or an occasional haircut, wave, or shampoo. Expenditures for supplies were also small. The average of $56 per family for these items is only about enough to buy the necessary soap, toothpaste, and toothbrushes, shaving supplies, cleaning tissues, and a moderate amount of low-priced cosmetics.

Chapter XII

EXPENDITURES
FOR RECREATION

TOTAL RECREATION

Every family spent something for recreation; the average outlay was
$355, but individual family expenditures varied greatly. Fifteen per
cent of the families spent less than $100; 43 per cent spent from $100
to $300; and 21 per cent spent $500 or more. All but one of the highest expenditures, and a considerable number of those in the range between $200 and $300, were made by families who purchased radios,
television sets, or expensive musical instruments such as pianos or
organs. As a whole, the families in the sample spent 6 per cent of
all their current consumption expenditures for recreation, and 86 per
cent of the group reported expenditures which amounted to less than
10 cents of each dollar spent for consumption goods. For the remaining 14 per cent, recreation expenses were a sizable proportion of
total consumption expenditures, amounting to as much as 31 per cent
for one family that purchased a piano, and 37 per cent for another
that purchased an organ.

Families with incomes above $6,000 spent 43 per cent more for
recreation than did those with lower incomes—an average of $415 in
contrast with $290—and these expenditures accounted for 6.4 per cent
of all their consumption expenditures as against 5.3 per cent for the
lower income group. The greatest differences in average expenditures
occurred in the purchase and repair of television sets, radios, and
musical instruments, where the upper group spent 71 per cent more
than those with lower incomes, and in paid admissions other than
movies, which were 82 per cent higher among the upper income families than for the lower bracket.

TABLE 76

Expenditures for Recreation, by Type of Expenditure

Families reporting expenditures

Expenditure class	Total recreation	Radio, TV, musical instruments (purchase and repair)	Toys and play equipment	Movies	Pets	Dues	Paid admissions (except movies)	Camera equipment and supplies	Sport goods and game equipment	Records and sheet music	Vacation recreation	Other
Families reporting												
Total..........	159	101	138	154	93	130	131	136[a]	80	109	75	62
Under $100	24	53	122	148	83	123	130	129	75	108	74	54
Under $25	0	36	51	91	44	88	85	105	49	91	53	37
$25 to $49	5	9	39	37	23	22	32	19	13	16	16	9
$50 to $74	11	6	25	12	10	10	10	2	6	0	3	8
$75 to $99	8	2	7	8	6	3	3	3	7	1	2	0
$100 to $199 ...	35	3	16	6	9	5	1	4	2	1	1	4
$200 to $299 ...	33	13	0	0	1	2	0	1	3	0	0	3
$300 to $399 ...	13	11	0	0	0	0	0	0	0	0	0	0
$400 to $499 ...	21	8	0	0	0	0	0	1	0	0	0	0
$500 and over ...	33	13	0	0	0	0	0	0	0	0	0	1

Average expenditures, by income class, ranges, and per cent reporting expenditures

	$355.35	$152.67	$36.88	$27.13	$23.76	$22.36	$18.83	$18.67	$17.75	$9.16	$8.40	$19.74
All families												
Mean	$355.35	$152.67	$36.88	$27.13	$23.76	$22.36	$18.83	$18.67	$17.75	$9.16	$8.40	$19.74
Median	264.99	10.00	25.50	16.75	4.00	10.00	12.75	9.13	.50	5.00	...	...
Families reporting												
Total												
Mean	355.35	240.35	42.50	28.01	40.62	27.34	22.86	21.83	35.27	13.37	17.82	50.62
Median	264.99	69.60	30.75	17.55	26.00	14.20	16.00	10.00	17.72	9.88	10.00	19.62
Range	27.45 to 2,545.92	2.50 to 2,437.56	.50 to 188.48	.20 to 180.20	.10 to 260.00	.60 to 284.00	.80 to 100.00	1.00 to 404.00	.50 to 250.00	.50 to 100.00	.50 to 100.00	1.00 to 767.50
Incomes under $6,000												
Mean	289.70	176.75	34.28	25.69	40.86	25.67	15.78	20.81	34.21	9.65	15.78	45.11
Median	215.10	59.68	25.50	18.32	26.52	12.50	12.75	9.26	8.00	8.78	10.00	24.00
Incomes $6,000 and over												
Mean	415.47	302.70	49.40	30.15	40.40	28.77	28.65	22.68	36.14	15.88	19.34	56.14
Median	298.65	226.61	34.80	16.99	26.00	16.50	23.50	11.50	25.90	10.00	100.00	10.00
Per cent reporting	100.0	63.5	86.8	96.9	58.5	81.8	82.4	84.9	50.3	68.6	47.2	39.0

[a] Includes 1 family with size of expenditure not reported.

TYPES OF RECREATION
EXPENDITURE

Radio, television, and musical instruments.—The largest recreation
expenditures were for the category which included radios, television sets,
and musical instruments. All but 1 family owned a radio, and most families
had two. Seventy-two per cent had some record-playing instrument; 39 per
cent owned a piano or organ; and 31 per cent had television sets. With the
exception of the television sets (74 per cent of which were bought or received
as gifts in 1950), most of these instruments had been bought in previous
years. There were some 1950 purchases of radios and musical instruments,
but almost half of the money spent for all the items in this general category
was used to buy television sets.

The average expenditure by the entire group of families for the purchase
and upkeep of all these instruments was $153, or 43 per cent of their total
recreation expenditures. Sixty-four per cent of all families reported expenditures and spent an average of $240 per family. Slightly more than one-
third of the families spent less than $25, and slightly more than half spent
less than $100. Most expenditures of less than $100 were for inexpensive
radios, record players, violins or other stringed instruments, or for the
repair of various instruments. Forty-five per cent of those with expenditures reported much larger amounts—from $200 to $2,438. This group included 34 families that purchased television sets at an average price of
$354; 68 per cent of the sets cost between $200 and $400, and all but one of
the rest cost from $400 to $590. The other 11 families with large expenditures included 1 family that bought an organ for $2,438, and several fami-
lies that purchased pianos or radio phonographs.

The only recreation items which were bought on installment in 1950 were
relatively expensive—costing $100 or more. Installment credit was used
for 38 per cent of the television sets and 42 per cent of the radio phonograph
purchases, as well as to buy three of the seven pianos acquired during 1950,
and in the purchase of an organ and an accordion.

Other types of recreation expenditures.—The average of $203 spent by
these families for all other types of recreation was used for many different
things. Almost all families went to the movies, and 82 per cent had expenditures for other types of paid admissions. Between 82 and 87 per cent bought
toys and play equipment or cameras, or paid organization dues; and from
47 to 69 per cent had expenditures for pets, sporting goods, records and
sheet music, and vacation recreation. The average sums spent by those reporting expenditures for any of these categories were never large—they
ranged from $13 to $42. Movies were the most common form of recreation,
with an average expenditure of $28; this was less than was spent for several
other types of recreation. An average of $24 went for toys and play equip-

ment, and $41 was spent for pets. For the other specified types of recreation expenditures, the average cost of each category ranged from $13 to $35. For each category, 88 per cent or more of the expenditures were less than $100; the vast majority were less than $50, and there were never more than 3 families who reported expenditures of $200 or more. Among all the categories, the largest sums spent were $404 for the purchase of camera equipment, and $750 lost in gambling.

Vacation.—In order to maintain comparability with the U.S. Bureau of Labor Statistics income and expenditure studies, only a small part of total vacation expenses—the sum spent specifically for recreation—is included in this recreation analysis. Forty-seven per cent of the families reported vacation recreation expenditures, at an average cost of $18. Seventy-one per cent of the expenditures were less than $25, and the largest amount spent was $100. There were, of course, other expenses connected with vacations, such as food, lodging, and transportation, but these items have been included with other family expenditures of the same kind.[1] Although it is not practical to determine what part of family automobile expenses should be allocated to a vacation, or to allocate certain other minor vacation expenditures, it is possible to combine most of the major expenses reported in other sections of the budget, and thus obtain a rough idea of vacation costs. Three-quarters of the families reported vacation expenditures, and they spent an average of $144—less than was spent for the combined category of radio, television, and musical instruments, but much more than was spent for other categories of recreation. These vacation costs ranged from $1.50 to $783. Forty-four per cent of the families spent less than $100, usually because they visited relatives or went camping where the only costs were fees for a camp site or for food which they prepared themselves. Twenty per cent of the expenses were more than $200, but only 2 families spent more than $500, both for trips across the country which cost between $700 and $800.

---

[1]Vacation expenditures are classified as follows: food, under food away from home; lodging, under housing away from home; automobile transportation, under automobile expenses; and plane or train, under "other transportation." Vacation items classified under other parts of recreation included, for example, film bought for taking pictures while on vacation, which is classified under camera and camera supplies. Vacation expenses for nonlocal events such as fees for admission to a zoo or for boat rental are included in vacation recreation as such.

Chapter XIII

EXPENDITURES FOR EDUCATION, READING, TOBACCO, AND MISCELLANEOUS ITEMS

EDUCATION

About three-quarters of the families included in this study reported some expenditure for education.[1] For the entire sample the average sum spent was $66, or 1.1 per cent of all consumption expenditures; for those who reported educational expenses, the average cost was $88. Nearly half of the amounts spent were less than $50, and a quarter were between $50 and $100. Thirty-one, or slightly more than one-fourth of the families with educational expenses reported expenditures of $100 or more, nineteen of which were between $100 and $200. The relatively high expenses in most of these 31 cases resulted either from tuition payments (usually at a college or university, but in some cases at private schools for younger children), or from music, dancing, or other private lessons.

READING

All families spent something for newspapers, magazines, or books (other than school books). The average expenditure was $49—only 0.8 per cent of total consumption expenditures. Slightly less than two-thirds of the families reported expenses under $50, and only 4 per cent spent more than $100. Most families spent only enough to have a daily newspaper, a magazine subscription or two, and perhaps an occasional book. The 7 families who spent more than $100 purchased both newspapers and magazines, and 6 of the 7 also spent $40 or more for books.

---

[1] Educational expenditures include tuition fees, expenditures for various kinds of private lessons, books and supplies, and student body dues. Food bought while at school or college is included with food away from home, and lodging while at school or college is included with housing away from home.

TOBACCO

Seventy-two per cent of the families reported expenditures for tobacco. The families as a whole spent an average of $57, or 1 per cent of total consumption expenditures. Those families that purchased tobacco had an average expenditure of $80. Slightly more than one-fourth of this group spent more than $100, and in these cases there was always more than 1 person who purchased tobacco—usually both the husband and wife.

MISCELLANEOUS

Miscellaneous expenditures included interest payments on loans,[2] bank charges, certain real estate expenses, legal expenses, funeral expenses, children's allowances not accounted for in other expenditure categories, and other miscellaneous costs. All but 12 families had expenses for one or another of these items. For the group as a whole the average expenditure for all the items combined was $71 or 1.2 per cent of current consumption expenditures; for those reporting expenses, the average was $76. Forty-five per cent of the families spent less than $25, 80 per cent less than $100, and 11 per cent between $200 and $550.

Twenty-two families reported expenses for real estate which was neither an owner-occupied home nor used for an unincorporated family business. This group of expenditures averaged $109 for those reporting, and although 54 per cent of the expenses were less than $50, 23 per cent were between $200 and $500.

Interest payments on loans were reported by 28 per cent of the families, with an average expenditure of $53 for those families incurring such debts. Only 3 families reported spending sums between $100 and $200, and only 1 paid more, reporting the relatively large sum of $534.

Seventy-eight of the families had expenditures for bank services and safe deposit box rental. The average sum spent by those reporting was $12, and 96 per cent of the expenditures were less than $30.

Expenditures for a wide variety of other items were reported by 55 per cent of the families. For all families in the sample, the average spent for these combined items was $31, and for those who reported expenditures it was $56; just over half the expenditures were less than $25, and 82 per cent less than $100. Twenty-nine per cent of these miscellaneous expenditures represented payments by 31 families for children's allowances which were not accounted for in other categories of expenditure; another 26 per cent was spent by 37 families for funeral expenses. A third item, reported only by 3 families but an important outlay for each of them, was the expense in connection with adopting a child. The 3 families spent an average of $249 for this purpose.

---

[2]Excluding installment charges, interest not due in 1950, or interest paid on an owner-occupied home.

TABLE 77

Expenditures for Education, Reading, Tobacco, and Miscellaneous Items

Families reporting expenditures

Number

Expenditure class	Education	Reading	Tobacco	Miscellaneous				
				Total	Interest on loans[a]	Bank services	Real estate[b]	Other[c]
Families reporting, total	118	159	114	147	44	124	22	88
Under $100, total	87	152	83	117	40	124	15	72
Under $50, total	57	101	31	90	29	123	12	61
Under $10	19	1	10	21	6	51	5	19
$10 to $19	11	4	6	31	7	56	2	19
$20 to $29	16	33	1	21	6	12	2	13
$30 to $39	4	33	9	12	5	4	2	6
$40 to $49	7	30	5	5	5	0	1	4
$50 to $99	30	51	52	27	11	1	3	11
$100 to $199	19	7	27	14	3	0	2	11
$200 to $299	3	0	4	5	0	0	3	2
$300 to $399	5	0	0	5	0	0	1	1
$400 and over	4	0	0	6	1	0	1	2

	Per cent							
Families reporting, total	100.0	100.0	100.0	100.0	100.0	100.0	100.0	100.0
Under $100, total	73.7	95.6	72.8	79.6	90.9	100.0	68.2	81.8
Under $50, total	48.3	63.6	27.2	61.2	65.9	99.2	54.5	69.3
Under $10	16.1	.6	7.8	14.3	13.6	41.1	22.7	21.6
$10 to $19	9.3	2.5	5.3	21.1	15.9	45.2	9.1	21.6
$20 to $29	13.6	20.8	.9	14.3	13.6	9.7	9.1	14.8
$30 to $39	3.4	20.8	7.9	8.2	11.4	3.2	9.1	6.8
$40 to $49	5.9	18.9	4.4	3.4	11.4	.0	4.5	4.5
$50 to $99	25.5	32.0	45.6	18.4	25.0	.8	13.6	12.5
$100 to $199	16.1	4.4	23.7	9.5	6.8	.0	9.1	12.5
$200 to $299	2.5	.0	3.5	3.4	.0	.0	13.6	2.3
$300 to $399	4.2	.0	.0	3.4	.0	.0	4.5	1.1
$400 and over	3.4	.0	.0	4.1	2.3	.0	4.5	2.3

Average expenditures, ranges, and per cent reporting expenditures

All families								
Mean	$65.62	$48.63	$57.30	$70.56	$14.79	$9.65	$15.04	$31.08
Median	25.00	42.00	54.60	26.21	...	7.80	...	2.50
Families reporting								
Mean	88.42	48.63	79.92	76.32	53.46	12.38	108.70	56.15
Median	50.00	42.00	78.00	30.00	34.83	11.57	37.50	24.00
Range	.50 to 696.50	8.40 to 190.72	.72 to 219.44	2.00 to 549.72	3.77 to 533.72	.50 to 74.40	3.21 to 484.89	1.00 to 426.40
Per cent reporting	74.2	100.0	71.7	92.5	27.7	78.0	13.8	55.3

a Excludes installment charges, interest not due in 1950 (even though paid in 1950), and interest paid on mortgages.

b Includes expenses for real estate not used for an unincorporated family business, and for land not occupied or rented, plus other miscellaneous expenses.

c Includes (in order of total spent) children's allowances, n. e. c.; funeral expenses (including flowers); adoption fees; personal insurance other than life, medical, or accident; legal expenses; money losses; wedding expenses; and other small items. n. e. c.

Chapter XIV

NONCONSUMPTION
EXPENDITURES

In addition to expenditures for family living, that is, "current consumption" expenditures, all families reported expenses for personal insurance,[1] gifts and contributions, and personal taxes.[2] These nonconsumption expenses complete the picture of total family expenditures during 1950.

The average of all expenditures by the families included in this study was $7,228, of which $5,957, or 82 per cent, was spent for current consumption, and $1,271 for nonconsumption items. Forty-two per cent of the nonconsumption expenditures went for personal insurance, 14 per cent for gifts and contributions, and 44 per cent for taxes.

PERSONAL INSURANCE

Every family reported some expenditure for personal insurance, at an average cost of $533. Only 1 family spent less than $100, and 68 per cent spent between $300 and $700. The four highest family expenditures ranged from $1,014 to $1,240. The families as a whole spent 7.4 per cent of their total expenditures for insurance; slightly under two-thirds spent between 5 and 10 per cent, and the highest proportion was 15.9 per cent. Families with incomes less than $6,000 spent an average of $457 for insurance and those with higher incomes $603. The larger dollar expenditures of the higher in-

---

[1] Except disability, health, or accident insurance, which was considered a current consumption expenditure.

[2] Including federal and state income, personal property, and inheritance taxes. Sales and excise taxes were included with the cost of goods purchased, and real estate taxes on owned homes were in the cost of housing. Real estate taxes on property other than homes occupied in 1950 were included with miscellaneous current consumption expenditures.

come group represented 7.7 per cent of their total expenditures in contrast
with 7 per cent for the lower income group.

The head of every family had one or more of the following types of retirement protection: Old Age and Survivors Insurance, a government retirement plan, or membership in a company-sponsored retirement plan which
was often carried through a commercial insurance company. All except
federal workers and those employed in the teaching profession were covered
by California Unemployment Disability Insurance, and all but 2 families
carried some kind of insurance through a commercial insurance company.

TABLE 78

Expenditures for Personal Insurance, by Type of Insurance and Family Member

Type of insurance	All families Mean expendi-ture	Families reporting expenditures				
		Number	Per cent all families	Expenditures		
				Mean	Median	Range
All personal insurance						
Family, total	$533.27	159	100.0	$533.27	$507.57	$89.27 to 1,240.44
Old Age and Survivors Insurance						
Family, total	37.33	135	84.9	43.97	45.00	4.88 to 71.10
Head	36.79	132	83.0	44.32	45.00	13.75 to 45.07
Other members ...	.54	11	6.9	7.78	5.33	.41 to 20.10
Government retirement						
Family, total	84.12	31	19.5	431.47	438.71	226.80 to 584.82
Head	81.37	30	18.9	431.28	438.36	242.00 to 569.60
Other members ...	2.75	3	1.9	145.72	134.35	76.00 to 226.80
Private company retirement						
Family, total[a]	110.11	99	62.3	176.85	173.00	69.00 to 344.56
California Disability Insurance						
Family, total	23.89	135	84.9	28.14	30.00	1.11 to 53.95
Head	23.54	132	83.0	28.35	30.00	1.11 to 47.52
Other members ...	.35	11	6.9	5.10	3.55	.27 to 17.40
Commercial insurance						
Family, total[b]	277.82	157	98.7	281.35	257.88	26.35 to 802.44

[a]Private company retirement payments were only reported by heads of families.
[b]Data on commercial insurance were not broken down by family members.

Data were not available to permit separate analysis of the types and costs
of the varied commercial insurance policies; however, it seemed certain
that most such policies were for life insurance, but a relatively small number were endowment policies or annuities.

Eighty-five per cent of the families reported contributions for Federal
Old Age and Survivors Insurance. Usually the contribution came from the
chief breadwinner, but in a few cases some other members of the family
were covered. At the time this study was made the worker's contribution to
Old Age and Survivors Insurance was 1.5 per cent of the first $3,000 of

TABLE 79

Families Reporting Expenditures for Personal Insurance, by Size and Type of Expenditure

Expenditure class	Total personal insurance		Old Age and Survivors Insurance		Government retirement		Private company retirement		California Disability Insurance		Commercial insurance	
	Number	Per cent	Number	Per cent	Number	Per cent	Number	Per cent	Number	Per cent	Number	Per cent
Families reporting, total	159	100.0	135	100.0	31	100.0	99	100.0	135	100.0	157	100.0
Under $50, total	0	.0	131	97.0	0	.0	0	.0	134	99.3	7	4.5
Under $30	0	.0	6	4.4	0	.0	0	.0	39	28.9	1	.6
$30 to $39	0	.0	0	.0	0	.0	0	.0	80	59.3	4	2.5
$40 to $49	0	.0	125	92.6	0	.0	0	.0	15	11.1	2	1.3
$50 to $99	1	.6	4	3.0	0	.0	1	1.0	1	.7	3	1.9
$100 to $199	5	3.1	0	.0	4	12.9	75	75.8	0	.0	49	31.2
$200 to $299	13	8.2	0	.0	5	16.1	19	19.2	0	.0	41	26.1
$300 to $399	22	13.8	0	.0	15	48.4	4	4.0	0	.0	25	15.9
$400 to $499	35	22.0	0	.0	7	22.6	0	.0	0	.0	12	7.6
$500 to $599	30	18.9	0	.0	0	.0	0	.0	0	.0	12	7.6
$600 to $699	21	13.2	0	.0	0	.0	0	.0	0	.0	4	2.5
$700 to $799	14	8.8	0	.0	0	.0	0	.0	0	.0	3	1.9
$800 and over	18	11.3	0	.0	0	.0	0	.0	0	.0	1	.6

annual earnings.[3] Therefore, because of the income qualifications of this study, practically all family contributions to O.A.S.I. were $45. A few, however, were more or less than this figure, either because those reporting had not worked a full year in covered employment, or because more than 1 family member had been covered at some time during the year.

Twenty per cent of the families reported payments to state or other government retirement systems. Again, most of the members of these systems were the chief breadwinners.[4] The average payment was $431, and none was less than $200 or more than $600.

Sixty-two per cent of the families made payments to company-sponsored retirement plans. The average payment was $177, with just over three-quarters between $100 and $200, and the highest $345. The size of the payment was based in most instances on the amount of salary earned, and/or the age when hired. One-hundred and twenty-nine of the breadwinners in the sample were employed by sixteen private concerns, and this entire group was covered by O.A.S.I. Ten of the concerns, employing 109 of the breadwinners, also had their own retirement plans, seven of which had voluntary, and the others compulsory employee membership. The seven voluntary plans were in firms employing 64 of the breadwinners, 57 of whom participated. Three of the nonparticipants had not been employed in their respective companies long enough to be eligible, and the other 4 evidently chose not to participate. One of these companies, employing 3 of the breadwinners, paid the entire cost of employee membership. Seven out of the ten plans were carried through commercial insurance companies; the remaining three were operated by the industries themselves, or by a bank acting as trustee. The remaining six firms, employing 20 of the breadwinners in the sample, had no retirement plans.

As was true of Old Age and Survivors Insurance, 85 per cent of the families reported payments for California Unemployment Disability Insurance, and in all but a few cases this protection was solely for the chief breadwinner. The California law provides for an employee-contribution of 1 per cent of the first $3,000 of annual earnings, and thus the sum paid by 46 per cent of the families was exactly $30. However, since the employer may if

---

[3] In 1951 the worker's contribution was based on the first $3600 of annual earnings. In 1954 the contribution rate was increased to 2 per cent, and in 1955 the maximum on which the contribution was based was increased to the first $4,200 of annual earnings. January 1, 1957, the worker's contribution was raised again to 2 1/4 per cent of the first $4,200 of annual earnings.

[4] The University of California academic retirement system has been classified as a state system, although it is administered by the Regents of the University, rather than by the state government.

TABLE 80

Expenditures for Commercial Insurance, by Income Class

	All families		Income class			
			Under $6,000		$6,000 and over	

Families reporting expenditures

Expenditure class	Number	Per cent	Number	Per cent	Number	Per cent
Families reporting, total...	157	100.0	75	100.0	82	100.0
Under $100	10	6.4	5	6.7	5	6.1
$100 to $199............	49	31.2	30	40.0	19	23.2
$200 to $299............	41	26.1	24	32.0	17	20.7
$300 to $399............	25	15.9	9	12.0	16	19.5
$400 to $499............	12	7.6	4	5.3	8	9.8
$500 to $599............	12	7.6	2	2.7	10	12.2
$600 to $699...........	4	2.5	1	1.3	3	3.7
$700 and over	4	2.5	0	.0	4	4.9

Average expenditures, ranges, and per cent reporting expenditures

All families						
Mean..................	$277.81		$228.92		$322.58	
Median	249.60		203.98		293.59	
Families reporting						
Mean.................	281.35		231.97		326.52	
Median	257.88		205.27		297.30	
Range	26.35 to 802.44		37.80 to 672.35		26.35 to 802.44	
Per cent reporting	98.7		98.7		98.8	

he wishes pay all or part of the required contribution himself, 29 per cent of the reported contributions were less than $30. One-quarter of the families reported contributions above $30, up to a maximum of $54. In a few cases these larger sums were the result of more than 1 family member working in covered employment, but in the main they represented individual contributions for coverage extending beyond what was required under the California Disability Insurance law.[5] In this study no attempt was made to determine what additional protection was provided by the larger contributions.

All but 2 families carried some kind of commercial insurance, and the average expenditure for all families was $278—slightly more than half of the average sum invested by all families in total personal insurance. The sums paid for these policies varied greatly, since they afforded many dif-

[5]The California law provides that employers may elect to insure the risks covered under the Unemployment Disability Insurance law with a private company or by self-insurance, but these so-called voluntary plans must provide protection which is greater than that which is required by the act. See Section 450.1 (a), p. 91; section 452.5, p. 93; section 456, p. 95.

ferent kinds and amounts of protection. A few families made payments of
less than $100 but 57 per cent of all payments ranged from $100 to $300,
and 16 per cent were between $300 and $400. One family in 5 spent larger
sums, up to a maximum of $802. Families with incomes of less than $6,000
spent an average of $232, and those with higher incomes paid premiums
averaging $327.

This group of families spent 7.4 per cent of their total expenditures for
insurance protection. If all the expenditure categories, both consumption
and nonconsumption, are placed in order of size, the sum spent for insurance is sixth from the top—lower only than the proportions spent for food,
transportation, housing, clothing, and taxes. Nearly half the average total
insurance expenditure represented payments either to state, federal, or
company retirement plans, and the remainder was used to purchase various types of individual insurance protection from commercial companies.
In most cases the sums spent for individual commercial policies provided
a substantial degree of insurance protection, since 62 per cent of the payments were $200 or more. The average commercial insurance premium
of $281 paid by these families was larger than that allowed for life insur-
ance in the Heller Committee budget for a salaried worker.[6] This budget
insurance plan with a premium of $229, together with federal Old Age and
Survivors Insurance, provides a family income of about one-half the total
budget excluding income taxes if the husband dies when the children are
young, and a reduced sum when the children are grown. Clearly, not all
families had this much protection; what their protection actually was depended upon the particular combination of insurance policies which they
were purchasing. Practically all breadwinners, however, had some protection at retirement, and also some additional protection for their families in case of death.

GIFTS AND CONTRIBUTIONS

All families spent something for gifts and contributions, averaging $177 per
family, or 2.4 per cent of total consumption and nonconsumption expenditures. Most families spent moderate amounts—36 per cent under $100, and
nearly three-quarters under $200. The highest quarter spent sums ranging
from $200 to $1,206, most of which included relatively large amounts
either for church contributions or for the support of persons outside the
economic family. Families with incomes less than $6,000 spent an average
of $169; those with higher incomes spent $184, or 9 per cent more, although
their total consumption and nonconsumption expenditures were 21 per cent

---

[6]The 1950 cost would have been the same as the cost in the 1953 and 1954
budgets.

greater. Thus the larger dollar expenditure of the higher income group represented 2.3 per cent of their total expenditures, in contrast with 2.6 per cent spent by the lower income group.

TABLE 81

Expenditures for Gifts and Contributions, by Type of Expenditure

	Total	Contributions				Gifts (cash or goods)	Cash support
		Total	Church	Welfare	Other		

Families reporting expenditures

Expenditure class	Number						
Families reporting, total.............	159	158	134	156	104	154	16
Under $100, total..	57	119	109	156	103	131	3
Under $20......	0	16	35	95	78	25	1
$20 to $39......	8	31	26	45	14	32	0
$40 to $59......	9	19	28	11	7	37	1
$60 to $79......	15	31	19	3	3	19	1
$80 to $99......	25	22	1	2	1	18	0
$100 to $199.......	61	25	16	0	1	18	9
$200 to $299.......	23	10	5	0	0	2	0
$300 and over	18	4	4	0	0	3	4
	Per cent						
Families reporting, total.............	100.0	100.0	100.0	100.0	100.0	100.0	100.0
Under $100, total..	35.8	75.3	81.3	100.0	99.0	85.1	18.8
Under $20......	.0	10.1	26.1	60.9	75.0	16.2	6.2
$20 to $39......	5.0	19.6	19.4	28.8	13.5	20.8	.0
$40 to $59......	5.7	12.0	20.9	7.1	6.7	24.0	6.2
$60 to $79......	9.4	19.6	14.2	1.9	2.9	12.3	6.2
$80 to $99......	15.7	13.9	.7	1.3	1.0	11.7	.0
$100 to $199.......	38.4	15.8	11.9	.0	1.0	11.7	56.2
$200 to $299.......	14.5	6.3	3.7	.0	.0	1.3	.0
$300 and over	11.3	2.5	3.0	.0	.0	1.9	25.0

Average expenditures, ranges, and per cent reporting expenditures

All families							
Mean	$176.79	$89.62	$60.14	$19.03	$10.45	$65.00	$22.17
Median	124.50	62.50	35.00	15.00	4.84	47.13	...
Families reporting							
Mean	176.79	90.18	71.36	19.39	15.97	67.11	220.38
Median	124.50	62.85	50.00	15.00	9.50	50.00	120.00
Range	22.00 to 1,206.38	5.00 to 735.40	1.00 to 712.40	2.00 to 86.00	.50 to 100.00	1.50 to 621.90	15.00 to 1,080.00
Per cent reporting ...	100.0	99.4	84.3	98.1	65.4	96.9	10.1

All but 1 family contributed something to a church, or to a welfare or other type of community organization, and their average expenditure was $90. Most of these contributions were small—half were less than $63, and three-quarters were less than $100. Contributions larger than $100 almost always included relatively large church donations, and all of the fourteen largest sums, which ranged from nearly $210 to $735, included contributions of $150 or over to churches.

The second largest of the expenditures were gifts of cash or goods to persons outside the economic family. All but 5 families reported such gifts, and the average sum spent was $65; 49 per cent spent less than $50, but 5 reported sums ranging from $214 to $622. There were also 16 families who provided some support for someone outside the economic family. These expenditures were insignificant for the entire group of families—$22 per family—but families who had these responsibilities often spent quite substantial sums. Nine families reported amounts between $100 and $200, and 4 spent between $315 and $1,080, usually for assistance to the mother of the husband or wife.

PERSONAL TAXES

Every family reported paying personal taxes, and the average outlay for this purpose was $561, or 7.8 per cent of total consumption and nonconsumption expenditures. Ninety-seven per cent of the average family tax bill went for federal income taxes.

All families paid federal taxes with an average payment of $546. Eighty-seven per cent of the bills were between $300 and $800, and 9 families paid larger sums, up to a maximum of $1,425. This group of 9 families had incomes before taxes ranging from $7,242 to $9,104. For all the families in the sample federal income taxes amounted to 7.6 per cent of their total expenditures; a little more than three-quarters were between 5 and 10 per cent; 1 in 10 was less than 5 per cent and slightly more than one-eighth of the payments ran from 10 to a maximum of 14.5 per cent of total expenditures. Although income taxes were affected by the number of dependents as well as by the size of other allowable deductions, as would be expected, families with incomes under $6,000 paid much lower federal taxes than those with higher incomes—averaging $452 as compared with $631. The lower income group spent 6.9 per cent of total expenditures for taxes, and the higher group spent 8 per cent. In this connection, it should perhaps again be pointed out that to be eligible for inclusion in this study the chief breadwinner's earnings were required to be between $4,800 and $7,500, and total family income not more than $10,000.

State income taxes were paid by 126 families, or 79 per cent of the total sample. The average state tax was only $14; 88 per cent of the payments were less than $25, and none was as much as $50. The average state tax paid by families with incomes under $6,000 was $9—not quite half as much as was paid by families with higher incomes.

Only 37 families reported what they paid in personal property taxes.

TABLE 82

Expenditures for Personal Taxes, by Size and Types

Expenditure class	Total personal taxes[a]		Federal income tax		State income tax	
	Number	Per cent	Number	Per cent	Number	Per cent
		Families reporting expenditures				
Families reporting, total..	159	100.0	159	100.0	126	100.0
Under $50, total	0	.0	1	.6	126	100.0
Under $25	0	.0	0	.0	111	88.1
$25 to $49	0	.0	1	.6	15	11.9
$50 to $99	1	.6	0	.0	0	.0
$100 to $199..........	2	1.3	3	1.9	0	.0
$200 to $299..........	7	4.4	7	4.4	0	.0
$300 to $399..........	23	14.5	24	15.1	0	.0
$400 to $499..........	29	18.2	28	17.6	0	.0
$500 to $599..........	31	19.5	38	23.9	0	.0
$600 to $699..........	36	22.6	31	19.5	0	.0
$700 to $799..........	19	11.9	18	11.3	0	.0
$800 to $899..........	6	3.8	4	2.5	0	.0
$900 to $999..........	2	1.3	2	1.3	0	.0
$1,000 and over	3	1.9	3	1.9	0	.0

Average expenditures, ranges, and per cent reporting expenditures

Families reporting			
Mean	$560.57[a]	$545.75	$14.17
Median	547.37[a]	536.23	12.64
Range	76.54 to	45.66 to	.37 to
	1,445.25[a]	1,425.25	48.00
Per cent reporting	100.0	100.0	79.2

[a]Total personal taxes include, in addition to federal and state income taxes, personal property taxes paid by 37 families, and an inheritance tax paid by 1 family. (See the text for further discussion of these two types.)

Undoubtedly, many more families paid these taxes, but reported them together with real property taxes. The average of those personal property taxes reported was only $10, with 95 per cent less than $25. Since the sums were always small, the fact that many undoubtedly did not report this tax separately would have only a very slight effect on the total family tax bills. As was true of other types of taxes, those families with incomes less than $6,000 paid less in personal property taxes than did the higher income brackets—an average of $6, in contrast with slightly more than twice that amount. Only 1 family reported any other kind of personal tax—$185 on an inheritance received the previous year.[7]

---

[7]There were 4 families who received inheritances in 1950 but reported·no inheritance tax in 1950, probably because the tax was paid before the money was received.

Chapter XV

INSTALLMENT BUYING

The use of installment credit in the purchase of automobiles and certain kinds of household appliances and furnishings, as well as television sets and musical instruments,. has been discussed in the chapters dealing with expenditures for these goods. No installment purchases were reported for other types of goods such as clothing or jewelry. The present chapter summarizes some of the detailed data considered earlier but is primarily concerned with the over-all use of this kind of credit by families in the sample, and with the extent to which installment debts, incurred both in 1950 and in earlier years, were liquidated by the end of 1950. The final section presents a comparison with data published in the Survey of Consumer Finances conducted by the Federal Reserve System in coöperation with the Research Center of the University of Michigan.

Sixty-four, or 40 per cent, of the families included in the Heller Committee study used installment credit to buy one or more items in 1950. Fifty-five families bought automobiles, and installment credit was used for twelve, or 22 per cent, of these purchases. One or more of the housefurnishings items listed on table 83[1] were purchased by 152 families, 30 per cent of whom bought at least one of these items on installment. Fifty families bought television sets, radios, or musical instruments, and 42 per cent used installment credit in making their purchases. Finally, 1 family used this type of credit to make repairs on a home, and another to buy books.

There were considerable differences in the frequency with which installment credit was used for the purchase of various items. Seventeen per cent of those who purchased furniture used this type of credit, and from 26 to 38

---

[1]Items for which installment credit was not used by any family in this study are excluded from tables 83 and 84.

TABLE 83

Number of Families with 1950 Purchases of Items Bought on Installment

Items bought on installment	Total families purchasing	Families purchasing on installment	
		Number	Per cent of total purchasing
All items	159	64	40.3
Automobiles	55	12	21.8
Housefurnishings, total	152	46	30.3
Furniture..........................	115	20	17.4
Textiles	108	1	.9
Floor coverings	63	11	17.5
Wool rugs or carpets	34	9	26.5
Other	42	2	4.8
Flatwear	30	1	3.3
Vacuum cleaners	28	9	32.1
Washing machines	26	7	26.9
Stoves..........................	17	2	11.8
Sewing machines	13	6	46.2
Refrigerators	13	5	38.5
Dryers	6	2	33.3
Ironers	3	1	33.3
Television, radio, phonographs, musical instruments, total	50	21	42.0
Television	34	13	38.2
Radio-phonographs................	12	5	41.7
Pianos or organs	8	4	50.0
Accordions	1	1	100.0
Home repairs or replacements.......	115	1	.9
Books	86	1	1.2

TABLE 84

Total 1950 Expenditures and 1950 Installment Expenditures for Items Bought on Installment

Items bought on installment	Aggregate expenditures		Installment expenditures	
	Total	On installment	Per cent of total expenditures	Per cent of total installment
All items	$169,972.41	$43,580.03	25.6	100.0
Automobile	72,764.85	16,957.61	23.3	38.9
Other, total	97,207.56	26,622.42	27.4	61.1
Housefurnishings	52,797.24	14,510.85	27.5	33.3
Television and musical instruments	22,414.41	11,769.32	52.5	27.0
House repairs and replacements........	20,646.20	250.00	1.2	.6
Books	1,349.71	92.25	6.8	.2

per cent of the purchases of wool rugs, washing machines, television sets, vacuum cleaners, and refrigerators were made on installment.

In 1950 a total of $169,972 was spent for those items usually bought on installment; $43,580 or 26 per cent of this sum represented installment purchases. These purchases accounted for 23 per cent of the total sum spent for automobiles, 52 per cent of the total expenditures for television,

TABLE 85

1950 Installment Expenditures, by Type of Expenditure

Expenditure class	All installment expenditures		Automobiles		Housefurnishings and other	
	Number	Per cent	Number	Per cent	Number	Per cent
Families reporting expenditures						
All families reporting......	64	100.0	12	100.0	55	100.0
Under $500, total........	33	51.6	1	8.3	36	65.5
Under $100..........	3	4.7	0	.0	3	5.5
$100 to $199........	8	12.5	0	.0	8	14.5
$200 to $299........	9	14.1	0	.0	10	18.2
$300 to $399........	11	17.2	1	8.3	13	23.6
$400 to $499........	2	3.1	0	.0	2	3.6
$500 to $999...........	17	26.6	2	16.7	14	25.5
$1,000 to $1,499........	4	6.2	3	25.0	2	3.6
$1,500 to $1,999........	6	9.4	4	33.3	2	3.6
$2,000 to $2,499.......	3	4.7	1	8.3	1	1.8
$2,500 to $2,999.......	1	1.6	1	8.3	0	.0
Average installment expenditures, ranges, and per cent of families reporting expenditures						
Families reporting						
Mean..................	$680.94		$1,413.13		$484.04	
Median	449.13		1,444.24		342.25	
'Range	92.60 to 2,586.22		352.45 to 2,586.22		92.60 to 2,437.56	
Per cent reporting	40.3		7.5		34.6	

radios, and musical instruments, and 28 per cent of the money spent for the types of housefurnishings and equipment for which installment purchase was used by any family.

Of the $43,580 spent on installment purchases in 1950, 39 per cent went for automobiles, 33 per cent for housefurnishings and equipment, and the remaining 28 per cent almost entirely for television sets, radios, and musical instruments. The 64 families who bought one or more items on installment spent an average of $681 for these purchases. Almost all these families spent more than $100; 48 per cent spent sums of $500 or more, and 22 per cent spent between $1,000 and $2,586. The largest installment purchases were reported by the 12 families who bought automobiles; three-quarters of these expenditures were $1,000 or more, and the average was $1,413. Fifty-five families who used installment credit for other kinds of goods spent an average of $484. One-fourth of these expenditures were between $500 and $1,000, and 9 per cent were larger sums up to a maximum of $2,438.

The liquidation of installment debt.—Every family that made installment purchases paid off all or part of these 1950 obligations, and by the end of

TABLE 86

Installment Debt Position of Families with Installment Purchases in 1950 and Prior Years

Items bought	1950 installment purchases								
	Total purchases			Paid in 1950			Owed 12/31/50		
	Number of families	Aggregate cost	Average cost	Number of families	Aggregate paid	Average paid	Number of families	Aggregate owed	Average owed
All items..............	64	$43,580.03	$680.94	64	$23,685.93	$370.09	61	$19,894.10	$326.13
Automobiles............	12	16,957.61	1,413.13	12	10,118.94	843.24	12	6,838.67	569.89
Other, total..........	55	26,622.42	484.04	55	13,566.99	246.67	52	13,055.43	251.07
Housefurnishings.......	46	14,510.85	315.45	46	7,531.20	163.72	42	6,979.65	166.18
Television, musical instruments...........	21	11,769.32	560.44	21	5,920.79	281.94	19	5,848.53	307.82
House repair	1	250.00	250.00	1	50.00	50.00	1	200.00	200.00
Books	1	92.25	92.25	1	65.00	65.00	1	27.25	27.25

Installment purchases before 1950 (excluding cars)

	Owed 1/1/50			Paid in 1950			Owed 12/31/50		
	Number of families	Aggregate owed	Average owed	Number of families	Aggregate paid	Average paid	Number of families	Aggregate owed	Average owed
All items except automobiles..	33	$7,130.18	$216.07	33	$5,598.96	$169.67	14	$1,531.22	$109.37
Housefurnishings	19	3,493.33	183.86	19	2,993.62	157.56	9	499.71	55.52
Television, musical instruments...........	9	2,166.17	240.69	9	1,480.42	164.49	5	685.75	137.15
House repair	6	888.18	148.03	6	782.72	130.45	2	105.46	52.73
Books	1	39.20	39.20	1	39.20	39.20	0	.00	.00
Miscellaneous	5	543.30	108.66	5	303.00	60.60	2	240.30	120.15

Summary of installment purchases (excluding cars), 1950 and prior years

	Owed 1/1/50 plus total 1950 purchases	Paid in 1950	Owed 12/31/50
Number of families	69	69	56
Aggregate amount	$33,752.60	$19,165.95	$14,586.65
Average amount	489.17	277.77	260.48

the year 54 per cent of the total 1950 installment debt had been paid off. Three families had paid off all these debts, and the remaining 61 owed an average of $326 at the end of the year. Thirty-four per cent of the unpaid balance was for cars, 35 per cent for housefurnishings and equipment, and most of the remainder for television sets, radios, and musical instruments.

The installment picture of these families would not be complete without examining their debt for goods purchased before 1950. (In this analysis installment purchases of automobiles bought before 1950 have been omitted because information was not obtained as to the amount of money owed on these cars at the beginning or end of the year.) At the beginning of 1950, 33 families owed $7,130, or an average of $216 per family, on these installment purchases made in prior years. In 1950 all these families paid off something on these debts, and by the end of the year 78 per cent of the total debt had been liquidated. Nineteen families had completed their payments, and the remaining 14 still owed an average of $109. The total 1950 installment debt (excluding automobiles), that is, the amount owed at the beginning of the year, plus the new debts incurred during 1950, amounted to $33,753. This amount was owed by 69 families, resulting in an average debt of $489 per family. During 1950 $19,166, or 57 per cent of the total 1950 installment debt (excluding cars) was paid off; 71 per cent of the payments were for 1950 purchases, and the remaining 29 per cent were payments on goods bought before 1950. At the end of 1950, 56 families owed $14,587, or $260 per family. Thus more families had installment debts at the end than at the beginning of the year, and the average sum was only $44 more.

COMPARISON. WITH
THE NATIONAL SURVEY
OF CONSUMER FINANCES

It is possible to compare certain of the data on the methods of purchasing automobiles, furniture, and household appliances, which were used by the families in this study, with the 1950 findings of the Survey of Consumer Finance. In this Federal Reserve survey the analysis of credit purchases of automobiles includes both installment credit and other borrowings. [2] Therefore, in order to compare the method of financing automobiles used by the families in the Heller Committee study with the findings of the Survey of Consumer Finances, it was necessary to add to the installment purchasers in the Heller Committee study those who borrowed money to buy a

---

[2] Federal Reserve Bulletin, June 1954, p. 571.

TABLE 87

Per cent of Families Buying on Installment in 1950, Heller Committee
and Survey of Consumer Finance Studies

Items bought on installment	Heller Committee	Survey of Consumer Finances	
	All incomes	All incomes	Incomes $5,000 to $7,500
Automobiles · · · · · · · · · · · · · ·	52.7	52.0[a]	· · · ·[b]
Furniture and major household appliances, total · · · ·	35.1[c]	51.0[d]	40.0[c]
Television · · · · · · · · · · · · ·	38.2	44.0[e]	· · · ·[b]
Refrigerators · · · · · · · · · ·	38.5	54.0[e]	· · · ·[b]
Washing machines· · · · · · · ·	26.9	42.0[e]	· · · ·[b]

[a]Federal Reserve Bulletin, July, 1951, p. 764.
[b]Not available.
[c]The families included in the Heller Committee figures are those who spent $100 or more for furniture and all buyers of major household appliances (including television, radio-phonographs, and musical instruments) as defined by the Survey Research Center. The $100 minimum on furniture purchases was set in an attempt to make the Heller Committee data at least roughly comparable with the Survey of Consumer Finances. This latter study asked the respondents whether they bought any "large items" of furniture on installment, and there was no definition in terms of dollars of what should be considered a large item. On the basis of the correspondence with the Survey Research Center it was decided that a reasonable degree of comparability between the two studies would be attained by setting a minimum of $100 for any item (including suites of furniture) bought by the Heller Committee families.
[d]Federal Reserve Bulletin, July, 1951, p. 770.
[e]Federal Reserve Bulletin, June, 1954, p. 573.

car. Thus the total number of families in the Heller Committee study who used credit to buy automobiles was 29.[3]

Slightly more than half of the car purchasers in both of these studies used installment or other forms of credit in buying their cars. The very close agreement of these figures must be interpreted with caution, in view of the small number of car purchasers in the Heller Committee sample. It might have been expected that credit purchases of automobiles by the families included in the Heller Committee study would have been less frequent than in the Survey of Consumer Finances because of the higher incomes of the families studied by the Heller Committee.[4] These families had a median income before taxes of $6,600, and only 4 families had an income of less than $5,000, whereas the median income before taxes in the Survey of Consumer Finances was $3,000, and 80 per cent reported incomes

[3]Although in the Heller Committee study, information was not requested concerning the specific purpose for which cash loans were made, in ten of the seventeen cases classified as obtaining cash loans for the purchase of a car it was specifically indicated that the loans were for this purpose; in the seven other cases internal evidence indicated that the loans were probably used to purchase cars.

[4]See Federal Reserve Bulletin, May 1955, p. 466, for recent evidence concerning the relationship between the method of financing the purchase of automobiles and income. Also see Federal Reserve Bulletin, July, 1951, p. 764.

of less than $5,000.[5] The fact that both groups purchased the same propor-
tion of cars on credit may be owing to chance variations in the Heller Committee sample. It is, however, possible that there may be differences in
the method of financing cars between the San Francisco Bay area and the
nation-wide sampling area covered in the Survey of Consumer Finances.

A comparison of the installment purchases of furniture and certain types
of household appliances shows that there were considerable differences between the Heller Committee and the Survey of Consumer Finances. Thirty-
five per cent of all purchasers of large items of furniture and major household appliances in the Heller Committee sample used installment, in contrast with 51 per cent of the buyers in the Survey of Consumer Finances.
However, when the Survey of Consumer Finances purchasers were analyzed
by income groups, it was found that 40 per cent of those with incomes between $5,000 and $7,500 purchased these items on installment—a figure
much closer to the one shown in the Heller Committee study.

Although the use of cash or installment credit for all household items
was available by income class in the Survey of Consumer Finances, the
various categories of housefurnishings and equipment for which installment
credit was used were not classified by income. Furthermore, certain categories were not comparable, so that a comparison of the method of purchasing in the two studies can be made only for certain items and for all income
groups combined. Installment credit was used by 38 per cent of the purchasers of television sets and refrigerators in the Heller Committee study,
and by 44 and 54 per cent respectively of the purchasers of the Federal
Reserve study. Washing machines were purchased on installment by 27 per
cent of the buyers in the Heller Committee study, and by 42 per cent in the
Survey of Consumer Finances study. These differences are undoubtedly related to the fact that families at higher income levels tend to use installment
credit less frequently than do those in the lower income brackets. If data
classified by income had been available concerning installment purchases
of the various categories of household equipment, there would almost certainly have been a closer relationship between the proportion using installment credit in the two studies.

---

[5] Federal Reserve Bulletin, June, 1951, p. 571.

Chapter XVI

CHANGES IN ASSETS
AND LIABILITIES

As a conclusion to this study it is important to discover whether the 159 families spent more or less than their total money receipts during 1950. If money income and other money receipts did not equal expenditures, the difference should have been accounted for by a net change in assets or liabilities. [1] This change represents the algebraic sum of total surpluses (increases in assets and/or decreases in liabilities) and total deficits (decreases in assets and/or increases in liabilities). An example of 2 families, 1 with a net surplus and the other with a net deficit, is given below.

---

[1]Because families are rarely able to give completely accurate accounts of either their income and expenditures or their net change in assets or liabilities, total disbursements and total receipts are very seldom equal. The unaccounted-for sum is called the "balancing difference," a term used by the U.S. Department of Labor, Bureau of Labor Statistics. (See Family Income, Expenditures, and Savings in 1950, Bulletin 1097 (revised) p. 5. In the Heller Committee study, if the information secured from the family met the tests of completeness and internal consistency, and the balancing difference was not more than 10 per cent of total income or expenditures, whichever was larger, the schedule was considered acceptable. Balancing differences could, of course, be either positive or negative; they were positive when reported income plus deficit exceeded reported expenditures plus surplus, and negative when reported expenditures plus surplus exceeded reported income plus deficit. In this study the average balancing difference for all families was a negative figure of $210, and other studies have shown that there is a tendency for a negative difference to predominate.

Family with a Net Surplus		Family with a Net Deficit	
Total Income	$6,000	Total Income	$6,000
Total Expenditures	5,300	Total Expenditures	6,700
Surpluses—Increases in assets and/or decreases in liabilities		Surpluses—Increases in assets and/or decreases in liabilities	
Bank Deposits greater than withdrawals	1,000	Bank Deposits greater than withdrawals	1,000
Debt paid to loan co.	600	Debt paid to loan co.	600
	1,600		1,600
Deficits—Decreases in assets and/or increases in liabilities		Deficits—Decreases in assets and/or increases in liabilities	
Sale of a lot	600	Sale of a lot	2,000
Unpaid balance on install- ment debt	200	Unpaid balance on install- ment debt	200
	800		2,200
Total Surpluses	1,600	Total Deficits	2,200
Total Deficits	800	Total Surpluses	1,600
Net Surplus	800	Net Deficit	600
Balancing Difference	-100	Balancing Difference	-100

The total expenditures of the 159 families were slightly more than their total income, after allowance was made for the balancing difference. (See table 3, p. 13.) The average excess of expenditures over income—that is, the average net deficit—was $57 for the entire group of families. Only 1 family reported no changes in assets and liabilities, and therefore had neither a net surplus nor a net deficit at the end of the year.

Most families reported several kinds of changes in assets and liabilities, some representing surpluses and others deficits, and the final net surplus or net deficit position of the family was determined by the larger of these two types of changes. In this study 85 per cent of the funds which contributed to surpluses were increases in assets such as bank accounts and money invested in a home or other real estate, and only 15 per cent were the result of liquidating old debts. Forty-one per cent of all deficits were decreases in assets such as spending past savings or converting investments into cash, and the remainder were debts incurred during 1950.

For all families in the study the average increase in assets was just over twice the size of the decrease in assets—$2,527 in contrast with $1,247. However, the decrease in liabilities, i.e., the liquidation of debts, amounted to only $447, whereas the debts which were incurred averaged $1,784. Thus

TABLE 88

Average Total Surpluses and Total Deficits, and Net Changes in Assets and Liabilities, by Income Class

	All families					Families reporting			
	Surplus (asset increases; liability decreases)		Deficit (asset decreases; liability increases)		Net change	Surplus (asset increases; liability decreases)		Deficit (asset decreases; liability increases)	
	Average	Per cent	Average	Per cent		Number reporting	Average	Number reporting	Average
All families									
Assets and liabilities, total...	$2,974.44	100.0	$3,030.98	100.0	-$56.54	151	$3,132.03	148	$3,256.25
Assets	2,527.36	85.0	1,247.00	41.1	+1,280.36	219	3,115.13	116	1,709.25
Liabilities	447.08	15.0	1,783.98	58.9	-1,336.90	109	652.16	117	2,424.38
Incomes under $6,000									
Assets and liabilities, total...	2,376.11	100.0	2,564.03	100.0	-187.92	72	2,508.12	71	2,744.60
Assets	2,007.18	84.5	1,047.40	40.8	+959.78	61	2,500.75	57	1,396.54
Liabilities	368.93	15.5	1,516.63	59.2	-1,147.70	51	549.78	55	2,095.71
Incomes $6,000 and over									
Assets and liabilities, total...	3,522.31	100.0	3,458.54	100.0	+63.77	79	3,700.66	77	3,728.04
Assets	3,003.68	85.3	1,429.76	41.3	+1,573.92	68	3,666.26	59	2,011.36
Liabilities	518.63	14.7	2,028.78	58.7	-1,510.15	58	742.18	62	2,715.94

the net increase in assets of $1,280 was more than canceled by the fact that there was a net increase in liabilities of $1,337, and therefore the families as a whole had a net deficit of $57.

In order to maintain comparability with the 1950 classifications of the Bureau of Labor Statistics, payments for all personal insurance were classified as expenditures. The small average deficit of the Heller Committee sample would have been changed to a surplus had insurance payments been included as assets, as they were in the 1934-1936 and 1941-1942 B.L.S. studies.[2] If they had been considered assets, the 159 families would have shown a net surplus of $476. The fact that these families were making average personal insurance payments of $533 indicates that the net deficit of $57 per family was no threat to the financial well-being of the families as a whole.

There was an almost equal division between families who reported net surpluses and those who reported net deficits. Seventy-seven families had a net surplus which averaged $1,069. One-third of these net surpluses were between $500 and $1,000; 62 per cent were more than $500, but only seven were more than $2,500—ranging up to a maximum of $8,789. Each of the 7 families with the highest surpluses increased assets by buying or making extensive improvements on a home, and 2 of them also added to their investments in stocks and bonds. The average size of the net deficit reported by 81 families was $1,127. Most such deficits were quite large: 41 per cent were between $500 and $1,500, and 27 per cent were even larger, with the highest being $6,247. This large deficit was in the main accounted for by a mortgage at the end of the year of approximately $13,400 on a new home, and also withdrawals of $4,400 from savings during the year. Moreover, because of the sale as well as the purchase of a home, this family had surpluses totaling only about $11,600.

It is important to understand the implications of both the surpluses and deficits reported by these families. A family with a net deficit spent more money than it received in current income and other money receipts. This does not mean, however, that families with deficits were necessarily sinking into debt. A deficit resulted either from a decrease in assets—which was merely the transferring of past savings or investments into funds available for expenditures in 1950—or from an increase in liabilities, representing a claim on future income. For example, in 1949, a family might have set aside $300 in the bank, with which to buy a television set in 1950. The withdrawal of that $300 in 1950 would appear as a decrease in assets for

---

[2]U.S. Department of Labor, Bureau of Labor Statistics, Family Expenditures in Selected Cities 1935-36, Bulletin No. 648; Family Spending and Saving in Wartime, Bulletin No. 822.

TABLE 89

Net Surplus or Deficit, by Income Class

	All families[a]				Under $6,000				$6,000 and over[a]			
	Net surplus		Net deficit		Net surplus		Net deficit		Net surplus		Net deficit	
Size of net surplus or deficit	Number	Per cent	Number	Per cent	Number	Per cent	Number	Per cent	Number	Per cent	Number	Per cent

Families reporting net surplus or deficit

Size of net surplus or deficit	Number	Per cent	Number	Per cent	Number	Per cent	Number	Per cent	Number	Per cent	Number	Per cent
Families reporting, total	77	100.0	81	100.0	34	100.0	42	100.0	43	100.0	39	100.0
Under $500	29	37.7	26	32.1	12	35.3	12	28.6	17	39.5	14	35.9
Under $100	7	9.1	4	4.9	1	2.9	1	2.4	6	14.0	3	7.7
$100 to $199	5	6.5	4	4.9	2	5.9	1	2.4	3	7.0	3	7.7
$200 to $299	8	10.4	7	8.6	5	14.7	5	11.9	3	7.0	2	5.1
$300 to $399	4	5.2	6	7.4	1	2.9	4	9.5	3	7.0	2	5.1
$400 to $499	5	6.5	5	6.2	3	8.8	1	2.4	2	4.7	4	10.3
$500 to $999	26	33.8	16	19.8	15	44.1	8	19.0	11	25.6	8	20.5
$1,000 to $1,499	8	10.4	17	21.0	2	5.9	9	21.4	6	14.0	8	20.5
$1,500 to $1,999	4	5.2	14	17.3	1	2.9	9	21.4	3	7.0	5	12.8
$2,000 to $2,499	3	3.9	3	3.7	1	2.9	2	4.8	2	4.7	1	2.6
$2,500 to $4,999	4	5.2	4	4.9	2	5.9	1	2.4	3	7.0	3	7.7
$5,000 and over	3	3.9	1	1.2			1	2.4	1	2.3	0	.0

Average net surplus or deficit, ranges, and per cent reporting

Families reporting[a]	Number	Per cent	Number	Per cent	Number	Per cent	Number	Per cent	Number	Per cent	Number	Per cent
Mean	$1,069.10		$1,127.28		$1,067.93		$1,204.57		$1,070.02		$1,044.04	
Median	655.25		932.12		584.17		1,102.72		660.19		813.68	
Range	17.66 to 8,789.01		2.52 to 6,247.16		39.00 to 6,560.14		97.50 to 6,247.16		17.66 to 8,789.01		2.52 to 3,562.50	
Per cent of all families	48.4		50.9		21.4		26.4		27.0		24.5	

[a] One family with an income over $6,000 reported neither a net surplus nor a deficit.

the family, and if this were the only entry in the surplus-deficit section, it would be reported as a net deficit for the year. Thus, although the family was certainly no less solvent in 1950 than in 1949, and had indeed been prudent in its planning, expenditures in 1950 exceeded income by $300. A second family might have bought a $300 television set on installment, with the entire cost to be paid after 1950. In this case the $300 would also appear as a net deficit (if it were the only entry) in the form of an increase in liabilities. The two types of deficit represent quite different situations in a family's financial life. In both cases the financial position of the family was less good at the end than at the beginning of the year, but only in the second case had the family mortgaged its future income.

Similarly, families with surpluses were not necessarily building up sizable money resources. Surpluses resulted either from an increase in assets or a decrease in liabilities. For example, 1 family may have added $1,000 to its savings account during 1950, and another may have paid off an installment debt incurred before 1950 for the purchase of an automobile. Both of these families were better off at the end than at the beginning of 1950, but only in the first case had the family added to funds available for spending in subsequent years; the second case merely represented the liquidation of an old obligation.

Surpluses: increases in assets and/or decreases in liabilities.—One hundred and fifty-one families reported some increases in assets and/or decreases in liabilities during 1950, but only 77, or slightly less than half the sample, had a net surplus at the end of the year. In the other cases total surpluses were outweighed by total deficits, resulting in a net deficit position. Assets were increased in a variety of ways, including the purchase or improvement of homes, or increases in bank accounts or in the ownership of stocks and bonds. Liabilities were decreased by reducing mortgages on owned homes or other real property, purchased before 1950, or by making payments on other debts incurred before 1950.

The most frequent type of increase in assets was improvements on owned homes, reported by 72 families at an average cost of $256 per family. Thirty-two per cent of these expenditures were less than $50, and 81 per cent were less than $400. As might be expected, a few families had expenses for major improvements, including 4 who reported spending from $1,020 to $2,590. Fifty families reported increases in cash in banks or on hand, averaging $567 per family. Such increases of course varied greatly—from $5 to $5,158. Sixteen per cent of these sums were $1,000 or more, but only one was more than $2,400. Sixty-seven families reported some stock and bond transactions during the year; 32 of this group spent more for the purchase of stocks and bonds than they received from the sale of such investments bought before 1950, thus increasing their assets by an average of $908 per family. Slightly

TABLE 90

Average Changes in Assets and Liabilities and Number of Families Reporting, by Type of Change

Assets

	Total families reporting change		Families reporting net asset increases			Families reporting net asset decreases		
	Number	Per cent of all families	Number	Per cent of all families	Mean	Number	Per cent of all families	Mean
Investments in owned homes								
Assessments	11	6.9	11	6.9	$111.79	...	...	...
Improvements	72	45.3	72	45.3	256.19	...	...	...
Purchases and sales[a]	17	10.7	14	8.8	12,557.91	3	1.9	$8,896.23
Investments in other real estate								
Assessments	3	1.9	3	1.9	177.83	...	...	...
Improvements	5	3.1	5	3.1	82.76	...	...	...
Purchases and sales[a]	12	7.5	9	5.7	13,750.17	3	1.9	2,733.33
Cash in bank, etc., or on hand	134	84.3	50	31.4	566.64	84	52.8	1,269.21
Money owed to family	42	26.4	28	17.6	782.16	14	8.8	872.93
Business investments	2	1.3	2	1.3	1,182.50	...	...	...
Stocks and bonds[b]	67	42.1	32	20.1	908.39	35	22.0	932.99
Sale of personal property, total	39	24.5	...	...	...	39	24.5	81.81
Cars	3	1.9	...	...	...	3	1.9	178.33
All other	38	23.9	...	...	...	38	23.9	69.89
Life insurance—settlement or surrender	10	6.3	...	...	...	10	6.3	870.37

Liabilities

	Number	Per cent	Families reporting net liability decreases			Families reporting net liability increases		
			Number	Per cent of all families	Mean	Number	Per cent of all families	Mean
Mortgages—owned home								
New or refinanced, 1950[c]	13	8.2	...	...	...	13	8.2	10,423.10
Principal payments, homes bought before 1950	77	48.4	77	48.4	620.18	...	...	...
Mortgages—other real estate								
New or refinanced, 1950[c]	7	4.4	...	...	...	7	4.4	10,485.98
Principal payments, property bought before 1950	5	3.1	5	3.1	516.46	...	...	...
Installment debts								
Cars	23	14.5	11	6.9	638.02	12	7.5	569.89
All other	71	44.7	26	16.4	114.79	45	28.3	247.67
Bills (including rent and taxes)	95	59.7	28	17.6	112.14	67	42.1	128.38
Money owed individuals, banks, etc.	66	41.5	18	11.3	411.46	48	30.2	1,000.39
All other liabilities	5	3.1	1	.6	200.00	4	2.5	36.68

[a]The net difference between the gross purchase price of real estate bought in 1950 and the gross sale price of real estate purchased before 1950.
[b]The net difference between the cost of stocks and bonds bought in 1950 and the proceeds from the sale of stocks and bonds acquired before 1950.
[c]Mortgages on real estate bought in 1950, or the amount of mortgage increase due to refinancing in 1950, minus any principal payments made on these mortgages during 1950.

more than one-third of these increases were less than $200; a like number ran from $200 to $500, and the remainder were all more than $600, up to a maximum of $6,570. The purchase of real estate resulted in much larger increases in assets than did any other type of investment or savings. Fourteen of the 15 families that bought homes which they occupied in 1950 increased their assets by an average of $12,558. These fourteen homes ranged in price from $8,675 to $22,500, with 71 per cent between $11,500 and $18,750. Nine families purchased other real estate, with an average investment of $13,750; the sums involved ranged widely—from $2,650 to $18,650, and the real estate purchased included several lots, as well as a house bought to rent, and homes to be occupied by the owners in 1951.

Surpluses also resulted from the reduction of liabilities through payments on mortgages or other kinds of debts. Seventy-seven families that purchased their homes before 1950 reduced the mortgages on those homes by an average of $620. Seven families made principal payments of less than $200 during the year; in five of these cases payments were low because the purchase price of the house was less than $7,000. Seventy-one per cent of the principal payments were between $200 and $500, and only 6 families paid $1,000 or more. This last group of families included 3 who wiped out mortgage debts of between $6,000 and $7,000 apiece when they sold their homes. There were also 5 families who reduced mortgages on other property with an average payment of $516.

Other types of debts were reduced by a considerable number of families. Eleven made payments averaging $638 on cars which had been purchased on installment before 1950. Twenty-six paid on other installment debts incurred in earlier years, and their payments averaged $115. Twenty-eight families reduced their outstanding bills by an average of $112; 71 per cent of these payments were less than $70, and only 1 family reported more than $385, as a result of paying a bill of $695 for housefurnishings. Eighteen families decreased their money debts to such agencies as banks and insurance companies, with an average payment of $411. Nine of these decreases were less than $200, and the two highest were $750 and $2,735.

In terms of the money involved, transactions related to real estate were the most important source of increased assets among these families. Nearly half of the total increase resulted from expenditures for purchases, improvements, or special assessments on owned homes, and 31 per cent came from the same group of expenditures for other real estate. The remaining increases included bank deposits or investments in stocks and bonds. Decreases in liabilities were also in the main related to real estate; 71 per cent of all the money involved in these decreases represented payments on mortgages—largely on owned homes. Most of the remaining money decreases went for payments on installment debts, or on money debts which were usually owed to such agencies as banks or loan and insurance companies.

Deficits: decreases in assets and/or increases in liabilities.—Although 81, or just over half the families reported a net deficit at the end of 1950, there were 148 families who reported some deficit during the year. Sixty-seven of this larger group had total surpluses which outweighed their total deficits, and as a consequence they ended the year in a net surplus position. The most usual way to decrease assets was to spend previously accumulated cash. Eighty-four families reduced their bank accounts by an average of $1,269. Although 52 per cent of these withdrawals were sums of less than $500 per family, nearly a third ranged from $1,000 to $10,500. Two of the four largest withdrawals were approximately $6,000 each, and the others were $8,800, and $10,500. These sums were reported by 3 families that made down payments of $6,000 or more on new homes, and a fourth that increased its stock holdings by $6,100. Thirty-nine families decreased assets by selling personal property—largely housefurnishings—and the average amount realized from these sales was $82. Only four such sales were for sums above $200: 2 families sold automobiles for $210 and $250, and 2 sold housefurnishings for $353 and $562. Thirty-five families received more money from the sale of stocks and bonds owned before 1950 than they invested in stocks and bonds during 1950. The average decrease in assets from these stock transactions was $933; 10 families had decreases of less than $200, but 9 reported decreases of more than $1,000, the highest of which was $7,979. Ten families surrendered insurance policies, with an average asset decrease of $870. The amounts received from these policies varied widely, from $100 to $2,372. Two families sold homes and did not buy new ones, and a third sold a home for slightly more than the cost of the one they purchased. As a result of these transactions the 3 families had an average decrease in assets of $8,896. Three additional families sold other real estate with an average asset decrease of $2,733.

In addition to drawing upon past savings or investments, many families increased their indebtedness during 1950. Sixty-seven owed an average of $128 more on bills for goods and services at the end of the year than they had at the beginning of the year. Fifty-five per cent of these outstanding debts were less than $100; 82 per cent were less than $200; and all were under $600, with the exception of 1 family that increased its bills by $1,160. Twelve families that purchased automobiles on installment increased their debts by an average of $570, and 45 increased other installment debts by an average of $248. Thirteen families financed the 1950 purchase of homes with mortgages, and the average increase in their liabilities as a result of these mortgage transactions was $10,423. Similar new mortgages (plus one refinancing of a mortgage) on other types of real property were reported by

TABLE 91

Average Total Surpluses and Total Deficits, by Source and Income Class

	All families				Families with incomes							
	Surplus		Deficit		Under $6,000				$6,000 and over			
					Surplus		Deficit		Surplus		Deficit	
	Net increase		Net decrease		Net increase		Net decrease		Net increase		Net decrease	
	Average	Per cent	Average	Per cent	Average	Per cent	Average	Per cent	Average	Per cent	Average	Per cent
					All assets							
Total assets	$2,527.36	100.0	$1,247.00	100.0	$2,007.18	100.0	$1,047.40	100.0	$3,003.68	100.0	$1,429.76	100.0
Investments in owned homes	1,229.47	48.6	167.85	13.5	1,085.30	54.3	...	...	1,357.83	45.2	321.55	22.5
Investments in other real estate	784.27	31.0	51.57	4.1	652.55	32.5	78.95	7.5	904.88	30.1	26.51	1.9
Cash in banks, etc., or on hand	178.19	7.1	670.53	53.8	103.21	5.1	694.40	66.3	246.85	8.2	648.66	45.4
Money owed to family	137.74	5.4	76.86	6.2	22.62	1.1	98.35	9.4	243.14	8.1	57.19	4.0
Business investments	14.87	.6	...	...	...	...	...	...	28.49	.9	...	...
Stocks and bonds	182.82	7.2	205.38	16.5	139.50	7.0	118.45	11.3	222.49	7.4	284.97	19.9
Sale of personal property	...	...	20.07	1.6	...	...	15.08	1.4	...	...	24.63	1.7
Settlement or surrender of life insurance	...	...	54.74	4.4	...	...	42.17	4.0	...	...	66.25	4.6

All liabilities

	Net decrease		Net increase		Net decrease		Net increase		Net decrease		Net increase	
	Average	Per cent	Average	Per cent	Average	Per cent	Average	Per cent	Average	Per cent	Average	Per cent
Total liabilities	$447.08	100.0	$1,783.98	100.0	$368.93	100.0	$1,516.63	100.0	$518.63	100.0	$2,028.78	100.0
Mortgages on owned homes	300.34	67.2	852.20	47.8	237.35	64.3	708.17	46.7	358.01	69.0	984.09	48.5
Mortgages on other real estate	16.24	3.6	461.65	25.9	19.92	5.4	402.63	26.5	12.87	2.5	515.69	25.4
Installment purchase of cars	44.14	9.9	43.01	2.4	28.46	7.7	49.77	3.3	58.50	11.3	36.82	1.8
All other installment purchases	18.77	4.2	70.09	3.9	25.49	6.9	48.65	3.2	12.62	2.4	89.74	4.4
Bills	19.75	4.4	54.10	3.0	19.54	5.3	43.84	2.9	19.94	3.8	63.48	3.1
Money owed individuals, banks	46.58	10.4	302.01	16.9	35.54	9.6	262.63	17.3	56.69	10.9	338.06	16.7
All other liabilities	1.26	.3	.92	.1	2.63	.7	.94	.1	...	...	.90	.0
Average, all surpluses ..	$2,974.44				$2,376.11				$3,522.31			
Average, all deficits ...			$3,030.98				$2,564.03				$3,458.54	

7 families, who increased their liabilities by $10,486. The mortgages on owned homes (less any 1950 principal payments) ranged from $5,049 to $16,762, and on other real property from $7,167 to $13,635. A few families increased other debts, but the sums involved were always small.

In terms of the money involved in deficits, the most important decrease in assets was the withdrawal of money from banks, which accounted for 54 per cent of all asset decreases. Most of the remaining decrease in assets came from the sale of stocks or bonds and real estate. Nearly three-quarters of the total increase in liabilities represented real estate mortgages, and 17 per cent represented debts to such agencies as banks, or loan and insurance companies.

Surplus and deficit by income levels.—When the families were divided into two income groups—those with incomes above and below $6,000, the lower group had an average net deficit of $188, and the upper bracket a net surplus of $64.[3] In both groups some families reported net deficits and some net surpluses; however, only 45 per cent of the lower income group, in contrast with 52 per cent of the upper bracket, reported net surpluses. The proportions of families in the two groups reporting the various types of surplus or deficit transactions were quite similar, although of course the sums of money involved differed considerably.

Among families with net surpluses, the average surplus of those with incomes below $6,000 was $1,068, and of those with higher incomes, $1,070. For families with net deficits, the average deficit was $1,205 in the lower income bracket, and $1,044 in the upper bracket.

For both income groups increases in assets were greater than decreases in assets, and increases in liabilities were greater than decreases in liabilities. However, in the lower group the $1,148 net increase in liabilities more than canceled out the $960 net increase in assets, whereas for the upper bracket the $1,574 net increase in assets outweighed the $1,510 net increase in liabilities. This resulted in the deficit of $188 for the lower group, and the net surplus of $64 for the higher income families.

Summary of the surplus-deficit positions of all families.—Since the average net increase in liabilities for the entire sample was larger than the average net increase in assets, the families as a whole ended the year 1950 with an average net deficit of $57.

A comparison of all increases and decreases in assets shows that for the sample as a whole more money was involved in acquiring assets than in liquidating them. The average net increase in assets was $1,280. Real

---

[3]If personal insurance payments during the year had been classified as increases in assets rather than as expenditures, both groups would have shown surpluses—$269 for those with incomes under $6,000; $667 for those with incomes of $6,000 and more.

estate, particularly owner-occupied homes, was the major asset in which increases surpassed decreases. A smaller though important asset which increased more than it decreased was the amount of money owed to the families. The only important asset which decreased more than it increased was money on hand or in the bank; as a whole, the families withdrew more money during the year than they deposited.

When all increases and decreases in liabilities are compared, we find that increases were greater during the year than decreases, and thus families financed some expenditures from sources outside of current income, by using either accumulated reserves or credit. The average net increase in liabilities was $1,337. Every specified type of liability contributed to the over-all net increase, and again real estate, particularly owner-occupied homes, was the most important type. More money was involved in mortgage debts incurred during the year than was used for principal payments on mortgages, although many more families made the latter transactions. Money owed to persons outside the family, such as personal loans, was the next most important type of liability in terms of the money involved.

In terms of surplus and deficit, surpluses—that is, increases in assets and/or decreases in liabilities—came most frequently from real estate (usually home purchase or improvement). Deficits (decreased assets and/or increased liabilities) were less concentrated; among the most frequent were bank withdrawals and increases in the amount of money owed to stores, lending agencies, or individuals.

Surplus and deficit by expenditure levels.—When the families were classified by size of expenditures for current consumption, rather than by income levels, it was found that those that spent less had a net surplus, and those with higher expenditures showed a net deficit. The total group of 159 families had an average expenditure of $5,957 for all current consumption items, and a net deficit of $57. There were 88 families who spent less than $6,000, and 71 whose expenditures were $6,000 or more. Sixty-nine per cent of the families who spent the lower sums reported a net surplus, but 22 per cent of the higher expenditure bracket had a surplus. The lower group had an average net surplus of $417, and the upper group had an average net deficit of $643. Thus there was evidence that a majority of the families in the upper expenditure group, either by spending accumulated reserves or by using credit, attained a level of living slightly higher than would have been permitted by their current income.[4]

----

[4]For a discussion of this subject in connection with an earlier study see U.S. Department of Labor, Bureau of Labor Statistics, Money Disbursements of Wage Earners and Clerical Workers, 1934-36, Bulletin 638, pp. 174-175.